Political Parties and Ideologies in Canada: liberals, conservatives, socialists, nationalists

Party is a body of men for promoting by their joint endeavors the national interest upon some particular principle in which they are all agreed. . . . It is the business of the speculative philosopher to mark the proper ends of government. It is the business of the politician, who is the philosopher in action, to find out proper means towards those ends, and to employ them with effect.

Edmund Burke
Thoughts on the Cause of the Present Discontents (1770)

Political Parties and Ideologies in Canada: liberals, conservatives, socialists, nationalists

by

William Christian
Department of Political Science,
Mount Allison University
Sackville,
New Brunswick

and

Colin Campbell
Department of Political Science
Mount Allison University
Sackville
New Brunswick

McGraw-Hill Ryerson
Toronto   Montreal   New York   London
Sydney   Mexico   Panama   Sao Paulo
Johannesburg   Düsseldorf   New Delhi
Singapore   Kuala Lumpur

UXORIBUS LAUDE DIGNISSIMIS
QUAE SAEPIUS NOBIS MAGNO
AUXILIO FUERINT

ISBN   0-07-077661-X   Hard cover
       0-07-077686-5   Soft cover

Library of Congress Catalogue Card Number 73-10792

Printed and bound in Canada

12345678910 AP74 3210987654

Table of Contents

Foreword

Recently we have heard a good deal about "the end of ideology". While the phrase obviously has many meanings, I wonder if it is not wrong when applied to the Canadian scene. My impression is that Canadian students at least are becoming more and more interested in ideological questions and in ideology itself. One could cite as an example the recent growth of popularity in Canadian universities of courses in the philosophy and doctrines of religion but the interest is evident also in courses in political science. I think that probably a number of teachers of courses in Canadian politics have noticed, as I have, that since the nineteen-sixties students have displayed an increasing interest in two fields in particular, social problems and political ideologies.

Despite this growing interest in the philosophical persuasions of our parties, there has been almost no attempt to describe them or to analyze them comparatively within a single book. We have had a number of very good monographs and articles on selected subjects — social credit, conservatism, liberalism, socialism, and nationalism — but we have lacked a work that brings together in one volume appraisals of the beliefs of our leading parties. As a result, successive generations of Canadian students have acquired the notion that our political parties are pragmatic creatures without philosophical underpinning.

Professor Christian's and Professor Campbell's book should disabuse readers of this concept. In fact, *Political Parties & Ideologies in Canada* serves a double purpose. It not only provides in one handy small book a comparative account of the political theories of several of our parties but it demonstrates, by pursuing the historical method, that our parties have had a greater measure of ideological conviction and been more faithful to it than many of us have acknowledged. After reading this book, it may be difficult for a critic to dismiss our parties as "merely the struggle for office, the madness of the many for the gain of the few," despite the fact that no less an authority than Sir John A. Macdonald uttered the remark. I suspect that most Canadians will be surprised — pleasantly, I hope — to discover that our parties really do stand for something, philosophically speaking.

It is also interesting, and perhaps significant, that this book comes from two younger Canadian scholars who have developed it from the material which they have prepared for a course in Canadian politics which they offer in their university. The authors and their students clearly belong to the new generation which is more concerned with theory than with bare facts. We may be passing into a more sophisticated era in which Canadian political theory is studied more intensively and in which, one can hope, indigenous political theories will be formulated.

In the interval, this book will serve a useful purpose by showing that Canadian politics is not as deficient in ideology as conventional wisdom casually assumes.

August 27, 1973　　　　　　　　　　　　　　　PAUL W. FOX
University of Toronto　　　　　　　　　　　　　General Editor

Preface

Canadian political thought, as a field of study, is just beginning. It is still possible to react to a project like ours as did a wise and humane friend when he asked whether we were going to study the Plato of Orillia or the Aristotle of Owen Sound. Yet on reflection it is clear that what has been lacking is not the political thought, but the conscious reflection about its nature and its adequacy.

A few words of caution about our approach are in order. Our claim that Canadian politics are ideological is bound to be misunderstood, simply because "ideology" as a term has many different meanings. Perhaps the most common is some variation of the Marxist theory that ideologies are created by the productive relationships prevalent in a society. Such theorists treat ideologies as Hobbes suggested words should be viewed: "For words are wise men's counters, they do but reckon by them; but they are the money of fools. . . ." This approach is indeed an interesting one, and would lead, in Canada, to a fruitful inquiry about the economic and social condition of the supporters of political ideas, similar to the activity in which psephologists engage when they study voting behaviour and political parties.

We have chosen, however, another accepted approach to ideology which, as Leonard Schapiro has put it in his recent book, *Totalitarianism,* "denotes a system of beliefs which relate to fundamental political aims" designed to "influence and direct the course of action of those who are within its sphere of influence". Such a use of "ideology" can extend from an official state ideology like Marxism-Leninism to the doctrines of the British Labour Party. It can further be used to describe the beliefs implicit or inherent in a nation, or even an inconsistent set of beliefs. But since these ideas are in the realm of thought, they can profitably be explicated, clarified and criticized. Because they change over time as a consequence of purposive human decisions, it is not only methodologically proper, but also interesting, to write their history. We therefore ask that our work be judged according to what we have set out to do, not according to understandings of ideology, however valuable, which we have not seen fit to adopt. If our book stirs up interest in this long neglected field, we hope that it will be academic in the best, rather than the worst, sense of the word.

The problems raised by journalists when they refer to "small-l liberals" have plagued us throughout this book. Clearly, Conservatism and Liberalism are easy; with capitals they refer to the doctrines of the Liberal-Conservative Party and its successors, and to the Liberal Party. However, more important for our analysis is the series of ideologies — conservatism, toryism, liberalism, socialism and nationalism — which we use for the purpose of analysis. In the appropriate chapters we have outlined what we think are the key ideas associated with these ideologies. These ideologies, except as noted in the text, we take to be of reasonably stable content; and our argument is that most liberals are in the Liberal Party, most conservatives in the Conservative Party and most socialists in the NDP. When we talk about the liberals in the Conservative Party, we mean only that there are those Conservatives who place a high value on individuals and on the enhancement of liberty. The greatest confusion arises in the case of the Liberal Party, which we argue comes closest to a party with a pure ideology. In some cases Liberalism and liberalism so closely coincide that it is difficult to decide whether to capitalize or not. On balance, unless we have wanted to make a specific point about the Liberal Party, we have not done so.

We have received much help in completing this manuscript. Mount Allison has not only presented us with a pleasant setting in which to teach and write; it has also helped us through the Dean's Fund and the Research Fund for the Social Sciences and Humanities. From the latter we retained the services of Mr. Peter German and Mr. Jim MacAulay as research assistants who have saved us much time by their diligent compilation of bibliography and index, and checking of footnotes. Miss Louise Smith acceded so cheerfully and efficiently to our demands on her typing skills as to make us feel guilty. Dr. W. B. Cunningham of the Economics Department gave us constant encouragement and much helpful criticism. Finally, we must extend our sincere thanks to Professor Paul Fox and Mr. Geoffrey Burn of McGraw-Hill Ryerson. Professor Fox shared our interest in this project almost from its inception, and his advice and enthusiasm have been of considerable help.

It is customary at this point to take the entire responsibility for the "work as it appears, such as it is". In a formal sense, this responsibility is clear, and needs no stating. However, in a very real sense, some of the deficiencies of this book stem from the fact that Canadians have not been sufficiently proud of their past and their uniqueness, nor self-conscious or critical about the political ideas that have guided their national life.

C. CAMPBELL
W. CHRISTIAN
Mount Allison University, Sackville.

Chapter I

The Appeal of Ideology

Most Canadians, throughout their history, have been proud of the fact that they do not think reflectively about the profound questions of politics. How many are there who would not share Sir John A. Macdonald's pride in his boast that he had felt it unjustified to "waste the time of the legislature and the money of the people in fruitless discussions on abstract and theoretical questions of government".[1] If they thought about the matter at all, Canadians would suggest that their politics were practical, pragmatic or common-sensical. They would reject with disdain any notion that ideology played a major role in Canadian politics.

There was even a time in the late 1950's and early 1960's when it was fashionable to herald the end of ideology or even to write the obituary of political philosophy.[2] Students of Canadian politics found nothing strange in such views. The famous "brokerage theory" of politics was taught to a generation of students. Its proponents believed that Canadian political parties, as part of the larger political system, played their proper role if they traded and balanced competing interests within the country. The stronger or more numerous predominated, and the weaker or less numerous either got enough to keep them reasonably content, or else were reconciled that they had lost a fair fight, waged according to the rules of the game.

The problem with this theory was that there were too many things it did not adequately explain.[3]

It treated the 1926 constitutional crisis as a series of domestic political manoeuvres and ignored the serious division about the fundamental issue of Canada's place in the Empire. The Bennett victory of 1930 was a deviation, and his New Deal a fraud in this view because they suggested that Canadian politics might chart a new course. Even the CCF and Social Credit could be written off as third parties, anomalies in a two party system. After all could not Mackenzie King treat the CCF as really "Liberals in a hurry" whose reason for existence as an independent political party would be undermined when the times were propitious for him to adopt so much of their platform as he found desirable. If both Liberals and Conservatives were honest brokers, addressing an appeal to all men of good will, what purpose could ideological parties serve except to distort the patterns of politics? For the brokerage theory of politics to work, the assumption had to be made that there were no significant ideological divisions in the country; otherwise there was no framework within which the parties could balance interests.

This attitude to Canadian politics has been aptly described as the Mackenzie King system. King was so adept at conciliation and compromise that he persuaded his rivals in the other parties to meet him on his own ground. He imposed a style of politics on Canada which took such deep roots that people mistook it for politics itself. Interest politics became the prevailing orthodoxy. For the greater part of the time from King's election as prime minister in 1921 to St. Laurent's defeat in 1957 liberalism accounted fairly well for most important features of social and political life in this country.

Yet the widespread success of Canadian liberalism never succeeded in eradicating competing ideologies. Since the late 1950's conservatism, socialism and nationalism have begun again, with increasing vigour, to add their contribution to the ideological rivalry in Canada. This change is indeed a healthy sign; the ideological diversity of Canada is, we believe, much preferable to the alternative style of consensus politics which often led to uniformity and stagnation.

Recent writers have begun increasingly to comment on this competition of ideas, but they have so restricted the scope of their inquiries that the subject matter about which they wrote seemed to bore them.[4] What they called ideology was really little more than disagreement about policy or about the importance of certain key institutions. They glossed over or ignored any important disputes about the quality of political life or the fundamental assumptions of politics. There are few treatments which even go so far as to suggest that Canadians should concern themselves with such matters.

Moreover writers who have treated Canadian ideologies in this way have patronized them. Canadian politicians have, on the whole, been Burke's philosophers in action. They have not given us an easily accessible theoretical compendium to study. As a consequence it has been easier to study ideologies with similar names in Europe or the United States, and then to assume that the

Canadian counterpart must be similar. The unique Canadian ideological mix which we discuss in the next chapter makes this treatment singularly inappropriate.

Of course it cannot be denied that Canadian ideologies are members of larger families; they do bear a family resemblance, at times striking, to their British and American counterparts and namesakes. There are two important reasons for this. First, when French and English Canadians alike came initially from Europe to the New World they did not and could not abandon all the political ideas that they had lived with in their homeland. Second, Canadians after all live in North America. They are British North Americans to be sure, but it is not surprising that they have sometimes reacted to their environment in a manner similar to their neighbours.

Moreover Canada has never been a closed intellectual circuit. Ideas which have been in the air elsewhere have found their adherents here. The writings of Lord Keynes and Sir William Beveridge influenced the way that Canadian Liberals thought about the state's role. The New Deal of President Roosevelt, the nostalgic radicalism of Barry Goldwater and the social conscience of the British Conservative Party have all made an impact on segments of the Conservative Party. Many of the leaders and theorists of Canadian socialism like Woodsworth, M. J. Coldwell and David Lewis were either born or educated in England; and the eyes of many CCFers were on the revision of socialist doctrine that the British Labour Party was carrying out in the mid 1950's. The lessons they drew were applied to the development of the doctrine of the New Democratic Party when it was founded in 1961.

This influence cannot be exaggerated. Canadians since the founding of New France have thought for themselves and have adapted to their own circumstances what they chose to borrow. To assert a similarity between, say, American conservatism and the ideology of a Canadian political party which also bears the name "conservative" is to be deceived by the primitive magic of names. As an approach it begs the question. We can only understand our political doctrines if we read the speeches of Canadian politicians and the platforms of Canadian political parties. We will never understand ourselves if we persist in turning our eyes across a border or an ocean.

Even if we accept that Canada has developed a unique set of ideologies, there is one further trap that must be avoided. We must be wary of becoming overly fascinated with external contrasts. There is a danger that if we concentrate too much on the differences between our ideologies and those of other countries we will gloss over the differences between them within Canada in the hope of making the contrast all the more striking. Indeed the brunt of our argument is that the ideological conflict within Canada is precisely what makes our politics unique.

Our point is brought out by the following illustration.[5] Suppose we are presented with a family photograph of ten members of the Churchill family. We notice that all its members bear a striking resemblance one to another. Our curiosity is aroused and we proceed to divide their faces up into ten of the most distinctive components (forehead, eyes, nose, etc.); from this investigation we draw up a comparative profile of all ten. On analysis we come to the conclusion that "no *two* members of the Churchill family need have any feature in common" for us to be able to say that all these "members of the Churchill family have the Churchill face".[6] Yet we would want to make two observations. First, it makes sense to talk about them as a family, because of the resemblance between the members. Second, we can intelligibly compare members of the Churchill family to non-members with the expectation of making a real comparison.

To approach Canadian political theory in this way, and to take seriously the integrity and coherence of Canadian political ideas, leads to valuable insights. Instead of beginning the analysis by a comparison of Canadian ideologies to their counterparts in other cultures or political traditions, it is appropriate to bring them together for a family photograph. When we do this — as this book sets out to do — we will note striking family features. Liberalism stands out as the least like the others. It is an individualist doctrine which attempts to expand liberty; but individualism was a major idea in nineteenth-century Canada, and it is not surprising to find that political conservatism in this country, which also took root in the mid-ninteenth century shares this individualism. Yet Canadian conservatism is also tory in its nature; which means that it is collectivist and hierarchical. Beside the tory we can see the socialist, sharing the former's collectivism, yet rejecting his defence of property and privilege, and preferring instead to pursue greater equality. And all can, for their varied reasons, be induced, if the circumstances are right, to agree with the nationalist that foreign domination is a dangerous threat. Yet nationalism's collectivism is often closer to the socialist conception of the composition of society than it is to the more individualist assumptions of either liberalism or, to a lesser extent, conservatism.

When these ideas are melded together, the resultant mixture is rarely thoroughly consistent. Yet each ideology takes on an increased identity. Conservatism, liberalism, socialism and nationalism share many similar core ideas, but the ideas, consistent or not, that they put them beside, create important, though at times subtle, nuances. The interaction of ideas, for example, suggests that a conservative and a socialist nationalist will have different understandings of the nation. Yet unless we were involved in a doctrinal squabble, we would be happy to describe them both as nationalists.

Once we have understood the similarities and differences, it might then be useful and illuminating to compare them with more distant relations. The fact which seems to have been neglected in previous treatments is that the four doctrines in question, although they are members of the same family, are not the same individuals. Although we could devise a composite photograph which has all the family characteristics, it is not true that this amalgam is more real than any of the actual features of which it is composed. It is possible to present a description which would take in all the main features which the rival ideologies hold in common and present this as evidence that there is no ideological division within Canada. To do so, however, is to fail to understand that there are two kinds of ideology operating in any political community.[7]

One is a type of ideology which expresses itself in the actual operating institutions. It is this kind of hidden wisdom which Edmund Burke exalted when he indicated that he would like to see political theory be derived from the constitution, rather than be imposed upon it.[8] If such a society is coherent — if it is operating to the satisfaction of its members who indicate this by showing neither a disposition to alter it in any fundamental way, or even a desire to offer comprehensive theories about the way in which it works — then the ideologies derived from it will be incomplete doctrines, mere expressions of salient features. The full theory will be contained in the actual functioning of the institutions, and will not need to be extracted. It is this particular kind of ideology which Canadian writers have emphasized implicitly in their studies of Canadian political thought.

A second kind of ideology is also present. This is the sort of doctrine which Michael Oakeshott describes as a "political crib". He argues that an ideology is "an abstract principle, or set of related abstract principles, which has been independently premeditated. It supplies in advance of the activity of attending to the arrangements of a society a formulated end to be pursued, and in so doing it provides a means of distinguishing between those desires which ought to be encouraged and those which ought to be suppressed or redirected".[9] As an illustration he compares an ideology to a scientific theory or hypothesis, which he suggests is not "a self-generated bright idea", but rather one which is heavily dependent on "the traditions of scientific inquiry from which it was abstracted".[10]

It could be suggested that ideologies are to politics what the drama critic is to a play, the performance of which he is evaluating. He extracts from the actual play the principles which he considers makes it successful drama, or which point to its failure. The canons of criticism, however, are not ideas independent of previous theatrical performances, but are the enduring central ideas of a tradition of dramatic writing. It may be possible to set them down in abstract form, as Aristotle does with the unities in his *Poetics,* but this abstraction remains dependent upon the actual practice of drama which preceded it.[11]

To return to Oakeshott's formulation, "a political ideology must be understood, not as an independently premeditated beginning for political activity, but as knowledge (abstract and generalized) of a concrete manner of attending to the arrangements of a society".[12] An ideology can be *indigenous* or *exogenous.* John Locke's *Second Treatise of Civil Government* was a classic example of both kinds of ideology. It was indigenous as "a brilliant abridgment of the political habits of Englishmen".[13] Locke took as his starting point the considerable success that seventeenth-century Englishmen had achieved in developing a working system of government that secured liberty for the subject by placing limits on the power and authority of the government; and the Revolution of 1688 and the subsequent Whig Settlement had firmly established this mode of politics. Locke's tardily published study provided a systematic handbook of inestimable value to later English writers whose task it was to formulate the application of traditional principles to situations unforeseen in 1690.

However, once Locke had set down his ideas in a form which *purported* to be a universally valid explanation of politics, it was open to thinkers in other countries to appropriate them, and attempt to apply them as exogenous theories to their own different situations. Thus, first the American, and then the French Revolutionaries in the late eighteenth century devised their *Bills of Rights* and *Rights of Man.* These documents appeared on the surface to be independently premeditated but in fact they owed a substantial debt to Locke's earlier formulations. Indeed, Locke's abridgement of the political practice of seventeenth-century England has not been without its influence in Canada, though it has had a good deal of company in recent years. Ideas for reorganizing our political life drawn from the experience of countries as diverse as Sweden, the United States and Communist China have been pressed on us by one group or another.

An ideology does not need to originate in political activity. Men can abstract from the practice of war, religion, or as Oakeshott believes Marx had done, from the conduct of industry. Ideologies have a certain usefulness to the extent that they highlight particular features of a country's political tradition and thus serve an educational function. However, as a guide or blueprint to the functioning or direction of a whole society they are quite deficient. For since they present or lay stress on only a few strands ("intimations") of a political tradition, they are apt to be seriously misleading. Curiously enough, Oakeshott's view of ideology as derivative of some concrete activity is similar to the Marxist view of ideology as merely a reflection of a particular set of economic or productive relationships. So Marx puts it in *The German Ideology:* "Men are the producers of their conceptions, ideas, etc. — real, active men, as they are conditioned by a definite development of their productive forces and of the intercourse corresponding to these, up to its highest forms. Consciousness can never be anything else than conscious existence, and the existence of men is their actual life-process."[14] Thus the Marxists see particular ideologies as the abstract expression or rationalization of the economic position of a particular group in society; and the dominant ideology at any point, the expression of the class interest of the ruling class, in the guise of the general interest of all.[15] The problem with Marx's own view, of course, is that ultimately it is itself uncommonly similar to ideology — an abstraction from a limited form of human activity, economic production, applied without reserve to all human activity.

Ideology need not, however, be wholly derived from an activity or practice; it could also come from thought or reflection — from philosophy. Thus, as we shall see below, Kedourie maintains that nationalism, for example, has its roots in certain philosophical notions about the nature of moral behaviour and of the state, ideas which were not formulated for any practical applications, but were dragged as it were into the political arena with the passage of "events which invested the philosophical issues with immediate and obvious relevance".[16]

Can we now come to an adequate understanding of the nature and role of ideologies?[17] We shall define an ideology thus. It is a doctrine or a set of ideas which purports to provide a comprehensive explanation of political arrangements. It will seek either to justify an existing state of affairs, and hence preserve it from change; or else it will seek to reveal inadequacies in the arrangements and consequently sketch the details of the new political system which will replace the old one. To this extent, ideology differs from social criticism, which is content to point out incoherencies, injustices, miseries and the like, without attempting to formulate solutions or new social orders. Ideologies provide model understandings of politics which facilitate attacks on or defence of existing institutions by analyzing the totality in terms of concepts such as liberty, equality, privilege or the collectivity, or activities — religious, economic, cultural — which have played a noticeably important role in the political tradition of the community, or in some other community with which the first has close intellectual ties.

Ideology will attempt to abridge the political practices of the community in conformity with the organizing central ideas. If these central ideas have been historically important to a segment of the community, they will, if a crisis of some sort leads to dissatisfaction with the existing political organization, provide an immediately appealing and familiar guide to the nature of the crisis and the outlines of a possible solution. For example, the farmers in Western Canada had long practised co-operation in the rough and isolated frontier communities in which they lived. This aspect of their life could be seen not only in their projects of mutual self-help, but also in such institutions as the communally organized telephone services. They also had a rough sense of equality as a consequence of the agricultural organization of the prairie wheat economy, consequent on the government's policy of offering equal plots of land to all settlers. As a consequence, when these farmers, among others, were faced with the droughts and the ruinous decline of agricultural prices in the depression of the 1930's, they were open to the proposals for regeneration put forward when the Cooperative Commonwealth Federation was founded in 1932. The collectivism and egalitarianism of that movement's socialism could not help but appear as sound principles upon which to re-establish the country's political life. Further west, in Alberta, the Depression further increased the collective sense that Albertans were oppressed by the operation of the Eastern financial system. The doctrines of Social Credit pointed out solutions to these grievances, and Albertans dutifully returned fifteen Social Credit MP's in 1935.

An ideology also serves to narrow the range of relevant social and political information. As European politics became increasingly democratic from the middle of the eighteenth century on, reformers there began to indict existing governments for their complexity. They claimed that governments were unnecessarily confusing to the common man, and that this gothicity only served to allow rulers to impose on the ignorance of the people. Complexity, they felt, led to quietism; it was critical to establish a new way of looking at politics, stemming from certain simple principles easily comprehensible even to the uneducated. Ideologies then were born, in order to establish which political institutions and beliefs were valuable, and which could be discarded. The organizing ideas, whether they were collectivism, privilege, equality, liberty, or any other, were set to their task of purification and simplification.

New modes of argument arose, and old ones were discarded. Arguments from religious practice were, for example, mandatory in the seventeenth century, and continued to be useful even in the nineteenth. Yet they are no longer accorded much tolerance in the face of the modern secular ideologies. The impatience and hostility shown to sects such as the Doukhobors and the Hutterites stems partly from the fact that these groups are unable or unwilling to defend their practices according to the rhetoric of the present age.

That ideology narrows the range of conceptualization can be illustrated by considering Canadian Liberalism. Although the Liberal Party has, for most of the century, enjoyed the overwhelming political support of the people of Quebec, it has not been the agent of their nationalistic aspirations. Liberalism, concerned as it is with liberty and with the conditions which permit its exercise, is little interested in the nation as a collectivity. There are two main ways in which the liberal can become a nationalist. First, nations under foreign control can be seen to suffer from a diminution of their national liberty. It was therefore the goal of Liberal governments to eliminate all traces of colonial subordination to the imperial centre. Second, the nation may be given credit, under certain circumstances, for fostering independent attitudes of mind, or because it is well organized as a productive unit, and produces a satisfactory economic condition of life for its members.

Quebec's nationalism is not conveniently analyzed under these rubrics. In the first place, the "foreign oppressors" from the Quebec nationalists' point of view have been, for the greater part of this century, the Liberals themselves. Yet Liberalism, like equity, makes no man a slave. Second, modern Liberals are sceptical about whether even Canada itself is a rational economic unit. A fortiori, Quebecers cannot be rationally calculating their best advantage when they contemplate going it alone.

An ideology settles such important matters because it provides answers to fundamental questions; or perhaps even more important, it establishes what questions shall be treated as fundamental. First, what are the basic units of which society is composed: individuals or nations; equal or privileged men; Christians or a secular proletariat? Second, what is the relationship between these units, or within them: Do men compete, or do they co-operate? are all men to have equal opportunities to achieve wealth and other forms of success, or are certain types of men allowed either an advantage or sole access? Third, what questions are acceptable about such a polity, and what techniques are allowed in answering them? In other words, what are the limits of thought and speculation? When does criticism become treason? When does religious freedom verge on blasphemy? Are these doctrinal questions, to be settled by reference to a text, such as the works of Marx, Lenin, or Mao; or are they questions to be settled mainly by more empirical, utilitarian standards?

An ideology which contains these elements will gain adherents and respectability if it is more successful than its competitors in advancing the cause of a sizeable group in society which had previously felt confused, puzzled or disoriented, especially if its economic or social position had been declining relative to other groups within society, or relative to other nations. To gain acceptance, an ideology does not have to be novel or unprecedented. The contrary is probably true. The more familiar it *seems*, the more effective it is likely to be. What is most effective is an old organizing idea put to a new use, or put to use in novel circumstances. Thus Social Credit was successful in Alberta, partly because it could harness the religious enthusiasm which Aberhart had developed through the Calgary Prophetic Bible Institute. The expectation of religious salvation through a belief in the Bible was transmuted into a belief in the efficacy of economic rehabilitation through the doctrines of A + B.

The choice between rival ideological understandings is "a choice between incompatible modes of community life".[18] Ideological changes are rare events. It is not often that a man who shared a liberal vision of society will become a nationalist, though we will argue in the next chapter that certain ideologies, such as conservatism and socialism have closer affinities one with another than either do with liberalism. To reject one ideology without adhering to another is a serious matter; it is, in effect, to abandon all hope of influencing political developments. Men co-operate in politics because they have certain strains in their ideological vision activated by skilful leaders. But a man who merely despairs gives up politics. Aberhart did not counsel his followers to await the millenium and abandon politics. He advised them in the first instance to influence the old parties, and later to found one of their own. The founders of the CCF did more than demand the eradication of capitalism; they offered a programme that would lead to the establishment of the co-operative commonwealth. Pierre Vallières went further than mere condemnation of the society in which he was raised; he sketched the outlines of a new and vital social organization which he promised to the people of Quebec.

The process through which men convert from one ideology to another is a difficult one. The eccentric American political theorist, Eric Hoffer, has suggested[19] that it is a phenomenon analogous to a religious conversion. This is a wise observation, because just as the latter change involves the replacement of one set of metaphysical and theological presuppositions for another, so does an ideological shift entail the replacement of one set of social and political beliefs for another. It was one of Burke's greatest insights to realize that this process cannot happen often. What he described as the "capital of nations and ages" involved both the concepts and institutions of society. In the intermediate stages of a revolution, existing institutions lose their validity and new ones have not arisen or been created. The vigour and creativity of the society is disorganized and diffused; and much social energy has to be spent in creating new institutions, rather than getting on with the business of living.

Because the change from one ideology to another involves a fundamental change in the understanding of society, and how it should be organized, the process of conversion can never be a strictly rational one. Nothing can be compared because the two visions are fundamentally incomparable. Rather all competing ideologies offer their own standards of evaluation; each, of course, coming off best according to its own lights. Thus a man whose own ideology has proven unsatisfactory, or ineffective, might accept a rival explanation of politics. Once he has done so, he will be able to understand, retrospectively, certain inadequacies in his former approach. Thus it was to be expected that Pierre Vallières' *L'Urgence de Choisir,* written after he had repudiated the FLQ and its terrorist road to independence for Quebec, would more or less satisfy the criteria that it dictated for itself; needless to say, it fell short of satisfying some of the criteria of men such as Charles Gagnon who remained loyal to the ideology Vallières formerly held. Vallières' arguments were unlikely to *convince* his old comrades, although his *example* might have shaken some of their convictions extensively enough for them to adopt his new course.

This effect was less likely in the case of the FLQ, since that organization was doctrinaire. However, adherents to less systematic ideologies often ally within one political party because thereby they reinforce their beliefs. The policy conferences which the Liberals and the Conservatives hold irregularly, or the NDP more systematically, help to provide a sense of community for those who share roughly similar viewpoints. The separate Waffle caucus in the NDP was more than just a symbol of the divisions within that party over doctrine. It was a manifestation of an ideological split, and it was also a means whereby that split could have been perpetuated.

Again it was Burke's insight to realize that political parties were most satisfactorily organized around men who were agreed on the common priciples by which they intended to promote the national interest. Political parties also provide useful means, where there is a degree of prior ideological agreement, of developing policies or programmes. These are the means of making the word flesh and can be used to show how the particular ideological understanding can give guidance in identifying and offering solutions for the important problems of the moment.

We do not intend to argue that the major political parties in Canada have ever been captured by one doctrinaire ideological point of view. Usually the choice between the Liberals and Conservatives has not been clear, due partly to their substantial agreement on many important values. Even the NDP and its predecessor, the CCF, have provided a home for a diversity of ideological positions, of which liberalism has, historically, been almost as important as socialism. This observation does not detract from our argument that there has been a conversation of ideologies in Canada and that this diversity has been a valuable source of new ideas about the Canadian polity which open up a wider range of political options than is available in a single-ideology country. Indeed when the complaint is raised that Canadian politics are monotonous or boring, the objection would more accurately be aimed at the monologue which occurs when liberalism attains such a dominant position that it no longer has to listen to its rivals.

However useful ideologies are in political discussion, they do have their weaknesses. Our position in this book is neither for nor against ideologies; we believe in their limited value, but we are fearful when they threaten to become the sole mode for understanding politics. Let us then look at some of the deficiencies of the ideological understanding.

An ideology can isolate a political group from many urgent problems that are either ignored by the ideology or for which the ideology cannot provide what is in its own terms an acceptable answer. We touched earlier on the problems that Canadian Liberalism has with Quebec nationalism. It lacks the conceptual category of a cultural nation, in the first place. In this respect Pierre Trudeau shares with John Diefenbaker the belief that the grievance felt by French Canadians arises because as individuals (unhyphenated Canadians) they have been denied the right to use their mother tongue. If the problem is identified in this way then bilingual cheques and bilingual civil servants are an adequate answer according to Liberal criteria, though they are totally inadequate by the collectivist principles the nationalist holds dear. The right to use the French language is not a powerful moral right belonging to the French-Canadian *nation* that finds its home in Quebec, but rather a utilitarian convenience which the state should provide for Francophone individuals on a utilitarian basis wherever there is a sufficient concentration of them to make the expense not unjustifiably large.

Canadian Conservatism also reveals certain critical inadequacies in this area which we are using as an example. The conservative disposition to resist systematic attempts to displace the holders of privileged positions encouraged some Conservatives to sympathize with civil servants who felt threatened by the Liberal programme designed to foster a bilingual civil service. Moreover the nostalgic aspect of Canadian Conservatism was of British orientation, and they objected vigorously that the increase in the proportion of bilingual civil servants was accompanied by a diminution of the symbols representing the old connection.

Ideology comes to this inadequacy because it is always intent on acting in the world. It is not disinterested, and ideologists take little time for that reflection which Michael Oakeshott said ought to be "without presupposition, reservation, arrest or modification".[20] Ideologies are not adhered to for their own sake, but rather for some practical end. Marx said in his *Theses on Feuerbach* that previous philosophers had only interpreted the world; the point was to change it. This Marxist attitude, which is widely prevalent in the modern world, is not an expression of a philosophical disposition to understanding for its own sake, but is preoccupied with action. Perhaps we can better interpret Marx if we read him as saying that previously men had been philosophers and now they should become ideologists — but that is an entirely different point.

The second weakness of ideology is that it tends to be rather smug and self-satisfied. It takes itself very seriously, and more dangerously, it takes at face value its own claim to be a satisfactory account of political experience. A more satisfactory understanding of politics is more tentative — and more ambitious. It will attempt to encompass all aspects of political experience, leaving nothing that is politically significant or politically relevant out of its explanation of the totality of political experience. It may be objected that such an enterprise is frightening in both its scope and difficulty. There would be justice in this complaint and the enormity of the task helps explain why most men prefer to accept ideologies. But nothing less than this constant intellectual dissatisfaction can lead to a philosophically gratifying understanding of politics. For this, among other reasons, politics is not really an activity for the young. Plato recognized this fact in his *Republic* with his insistence that the potential ruler undertake a long, arduous process of formal education and experience before he would be deemed fit to rule in the state. Nor is this requirement limited to classical political thought. Both the Canadian and American constitutions insist that members of the Senate shall be at least thirty years old, and the American constitution goes on to specify an even higher age for the chief executive officer of the state. Ideology is the short cut that busy or lazy men take to avoid the rigours of philosophy; but one must be clear that it is partial, that it is an arrest in experience.

The third weakness of ideology is that it is not sufficiently self critical. "Truth" in the words of Francis Bacon, Lord Verulam, "comes more easily out of error than confusion." What may be true for truth is not necessarily so for action. "[P]art of the task of political theory is to clarify concepts, to engage in analysis and make distinctions."[21] Ideologies purport to make direct sense out of the empirical world. They rarely engage in the second order activity in which philosophy excels — that of making a world of ideas increasingly more coherent. The philosopher thinking about thought is not an expert, and political philosophy is not a discipline or training which suits anyone to offer advice on weighty political problems. A political philosopher is not specifically trained to take part in the world of practical activity. Because of this, the philosopher is not prepared by his study alone to "advise the Prince". As Hegel wrote in 1820:

> One word more about giving instruction as to what the world ought to be. Philosophy in any case always comes on the scene too late to give it. As the thought of the world, it appears only when actuality is already there cut and dried after its process of formulation has been completed. The teaching of the concept, which is also history's inescapable lesson, is that it is only when actuality is mature that the ideal first appears over against the real world in its substance and builds it up for itself into the shape of an intellectual realm. When philosophy paints its grey in grey, then has a shape of life grown old. By philosophy's grey in grey it cannot be rejuvenated but only understood. The owl of Minerva spreads its wings only with the falling of the dusk.[22]

The limitation on philosophy as a practical activity, as something "useful" should not be exaggerated. It is no crime not to be a prophet; it is a great crime to offer oneself as a prophet and to turn out to be a false one. Even though philosophy offers no special insights into the future, there is a lot to be said for studying politics in this manner. As a modern writer has put it: "For in the theatre of politics, the political philosopher is a kind of dramatic critic. He may grow fretful in the stalls and yearn to mount the stage himself, but just as critics are notoriously bad actors, so philosophers make wretched politicians. . . ."[23]

The job of the political philosopher is, then, to sit reflectively in the audience, watching the political actors. (The metaphor is to be taken seriously, because politicians, like stage actors, put on performances, some of which are good, some mediocre and some very bad indeed.) When he hears a politician finish a defence of the special interests of farmers, fishermen, manufacturers or French Canadians, with the assertion, "And that's my philosophy!", he is quick to respond, "if that's a philosophy, it is a shamefully inadequate one." It would be naive to imagine that politicians deliver every speech in terror of the judgments of political science departments across the country; the influence of academics is more diffuse and less direct. But a book such as George Grant's analysis of the problems of Canadian sovereignty, *Lament for a Nation,* has had a powerful impact because it caught the attention of the opinion reflectors, who in turn transmitted these arguments to the public at large.

But as arguments become summarized and simplified, they become a new ideology, or are added to an old one. They become new weapons in the political battle. Philosophy can always be corrupted or abridged into ideology, but the philosopher must always be there to make sure that somewhere the unsullied philosophic understanding is preserved untarnished. "Without political philosophy politics might well go on as merrily as ever. But the trouble is that it would not be understood, it would be a practice without consciousness of the norms which inform its activity, ignorant even of its own identity or nature. If the day ever comes when political philosophy is really dead, the triumph of information over knowledge will be complete."[24]

Ideologies are to political philosophy what the Readers Digest condensed book is to the original — a pale imitation for the man of affairs. But as Maurice Cranston has observed, one of the many disagreeable features of the twentieth century is that it is an age of dogma; and ideological disputes are to us what religious controversies were to earlier ages, or continue to be in Northern Ireland. Political philosophy has a twofold interest in ideologies. First, ideologies are sometimes corruptions of philosophy, and philosophy has constantly to purify and repurify. Second, ideologies are part of the world of political experience, and as a consequence, if philosophy is going to account comprehensively for *all* the phenomena relevant to an understanding of politics, it has to enfold ideologies in its coherent account of the whole.

What then are we to conclude from all this? It seems likely that ideologies are of complex parentage. If this is so, they may well embody abstractions from both practical activity and from philosophic reflection. This of course does not alter the essentially limited or partial nature of ideologies and the correspondingly constrained view of the world which they present. Nor does it alter the practical nature of ideologies — they are meant to have an effect in and on the course of events. Before we can turn to a description and analysis of the four ideologies we think most important in Canada, we shall turn to consider Canadian ideologies from an historical and social perspective.

[1] Quoted in H. Macquarrie, *A Brief Record of the Progressive Conservative Party of Canada* (n.p., n.d.), p.1.

[2] Daniel Bell, *The End of Ideology*, (Glencoe: Free Press, 1960). P. Laslett, *Politics, Philosophy and Society*, First Series, (Oxford: Basil Blackwell, 1956) p. vii.
See also S. M. Lipset, "Ideology & No End", *Encounter*, XXIX, No. 6. pp.17-22.

[3] Gad Horowitz, "Towards a Democratic Class Struggle," *Agenda 70*, T. Lloyd and J. T. McLeod, eds. (Toronto: University of Toronto Press, 1968) pp. 241-255.

[4] *See, for* example, R. A. Khan, S. A. MacKown, J. D. McNiven, *An Introduction to Political Science*, (Georgetown, Ontario: Irwin-Dorsey, 1972) pp. 340-451.
Also, W. L. White, R. H. Wagenberg, R. C. Nelson, *Introduction to Canadian Politics and Government* (Toronto: Holt, Rinehart & Winston, 1972).

[5] Renford Bambrough, "Universals and Family Resemblances," *Proceedings of the Aristotelian Society*, (1960-61), pp.207-22.

[6] *Ibid.*

[7] S. Wolin, "Paradigms and Political Theory," in *Politics and Experience*, B. C. Parekh and P. King, eds. (Cambridge: Cambridge University Press, 1968), p. 149.

[8] Burke, in *Parliamentary History*, XXIX, (London: 1817), p.1324.

[9] "Political Education," by Michael Oakeshott, in *Rationalism in Politics* by Michael Oakeshott (c) 1962 by Michael Oakeshott, (Methuen & Company Limited, London) (U.S.: Basic Books, Inc. Publishers, New York) p. 116.

[10] *Ibid.*, p. 119

[11] M. W. Cranston, "Politics and Ethics," Inaugural Lecture, mimeo, 26 X 1971.

[12] Oakeshott, p.120.

[13] *Ibid.*, p.121.

[14] Karl Marx, *The German Ideology*, R. Pascal, ed. (New York: International Publishing Co., 1947), p.14.

[15] *Ibid.*, pp.40-41.

[16] E. Kedourie, *Nationalism*, (London: Hutchinson, 1961) p. 10.

[17] Much of the following discussion is indebted to T. S. Kuhn, *The Structure of Scientific Revolutions*, (Chicago: University of Chicago Press, 1962), but since the debt takes the form of a free gloss, rather than a direct borrow-

ing, it will have to suffice here to note the source of inspiration for many of the following ideas.

18 Kuhn, p.93.
19 Eric Hoffer, *The True Believer*, (New York: Harper Bros., 1951).
20 M. Oakeshott, *Experience and Its Modes*, (Cambridge: Cambridge University Press, 1966), p. 2.
21 John Rees, *Equality*, (London: Macmillan, 1971), p.58.
22 G. W. Hegel, *Philosophy of Right*, translated by T. M. Knox, (Oxford: Oxford University Press, 1967), pp.12-13.
23 M. W. Cranston, "Politics & Ethics," Inaugural Lecture, mimeo.
24 *Ibid.*

Chapter II

The Canadian Setting

We have suggested that ideologies present limited or incomplete explanations of politics; and that ideologies can be distinguished one from another in terms of the central or organizing idea or ideas around which each is constructed. Thus concepts such as liberty, equality, privilege, individuality, collectivism or nationality have been used, alone or in tandem, as the focal points of political ideologies. We have further argued that there are four main ideologies to be found in present-day Canada: liberalism, conservatism, socialism and nationalism. Now a number of important questions arise out of this assertion: why, for example, should there be four ideologies? Why not six, or ten? Or perhaps more significantly, why not only one? A satisfactory answer to this raises the further query — why these four in particular? Why not fascism or communism or Maoism? Even when this is disposed of, the relationship of these political ideologies to practical politics in Canada, to political parties and elections is still unclear. We have, for example, a Liberal Party, a Conservative Party, and, in the NDP (in part anyway) a socialist party, but we have no Nationalist Party, though we have politicians of various stripes who call themselves nationalists.

The answers to a good many of these questions are to be found by looking at the past. Our ideologies, like our political parties, or any other part of our political tradition did not first appear in their present form. Rather they developed from the slow marriage of European ideas and the Canadian environment, an environment which at first was almost literally a clean slate, but which became progressively more complicated and sophisticated as the marriage bore fruit. This process of development is similar in its pattern to the theory of Canadian economic development propounded by the Canadian economic historian Harold Innis.[1] He argued that successive waves of European technology acting on the Canadian environment had produced a steadily more sophisticated and distinctive Canadian economic system. Thus the techniques of making felt hats from beaver pelts produced the fur trade, the development of fishing vessels able to cross the Atlantic, and the process of salting cod led to the growth of the fisheries, and in due course the introduction of railway technology made possible the development of the wheatfields of the West.

These are only a few examples, but they are sufficient to make the point that these imported techniques produced over time an increasingly complex and distinctively Canadian economy. The process was cumulative and self-perpetuating; the influence of external developments declined. The growth of railway technology, for example, created conditions which raised demand for iron and steel products sufficiently to warrant the growth of a Canadian steel industry.

A similar process is evident in the history of political ideas in Canada. Successive waves of immigrants brought different political ideas with them. Each has made a contribution to the ideological richness of Canada and on the other ideas with which it co-exists, creating an increasingly complex and distinctively Canadian matrix of political ideas.

This description barely scratches the surface. The difficult question is to establish exactly what political ideas came to our shores, and which of these took root. And this is not a simple question, for the reception of a political idea, in a practical sense, depends not only on its inherent ideal characteristics, but also on contemporary social and economic circumstances. To give an extreme example: Marxist socialism had very little appeal to the predominantly rural and prosperous Ontario of late Victorian times; to the Ontario of the 1930's, increasingly urban and industrial, and stricken by the Great Depression, it was a very real option to many.

To turn then to the "raw materials" of the Canadian political tradition, the European exports of ideas, what we must first realize is that the goods exported represent only a part of the total stock; that is, what we in Canada have received from Europe is only a part of contemporary Europe's political tradition. There are two reasons for this. In the first place, many settlers came to Canada at times when the political ideas of their home countries were in nothing like their present form, from pre-Revolution France or pre-industrial Britain. In the second place, those who chose or were forced to emigrate constituted by no means a perfect microcosm of their home countries. Louis Hartz[2] has made this point well in *The Founding of New Societies*: the new countries thrown off by Europe were only, in ideological terms, "fragments" of their parents. Hartz' argument, in its outline, is that the European countries exhibited a diversity of ideological beliefs which produced a dialectical process of development in their political ideas. In his view Europe entered the modern age dominated by feudal, or in their British form tory, ideas about the nature of society. The tory viewed society as a collective whole, an organic unity, and held that within this whole different groups or classes of people had distinct but harmonious functions. In particular one group, by its education, experience, birth and property, was especially fitted to govern, and all classes in society would prosper if it was allowed to carry out its assigned role. The proper attitude for the rest of society was obedience. This tory ideology directed attention to collectivism (stress on the group rather than the individual) and privilege (rule by those endowed with property and high birth) as the salient features of social and political life.

As new political ideas developed in Europe and were embodied in, and gave form to, the Puritan Revolution and the growth of a capitalist economy, they came into conflict with the older views. Hartz labels these newer ideas "bourgeois" or "liberal" (the more common British term); their distinguishing characteristic was their emphasis on the importance of the individual and the necessity and benefits of individual freedom. Protestant theology exalted the individual nature of the relationship of man to God and downgraded the authority of collective institutions such as the church. Similarly, a capitalist economy encouraged individual enterprise and initiative and rebelled against more collectivist economic organizations like the mediaeval guilds and collectivist economic theories like mercantilism. Politically, liberal individualism found its clearest expression in the writings of Thomas Hobbes and John Locke who were understood to argue that society was essentially an atomistic collection of individuals, and that government was a device to serve primarily individual ends, rather than group or collective ends. Along with this went, in varying degrees, arguments for individual freedom of conscience, expression and so on. Thus, liberalism is characterized by the ideas of individuality and liberty.

Hartz' point is that this new way of looking at politics and society did not supersede or eliminate the older way in Europe but rather came to exist alongside of it. The resulting conflict of ideas was fruitful in at least two respects. First, because neither became completely dominant, and thus able to shut out competition, the way to further development was left open. Second, the stock of "raw materials" for this future growth was that much greater. Out of this conflict developed socialism, the latest major European ideology joining elements of both its warring parents, the collectivism, or concern for the communal or group aspects of human life, of the feudal or tory tradition, and the liberal ideas of individuality and liberty in the form of the idea of equality. Thus, the socialist believes the moral liberty of the individual can only come about not through the liberal expedient of removing external restraints on individual action, but through the positive action of men, acknowledging their fundamental equality and working collectively through the state.

As we have said, Hartz argues that the new societies which developed from European settlement, such as the United States and Canada, did not reproduce in themselves this condition of ideological diversity and consequent process of development. New France was settled at a time when "feudal" or collectivist-hieirarchical views were dominant in France, particularly among the peasants and artisans, from whose ranks the settlers were drawn. Liberal French political thought developed later, after emigration to New France had been stopped by the Conquest, and so the whole process of ideological development was disrupted by the absence of liberal ideas except in an alien, English form.

Hartz' original argument was directed (in *The Liberal Tradition in America*) more specifically to the United States, and is most applicable to it. However, a closer examination of it helps dispel the unfortunate myth that Canadian political ideas are simply a more moderate version of the American. Setting out the American ideological tradition this way facilitates comparison. His conclusion that the United States is a one-ideology country is supported by two main arguments. His first argument is that the early settlers in the American colonies were predominantly liberal or bourgeois in their political beliefs. Indeed, the individualistic and sometimes libertarian views they held about religion and government were often the cause of their departure from a homeland which, in the seventeenth century, was still powerfully affected by tory beliefs. Thus, the society that developed in the United States represented in the main only a "fragment" of its parent — the liberal or bourgeois fragment. Furthermore, such non-liberal elements as were present were driven out at the Revolution or routed in the Civil War — the Tory Loyalists in the former, the quasi-feudal Southern planter aristocracy in the latter.

The second prong of the argument is that ideological uniformity, once achieved, became self-perpetuating by creating a climate of ideological intolerance which repels all foreign ideas. Specifically, liberal ideas of individualism, economic free enterprise and hostility to government initiatives in society or the economy so dominated in the United States that they became identified as an integral part of the American national identity. That is, to be an American came to mean to favour liberal ideas, to accept liberalism as part of the "American Way of Life". Conversely to believe in some other system of political ideas was to reject, in an important area, the United States itself; in short, to be un-American. This, Hartz argues, placed irresistible social pressures on new immigrants to conform to these liberal ideas, and to abandon in particular, both feudal or tory ideas of privilege and socialist collectivism.

Hartz' argument goes a long way to explain the dominance of liberal individualist thought in the contemporary United States, though there are factors, such as the incongruity of privilege or hierarchy in a frontier society, or the immense natural wealth of the country which allowed it to proceed through the early stages of economic growth without great hardship for its citizens, which may also have had their effect. His argument makes intelligible the hostility, verging at times on paranoia, that American society has demonstrated toward socialism, or even milder forms of collectivism. It also explains the desire of the United States to "export" American ideas and institutions to totally dissimilar cultures in the four corners of the globe. These are simply the reaction of a culture which cannot accept non-conforming ideas, or understand why others would willingly do so. The confidence and assertiveness with which this was done, and which Canadians sometimes reproach themselves for not having imitated, reflects the certainty of Americans that no alternative was worth considering. The increasing realization during the twentieth century that others are profoundly different and prefer to remain so has been in many ways a traumatic experience for Americans.

Now what is the importance of this for Canada? Perhaps our starting point should be the attempts of some writers to "export" an unmodified Hartzian explanation of American ideology to Canada and argue that Canada is virtually the same in this respect as the United States. One such is Hartz' collaborator in *The Founding of New Societies,* Kenneth Macrae, who sees Canada as basically uniform in ideology, sharing with the United States a common North American liberalism. Another Canadian historian who likewise stressed the essential sameness of American and Canadian political values was the late F. H. Underhill.[3] Although Underhill was a principal author of the *Regina Manifesto* of 1933, with its call for the eradication of capitalism expressed in Marxist rhetoric, it became evident that the benchmark he preferred for evaluating political change was the reformist capitalism of the Roosevelt New Deal. This essentially continentalist way of thinking about North America is also shared by many Canadian economists, who see

Canada not as a single economic unit, but as a series of regions, each of which is part of a transborder north-south economic unit. Thus, the "natural" economic affinity of the Maritimes is with New England, Ontario and Quebec with New York and the industrial Midwest, the Prairies with the American prairie states, and British Columbia with California.

This continentalist school of thinking about politics, history or economics is opposed by a vigorous nationalist school which concentrates not on those aspects of Canadian life that are shared with the United States but those which are peculiar or distinctive to Canada alone. One of the most important of these is the Canadian relationship to Europe and to European ideas. Thus, we shall look first at a nationalist interpretation of the Hartz thesis. As we have seen, Hartz argued that American society was completely permeated by the ideology of liberal individualism, and the continentalist Macrae extended this judgment to Canada, arguing that it too was a liberal "fragment", though with "minor imperfections". Gad Horowitz' now famous reply[4] was that these flaws or imperfections in the otherwise pure liberalism of Canada were by no means minor or insignificant: they were in fact sufficient to invalidate Macrae's argument and establish a specifically *national* political identity. What then are these flaws or imperfections?

As we have seen, the United States "purified" itself ideologically by escaping or expelling its tory elements in the past, and thus innoculating itself against the development of socialism in more recent times. In Canada, on the contrary, Horowitz saw evidence of significant tory and socialist thinking sufficient to produce a situation of ideological diversity closer to that of Western Europe. That these rivals do not have to dominate or completely displace liberalism is quite clear, for all of the Western nations have strong, and often dominant strains of liberal individualism in their political makeup. What distinguishes the United States is the *exclusive* position of the liberal ideology, and all that is needed to differentiate Canada, certainly in a North American context, is to demonstrate a meaningful ideological diversity.

It is not difficult to find sources for tory ideas in Canadian history. Leaving aside French Canada with which Horowitz does not deal there are the Loyalists who rejected the American Revolution, and the massive wave of British immigration in the nineteenth century. Horowitz' point is that although the people in these groups were by no means unalloyed Tories, they were sufficiently unliberal to produce a different political culture. The evidence Horowitz cites is persuasive:

> Such well-known features of Canadian history as the absence of lawless individualistic-egalitarian American frontier, the preference for Britain rather than the U.S. as a societal model, and generally, the weaker emphasis on social equality, the greater acceptance by individuals of the facts of economic inequality, social stratification, and hierarchy.[5]

This doubtless contributes to the greater willingness of Canadians (compared to Americans) to defer to constituted authority and the value that is placed on the maintenance of order and stability in society (witness the reaction to the October crisis and the proclamation of the *War Measures Act*).

These tory ideas have also contributed to the long-standing Canadian tendency to use the power of government to effect certain common goals or objects; and moreover to use it with equanimity, and often with enthusiasm. This can be seen in a multitude of instances from the railway and canal building of the last century to the initiation of public enterprises such as the CBC, Air Canada, Ontario Hydro and the prairie telephone systems in more recent times.

This difference in attitude is crucial, and cannot simply be explained away, as Macrae attempts to do, by arguing that Canada is smaller and poorer than the United States and cannot indulge itself in fixed principles on this sort of issue. The question of government intervention in economic matters has simply not been a matter for deep heart-searching by Canadians because of a differing set of political values. This is underlined by George Grant's observation that a good deal of such government intervention has been set in train by Conservative governments: (Ontario Hydro, the CNR, the Bank of Canada, and the CBC for instance); for the Conservative Party is the resting place for tory influences, and such action on its part is proof of their existence. Furthermore, it highlights the differences with the United States because American conservatism is so diametrically opposed on this point.

The presence of this tory strain in Canada in turn contributed, in Horowitz' view, to the growth of socialism in Canada, a development which further set us apart from the Americans. This, he argues, might have happened in one of two ways. On the one hand, the existence of a collectivist toryism provided the potential within the Canadian political culture for a collectivist socialism:

> Since toryism is a significant part of the political culture, at least part of the leftist reaction against it will sooner or later be expressed in its own terms, that is in terms of

class interests and the good of the community as a corporate entity (socialism) rather than in terms of the individual and his vicissitudes in the competitive pursuit of happiness (liberalism).[6]

On the other hand, it helped to keep Canada open to imported socialist ideas because through collectivist toryism, socialism had a ready-made point of contact, or introduction to Canadian society. It was not an exotic foreign growth; it "fitted" into the Canadian ideological structure. This was important, because socialist ideas had no such point of reference in the United States; they were, as we have seen, profoundly un-American, and as such were rejected. To become true Americans, immigrants had so to speak, to check their socialist ideas at the Statue of Liberty. In Canada on the other hand socialist ideas were implied, or potentially present, in the existing situation. In addition the fact that liberalism did not reign unchallenged in Canada prevented the sort of identification of ideology and nation that prevailed to the south, and opened the way for fresh developments.

Horowitz attempts to assess the weights of the two factors by using one of the more unfortunate of Hartz' notions, that of the "congealment" of the culture. Hartz argued and Horowitz accepted, that a new society will "congeal" or jell at some point, forming a peculiar national mould which would assimilate all future imports of men and ideas to a fixed national shape. The idea is an obvious reflection of the American experience of an ideologically intolerant and assimilationist society; it is applied uncritically by all the Hartzians to Canada. In fact there is no reason why any society should necessarily "congeal" at any particular point; although when a society is in its formative stages it may be more open to outside influences. We feel that this openness is a matter of degree however, and that while Canada is a good deal more settled in this respect than it was, say in 1825, it is still open to outside ideological influences. This is relevant to our discussion of Canadian socialism because the notion of congealment, as used restrictively by Macrae, tends to rule out any outside ideological influence after the early nineteenth century; and as used more indeterminately by Horowitz means nothing at all. It is best forgotten; the model of development we referred to at the outset is more appropriate to Canada. Excluding cataclysmic changes, succeeding imports of political ideas, like imports of technologies, will probably have lesser effects on a country which has been developing over a long period of time, than on an entirely undeveloped one; but it is unlikely they will have no effects at all. The United States, with the peculiar mechanism it has erected to sift out nonliberal ideas, is distinctly atypical in this respect in the context of the Western world. Thus Canadian socialism has profited not only from the openness of the Canadian political culture to collectivist as well as individualist politics, but from a continuous influx of immigrants, predominantly but by no means exclusively British, bearing collectivist ideas and loyalties, an influx which may well have had as much effect in the 1950's as the 1850's.

It might be useful at this point to sum up what our examination of the Hartz-Horowitz approach has told us about ideologies in Canada. In the first place we have identified three distinct ideological approaches to politics which in one way or another have been available for "export" to Canada: liberalism, organized around the two concepts of individuality and liberty; toryism, built upon collectivism, and hierarchy or privilege; and socialism, sharing the tory's collectivism, but seeking to replace privilege by equality. Second, we have seen that all three have found a place in the Canadian political culture, though not of equal strength. Third, we have seen how this ideological diversity — the existence of tory and socialist elements in a dominant liberalism, sharply distinguishes Canada within North America.

There still remain, however, some important unanswered questions. For example, we have now listed three ideologies, liberalism, socialism, and, the main beneficiary of toryism, conservatism; but is this list exhaustive? In fact, at least one more ideology, nationalism, has had and is having an important effect on Canadian politics and deserves consideration. Nationalism as a consciously thought-out political doctrine is certainly another European import; yet it draws on sentiments which are less coherently expressed and more universal: feelings of patriotism or xenophobia, for example. Nationalism too is less comprehensive in scope than the other ideologies — the number of practical political questions for which it provides answers is certainly smaller than its broader rivals. Consequently, it is almost always found in combination with one of them. A nationalist in Canada is usually a conservative, liberal, or socialist as well; but the reverse does not hold. Thus, looking at nationalism in a study such as this requires a process of abstracting nationalist elements from the wider groups of ideas in which they are found. For instance, the Waffle faction within the NDP claimed to be both nationalist and socialist, and the student of Canadian nationalism must disentangle the two for purposes of analysis.

To be sure, any study of this nature requires this sort of abstraction, for the philosopher's tidy schemes of ideas descend a good deal from their original clarity when they are worked out in practical political life, and for purposes of analysis at least some order and clarity must be restored. This is a particular problem in Canada, because the dominant liberalism pervades most areas of political thought and practice to one degree or another. Indeed, as we remarked before, the pervasiveness of liberalism has led some commentators to lose sight of its competitors, and even to forget that liberalism itself is an ideology. To return to nationalism, it is worth noting briefly the range of nationalist belief and opinion. Nationalism might be provisionally defined as the belief that political boundaries should coincide with the territory occupied by a particular "nationality" or "nation" — in short, belief in the "nation-state" — and nationalist policies seek either to achieve this end, or to protect it once arrived at. There are two important criteria for distinguishing different varieties of nationalist ideas, which grow out of this definition: one is the means of defining the "nation" or "nationality"; the other the depth of commitment to the ultimate nationalist end, the priority which achievement or protection of the nation-state is given in relation to other political ends such as equality or liberty.

What might be called classical European nationalism has defined the nation in terms of linguistic and cultural uniformity and has tended to give the demands of the nation rather than the individual a high priority. English-Canadian nationalism has followed a quite different path. While flirting with the notion of making Canada a unilingual anglophone state for a time in the late nineteenth century, it has steadily moved away from this position in more recent years. For the ideal of linguistic uniformity implied a closer union with one or other of the great English-speaking countries, Britain or the United States, and while both projects had their advocates, Canadian nationalists have at various times rejected both courses of action. On the contrary, nationalists have come to welcome and even to prize Canada's bilingual and multiethnic makeup as a factor which clearly distinguishes Canada from the United States. In any case, the pursuit of linguistic uniformity would disrupt the foundation of the present Canadian state. English Canadian nationalism has therefore rejected language and adopted instead political institutions, culture and more recently economic matters such as ownership of industry and natural resources as the focal points of its concern. It has also differed from European nationalism by giving the demands of the nation a lower priority than individual concerns. This watering-down of the demands of the collectivity, the nation, is not surprising in view of the dominant liberalism of English Canada.

This divergence from the European model has not been so

marked among the more ethnically uniform French minority, and there has been a strong strain of French-Canadian nationalism stressing both linguistic uniformity, and the need to reconstruct the political arrangements of French Canada along linguistic lines. The absence of a strong liberal strain in French Canada has also allowed a higher priority to be given the ends of the French-Canadian nation. Our discussion so far has been largely concerned with the process by which the ideological structure of English-speaking Canada was built up, a process which was made up of successive waves of immigrant-borne ideas, and the effect each new wave had on the existing structure.

Now this is not what happened in Quebec, for, as we noted, the last significant Francophone immigration to Quebec took place before 1760, and bore a single, "feudal" and conservative set of political ideas. Succeeding ideological influences on French-Canadian thinking were foreign or external to French Canada in a way not experienced by the rest of the country. In particular, they were the ideas of a conqueror. This, taken with the fact that these new ideas were heavily liberal and Protestant in nature, and thus repugnant to New France's conservative Catholicism ensured that their reception would not be entirely congenial nor their acceptance assured. Thus, the ideological situation in Quebec was rather more like that in the United States or Latin America than in the rest of Canada, with the close identification of a particular ideology with the society itself, and the consequent intolerance of, and rejection of any differing beliefs. This sort of intolerance has a long history in Quebec, from clerical attempts in the nineteenth century to destroy the free-thinking *Rouges,* to the Duplessis *Padlock Law* of 1937.

However, the attempt by Quebec to close itself off from its different and more diverse partner in British North America was never successful to the same degree as the United States, for Quebec simply did not possess the requisite political and economic power to enforce its wishes in this area. It was forced to tolerate an ideologically alien minority within its borders, and impelled by a mixture of choice and circumstance to enter into a federal union with an alien majority. Quebec was thus unable to escape entirely from the presence of its unwelcome rivals, and a process of ideological development, slower at first and less even in pace, took place.

Liberal ideas entered Quebec in two channels. In the form of economic liberalism, in ideas of individual free enterprise and entrepreneurship, it came with the British and American merchant community that set itself up in Quebec after the Conquest (which in turn was merely an extension or outpost of the burgeoning business liberalism of Britain and English North America).[7] In other words, the conservative, Catholic and rural society of Quebec was brought into much closer contact with the dynamic and secular capitalism of English North America. The predominant response of Quebec was to reject the new ideas and retreat behind the ramparts of tradition into the so-called "siege" or "fortress" mentality. This reaction was in part due to the understandable distaste of a Catholic society for the capitalist ethos, and in part to the differences of attitude and education which made equal participation difficult. In a negative sense this reaction meant a tenacious defence of Quebec's conservative ideology and values, and a refusal to adapt existing institutions such as the church-controlled education system to the new challenge. Thus was perpetuated the long neglect of technical, commercial and scientific education in French Canada. More positively, attempts were made to provide a workable alternative to a commercial and increasingly urban and industrial society by encouraging agriculture and rural settlement, through the colonization movements of the nineteenth and early twentieth centuries, promoted both by church and state.

Political liberalism too fell at first on stony ground in Quebec. The demands of the English minority for representative institutions, granted in 1791, met little francophone response, and the new institutions were used (or abused) by the *Canadiens* for nationalist or conservative ends. The rebellions of 1837 in Upper and Lower Canada are often equated as attempts to bring a greater degree of liberal-democracy into the existing governments. This is a serious over-simplification. Mackenzie and his followers indeed seem to have had this aim but the *Patriotes* were fighting not for self-government *per se,* but for freedom from anglophone rule — the immediate issue in question was merely the occasion presented by circumstances. Somewhat later in the century, the *Rouge* group developed, influenced by European liberalism and sharing to some degree its anticlericalism (though apparently not its religious scepticism). The latter won it the bitter hostility of the church and effectively prevented it from any real political success. Political liberalism only achieved respectability in Quebec with Laurier's repudiation of continental liberalism and its antireligious bias in favour of the more moderate British variety.

In the long run, French Canada was not able to maintain its isolation. George Grant has pointed out[8] the disadvantages of a conservative society defending itself against the dissolvent effects of a dynamic, technologically sophisticated liberal society, and Quebec had the further disadvantage of only possessing the very limited political sovereignty it is granted as a province in the Canadian Confederation. Quebec was able to protect its educational system from technological and liberal values, but it was not able to prevent the expansion of the North American economic system into the province. So, urbanization and industrialization proceeded apace, a process which the French Canadians were not trained to master The result was the anglophone domination of the Quebec economy which is so much an issue today. The people of Quebec had not only lost the battle, but were unable to make the best of their defeat, by seeking the maximum benefit from the victorious system. The frustration resulting from this situation is one cause of the so-called Quiet Revolution of the 1960's and of a good deal of the social and political unrest in Quebec today. The triumph of liberal capitalism forced French Canada to abandon the "feudal" or conservative ideology of the past, at least as the dominant ideology of Quebec in the search for a more effective and comprehensive alternative.

One answer to this dilemma has been to accept and come to terms with the invader; to accept liberal values, and to develop Quebec as a liberal society like the rest of North America. Leading among the advocates of this approach are, understandably, Laurier's heirs in the Liberal Party in both its federal and provincial wings. Intellectual liberals like Trudeau and Pelletier, who argued for liberal ideas and policies against the Duplessis regime from a political wilderness in the 1950's have since come into their own. On a more prosaic level, politicians such as Lesage and Bourassa have attempted to integrate Quebec more effectively into North American capitalism, and enable Quebecers individually to compete on more equal terms, by widespread reforms and new initiatives in a wide variety of government activities, from education, to transportation, hydroelectric, and other economic development.

It is hardly necessary to detail these changes, which are designed to enable the province and its people to participate with the maximum reward in a liberal capitalist economic system. However, if, as we have suggested, liberalism is concerned with the ideas of individuality and liberty, the liberalism of Quebec is by no means the purest of its kind. While anglophone liberals were quick to praise the steps taken in the Quiet Revolution to reduce political corruption, secularize education, stress technical and business training and encourage economic development, they were sometimes shocked by measures which seemed to favour neither individuality nor liberty. Nationalist or separatist policies which favoured a collectivity, the French Canadian *nation,* and government intervention in the economy (the best example, the nationalization of the electricity companies in 1962) which to some seemed to threaten economic liberty. This should not, however, surprise us, for the idea of community or collectivity is, as we have seen, deeply rooted in Quebec's past and has clearly tempered the liberalism imported from the English world. This continuing effect of the past is evident then in both nationalism and socialism in French Canada.

The old conservative or "feudal" ideas continue to exist not only in their effect on liberalism or socialism but in their original form, in the remnants of the Union Nationale, in many aspects of the Créditiste movement, in elements of the Liberal Party and even the Parti Québecois. They are found primarily in attacks on what might loosely be called the permissive society, and support for authority and order in the community. As in the past, this element of conservative thought in Quebec has no real answer to the challenge of economic liberalism. Its economic ideas do not extend beyond more government aid to farmers and small businessmen, a rather simple populism.

That socialism should arise in Quebec in conjunction with, or following upon, the incursions of liberalism and capitalism is hardly surprising from a Hartzian viewpoint. For socialism is the primary collectivist answer to modern industrial society, and Quebec's stock of political ideas includes a strong collectivist element. This collectivism is deeply imbedded in Quebec's institutions: from the earliest days of New France, the government actively intervened on a broad scale in economic affairs; in later years this activity declined, except for promoting colonization, but government action in social and cultural affairs remained. The church, by its nature a collectivist institution, has long encouraged community enterprise, whether in establishing charitable or educational institutions, or in more specifically economic terms, in encouraging land settlement and parish credit unions.[9]

Socialists then have drawn on this collectivist tradition in concluding that state action is the correct response to modern industrial society, and indeed this tradition has affected many liberals. Quebec's collectivist past provided receptive and fruitful soil for socialist ideas once the invasion of liberal capitalism had broken the monopoly of the old conservative ideology. Thus Quebec, like English Canada, has developed a lively, and sometimes explosive ideological diversity, though later in time and with more disruptive results. Indeed, the situation in Quebec is quite outside of any brokerage theory of politics.

Thus, Canada has developed largely by historical accident a system of political ideas distinctive in North America for its variety and diversity. We have looked briefly at the origin and nature of the more important of these in order to place them in this system, to locate these ideas in their Canadian setting. In the chapters that follow we shall examine each in turn by itself and in detail.

One further question might be asked: is this situation of ideological diversity good? It might be objected that, like the division between French and English, it divides and weakens us, and by placing one set of ideas in opposition to another, deprives us of the certainty that fathers decisive action. We are "sicklied o'er with the pale cast of thought" unlike the ubiquitous Americans. The answer of the historian or the patriot to this is simple: the situation is defensible simply because it is specifically *ours;* some other state of affairs might be preferable, but it would not then be Canada. In short, Canada's existence is its own justification. For the philosopher, who cannot take into account such considerations of contingency or sentiment, the justification is different, and we have suggested it already. Ideologies, we have argued, provide only limited or partial views or explanations of reality. The philosopher seeks a view without partiality or limitation, and this is more likely in a situation of ideological diversity, where the competition of ideas points out the weaknesses of each system, and the absence of an exclusive ideology fosters such questioning.

[1] Innis is best known for such works as *The Fur Trade of Canada* (Toronto: The Ryerson Press, 1927), *The Cod Fisheries* (Toronto: The Ryerson Press, 1940), *A History of the Canadian Pacific Railway* (1923), *The Bias of Communication,* and *Empire and Communications* (1950).

[2] *See also* Hartz' *The Liberal Tradition in America* (New York: Harcourt, Brace, Jovanovich, 1955).

[3] *See,* for example, Frank H. Underhill *In Search of Canadian Liberalism* (Toronto: University of Toronto Press, 1960).

[4] Gad Horowitz, *Canadian Labour in Politics,* © University of Toronto Press 1968, Toronto and Buffalo, Chapter 1.

[5] *Ibid,* p. 10.

[6] *Ibid,* p. 16.

[7] For an interesting, if heavily coloured view of this system, *see* Pierre Vallières, *White Niggers of America,* translated by Joan Pinkham, (Toronto: McClelland and Stewart, 1971), pp.123-42.

[8] In George Grant, *Lament For a Nation* (Toronto: McClelland and Stewart, 1965).

[9] The Manifesto of *Le Parti Acadien* (Petit Rocher, N.B.: 1972) in New Brunswick is a classic example of this mixture of traditional collectivism and socialism.

Chapter III

Canadian Liberalism

By the middle of the eighteenth century liberal political ideas had already attained a secure, though perhaps not dominant, place throughout the English-speaking world. The liberal emphasis on individualism — the belief in the primacy of the individual over the collectivity — together with its concern for liberty had already triumphed in the American colonies where it produced the now familiar declarations of liberal principles in defence of the American Rebellion. In Britain liberal ideas were increasing in political influence and were being reinforced by persuasive arguments in favour of economic individualism like Adam Smith's *Wealth of Nations.*

The ideological conversation which now forms an established part of the Canadian political tradition was first begun in this country in 1759. Liberal political and economic ideas entered Canada with Wolfe's army, and were secured by the *Treaty of Paris* which ceded Canada to Britain. Not only did British policy guarantee religious toleration in the new colony, but the pressure from the growing British and American merchant communities in Canada led eventually to the establishment of more liberal political institutions. Although the political ideas that the English-speaking merchants and settlers brought with them in the late eighteenth and early nineteenth centuries were, as Horowitz has argued, not exclusively liberal, they were predominantly so. Even the United Empire Loyalists, as we shall argue in the next chapter, were Tories who had accepted the Whig principles of 1688.

These liberal ideas at once ran against two main obstacles, and with this conflict, liberal politics, whose aim it was to impose a particular ideological understanding on Canada, were born. The first barrier to the realization of liberalism in Canada was external, arising from Canada's colonial subordination to Britain. In particular liberalism was initially checked by the form of colonial administration the British North American colonies enjoyed at the time, which placed executive power in the hands of an appointed governor and council who exercised it without responsibility to an elected assembly. This lack of popular control became increasingly the focus of resentment against the infringements of the liberties of the citizen it created. As a result groups of "Reformers" emerged in the colonial assemblies who sought greater local control of the executive; these men were the first ancestors of the present-day Liberal Party.

The second factor was purely internal: the social, religious and political ideas of the French Canadians. Here, as with the issue of autonomy, a direct ideological clash occurred. The *Canadiens* who, as we have seen, had inherited deeply conservative or feudal ideas, were simply not all that interested in individual liberty. While English-speaking liberals wanted reform to free themselves from impositions of the local oligarchies and the imperial government which hampered individual liberty, such as the attempt to establish the Anglican Church, the French wanted control over the colonial government to protect the collective interests of French Canadians. This goal was often in direct conflict with the individual liberties of English Canadians. For example, the French majority in the Assembly of Lower Canada obstructed efforts by English Canadians to further economic development, which was seen at the time as a pre-eminently liberal endeavour. Also, they peristed in supporting a *de facto* establishment of the Roman Catholic Church, which liberals saw as an infringement of individual Protestant rights and an improper exercise of the functions of the state.

This clash of French social conservatism with English liberalism had already helped to bring about the division of the colony of Quebec in 1791 into Upper and Lower Canada; but this had only partially solved the problem, for an English minority remained in Lower Canada. English liberals were thus placed in a paradoxical situation, for the achievement of the liberal goal of more local self-government would, in Lower Canada, result in the rule of the very nonliberal French. The racial conflict to which these ideological differences contributed came to a violent head in the rebellions of 1837, and resulted in the subsequent mission and *Report* of Lord Durham. The insurrections and Durham's reflections upon them bear examination for the light they shed on the nature and subsequent development of Canadian liberalism, as well as the immediate antecedents of the Liberal Party.

In Durham's view the troubles in Canada had arisen from a fierce ideological struggle between the French on the one hand, an "uninstructed, inactive, unprogressive people" in an "old and stationary society"[1] and the English on the other, representing the "liberal and enlightened movement"[2] of "a new and progressive world".[3] In this conflict the sympathies of Durham, a prominent English liberal, were clearly on the side of the English minority which sought changes in land tenure, and a more comprehensive programme of public works, both of which would give freer rein to the individual initiative and enterprise which the liberal values of the English settlers encouraged.

Durham's aim, in the long run, was to create an ideologically uniform colony. To do so he would have to persuade the imperial government to destroy the profoundly conservative society of Quebec, based as it was on French political, economic and social institutions dating from the settlement of the seventeenth century, which "more than those of any other European nation, [were] calculated to repress the intelligence and freedom of the great mass of the people".[4] Durham was clear that "the sympathies of the friends of reform are naturally enlisted on the side of sound amelioration which the English minority in vain attempted to introduce into the antiquated laws of the Province".[5]

The English "immigrant and enterprising population" had quickly secured a dominant position in the commercial life of the province and a strong position in its agriculture.[6] They naturally[7] sought, according to Durham, a government whose chief business it was "to promote, by all possible use of its legislative and administrative powers, the increase of population and the accumulation of property".[8] But this mercantile orientation of the English conflicted ideologically with the presuppositions of the French who saw Quebec "not as a country to be settled, but as one already settled" and who preferred its government "to guard the interests and feelings of the present race of inhabitants".[9]

If Durham were right that the conservatism of the French Canadians brought them into conflict with "the whole English population",[10] it shows how deeply and widely liberal assumptions were shared by the English population. Faced with a choice between a liberal policy — responsible government — that would only serve to protect and perpetuate a static, nonliberal society, and a nonliberal policy which nonetheless promised liberal ends, the English of Lower Canada unhesitatingly chose the lesser evil and made "common cause with a government which was at issue with the majority on the question of popular rights".[11] Their predicament was all the greater in comparison with the English in Upper Canada, who did not face this ideological division over the nature of society.

Canadians in Upper Canada largely agreed that society should be organized to secure a high degree of individual liberty and enterprise, and the various groups in the Assembly had generally co-operated, in spite of lesser ideological differences, to enact measures directed to this end. Without the distraction of a common ethnic and ideological enemy, Upper Canadians were more concerned with the smaller distinction within the colony between tory and liberal, differences which had been pushed into the background in Lower Canada. These distinctions were not unimportant; on the contrary, they are, as Horowitz argued, the source of a good deal of Canada's ideological diversity. But they must be seen in the context of a strong and persistent undercurrent or substratum of liberalism, a context which the comparison we have just made between the Upper and Lower Canada of Durham's day illustrates clearly. And the presence of liberal ideas in such strength is hardly surprising, given the strength of liberalism in the United States and Britain whence the English-speaking population originated. This liberal substratum gives a distinctive flavour to both conservatism and socialism in this country as we shall argue in some detail when we consider those ideologies. More importantly for our purposes here, it provides the solid foundation for the further development of liberal ideas. For the commitment to individual liberty which is discernible in the English settlers' support for a society which would allow them to employ their initiative and energies to the greatest possible extent, is the main distinguishing mark of the liberal ideology.

The presence of ideological and ethnic conflict in Lower Canada, pushed the English there into an equivocal position, as they opposed the extension of personal liberty in the political sphere, in the form of responsible government, as long as it would place power in the hands of the conservative French majority. In Upper Canada, the existence of a general consensus on economic development allowed more subtle differences to come to the fore, on specifically political issues like the absence of responsible government. A relatively small group, composed of longer-settled and more wealthy residents, and known popularly as the Family Compact, dominated the government, and enjoyed a powerful and privileged position in the colony: "The bench, the magistracy, the high offices of the Episcopal Church, and a great part of the legal profession are filled by the adherents of this party; by grant or purchase, they have acquired nearly the whole of the waste lands of the Province; they are all-powerful in the chartered banks, and, . . . shared among themselves almost exclusively all offices of trust and profit . . . ."[12] The most visible sign of their privileged position was the concerted attempt made to establish the Anglican Church in Upper Canada, endowing it with large tracts of strategically-placed land, the Clergy Reserves.

Many in the colony felt that the possession of such privileges by a minority group constituted a denial of political liberty, for it effectively excluded them from participation in government. Hence their demand that the government should be responsible to the legislature, and thus responsive to the wishes of the majority party. On these grounds, the liberal attack of the Reform Party was mounted, and eventually resulted in the violence of 1837. Despite the attachment of the greater part of the population to the cause of reform, Mackenzie's rebellion was a dismal failure, for there were significant differences among the reformers on the extent to which changes should be made. The more extreme wished to import the American practices of direct election of judges and the executive to increase popular control of, and participation in government, and were willing, like Mackenzie, to resort to rebellion in the last resort.

The greater number took a more moderate position, favouring responsible government on the British model, but wishing neither to imperil the imperial connection by rebellion nor to contribute to the "revolutionizing"[13] of the province by overly radical measures for popular control. They preferred to "assimilate the Government of Upper Canada, in spirit as well as in form, to the Government of England, retaining an executive sufficiently powerful to curb popular excesses, and giving to the majority of the people, or to such of them as the less liberal would trust with political rights, some substantial control over the administration of affairs".[14] George Brown, for example, one of the founders of the Liberal Party, and an important Reform figure from the late 1840's, was bitterly opposed to any extension of American-type radical democracy to Canada. His experience of such measures in New York led him to state that the newspaper he intended to found in Toronto would be "thoroughly conservative"[15], conservative that is by American standards.

This conserative streak has not been uncommon in Canadian liberals, and is undoubtedly one reason why other liberal movements like the Progressives have sprung up outside the Liberal Party, and why some liberals continue to find their political home in the NDP. It is significant that this tory strain was brought largely by British immigrants like Brown or Alexander Mackenzie, men who reflected something of the ideological diversity of British society. Their ideological stance found fertile soil in a land which had attracted so many of their compatriots and which, partly as a consequence, had a strong conservative strain. It illustrates well the impossibility of obtaining a perfect fit between political ideas and political parties in Canada.

The Union of the Canadas in 1841 led to a curious alliance. The Reformers were joined by the mass of conservative French Canadians in an attempt to curb the privileges of the Family Compact and the Chateau Clique, though now as in the 1830's their aims were at ideological opposites. Despite the rhetoric at many a Reform banquet, this alliance necessarily remained a marriage of convenience. The apparent natural allies of the French conservatives, the *Bleus,* were the English Tories; but two factors stood in the way of this coalition. In the first place, the English never entirely lost their suspicions that the French who had rebelled against the Crown were disloyal to the British connection. In the second, they were divided on the question of responsible government. For the English Tories this meant an end to at least some of their privileges, but for the *Bleus* it allowed them to establish their own system of French and Catholic privilege.

As time passed the first of these diminished, and with the accomplishment of responsible government in 1848-1849, the rationale for the alliance of the 1840's was undermined. The early 1850's saw a fundamental re-alignment of political forces that laid the foundations for the present Liberal and Conservative Parties. The question that brought matters to a head was the vexed issue of the separation of church and state. The Reformers viewed state churches as unforgiveable infringements on the liberty of conscience, and supported voluntaryism, the principle that each church or sect should be supported in all its activities solely by the voluntary aid of its adherents.

By 1850 they had largely defeated attempts to establish the Anglican Church in Canada West, when they were faced with a powerful attack from another quarter. Increasing demands from Roman Catholics for various forms of state recognition or assistance were met with warm support from the majority of French Canadian members of the legislature. These demands were for a full scale separate school system in Canada West and for public incorporation of a variety of Catholic bodies and institutions in Canada East. The support for these measures from their erstwhile allies in Canada East was disturbing to many of the Reformers but hardly surprising in view of their conservative and Catholic disposition. What made it particularly galling was that the most contentious issue, that of separate schools in Canada West, was being decided largely by the solid French bloc from Canada East who held a powerful position in the legislature of the United Province. Furthermore, since the seats were divided equally between the two Canadas despite the now superior population of Canada West, the members from Quebec were in a privileged position, and were using it to create yet more privileges for their co-religionists. Thus, to their protests against separate schools, the reformers again took up the cry for political reform, this time in the call for representation by population.

The protest against the domination of the nominally Reform government by the conservative French came first from the more radical reformers from Canada West, the Clear Grits. These included most of the more extreme radicals from 1837, and their agitation for American-style democracy at first alienated Reform members like Brown. However, the strength of the church-state issue was so great that many of the English Reformers, Brown at their head, finally broke with the Reform government. When the crisis surrounding the disintegration of the last Reform government (the Morin-Hincks ministry) in 1854 cleared, a new political configuration had appeared. The conservatives French-Canadian *Bleus* were allied with English conservatives led by John A. Macdonald, and some of the moderate Reformers whose reform aspirations had been satisfied by responsible government. This marked the beginning of the Liberal-Conservative Party, which today exists as the Progressive Conservative Party, whose development we shall follow from this point in Chapter IV.

This was opposed by another coalition, liberal in policy, and soon to be Liberal in name. United by a common commitment to equality of status and opportunity for each individual, expressed in their opposition to any church-state link and support for "Rep. by Pop.", were two unequally matched partners. In Canada West the Clear Grits allied with many of the English Reformers, strongest in Western Ontario, to provide the great bulk of the party's support. Although the initial commitment of the radical Grits to separation of church and state had been vindicated, other aspects of their radicalism had been muted by the influx of Reformers like Brown, who as we have seen, resolutely maintained his opposition to any overly-radical democratic policy. The centrist, middle-of-the-road position established by Brown and his supporters has remained a hallmark of the Liberal Party to this day.

This group from Canada West was joined by English Reformers from Canada East, and a rather different group of French-Canadian radicals, the *Rouges*. These were the descendants of the *Patriotes* of 1837, and Papineau himself for a time was involved in their leadership. Their position in some ways was very similar to that of the radical Clear Grits of Ontario. They favoured much more radical, American-style political reform than Brown, and were also resolutely opposed to any church-state connection.[16] They were very much a minority group in French Canada and were bitterly opposed by the church and a substantial portion of the population. This weakness posed a serious problem for the Liberal Party which was not really solved until Laurier's time.

It would be wrong to suggest that the division of 1854 was entirely a product of ideological differences, for many more pragmatic concerns pressed on men's minds.[17] Nevertheless, we are arguing that clear ideological divisions *did* exist, and that they played an important role in this realignment of parties.

The two main principles on which the liberal ideology was based, the commitment to liberty — freedom from restriction — and the belief in individualism — the desire for a society in which individual initiative, opportunity, and enterprise were given the fullest possible scope — continued to guide Reform politics after 1854. This is particularly evident in their response to the principal question of the day, the constitutional problem in the Province of Canada. The Reformers of Canada West chafed under the rule of Conservative Governments which owed their existence to the support of the *Bleus,* especially when they supported church-state links in the form of separate denominational schools in Canada West.

The repeal of the *Corn Laws* in Britain marked the triumph of early Victorian business liberalism, the principles of which were a strong influence on liberals in Canada. Thus they reacted with alarm at the disturbing tendency of the Conservatives to meddle in economic measures which, by liberal doctrine, ought to have been left to the operation of the natural laws of economics. Reformers thus opposed the sharp increase in protective tariffs in 1859 because it would tend to channel the import trade of Canada West through Montreal, rather than its "natural", and cheaper route through the United States.[18]

Similarly they supported the reciprocity agreement of 1854, and became increasingly anxious in the early 1860's as its future became more doubtful. The liberals in Canada West objected vigorously that this conservative tendency to subordinate economic rationality to politics favoured the sectional interest of Canada East; and more, it was a direct attack on the economic liberties of the inhabitants of the western province. This commitment to *laissez-faire* has continued, in various degrees, and different forms, in the Liberal Party to the present day. Perhaps the most important of these has been the Liberal desire to maintain close economic ties with the United States as the "natural" market for Canadian products.

The Reform platform for the first Dominion elections in 1867 asserted the "duty" of the Canadian people to "cultivate the most friendly relations with the neighbouring people of the United States, and especially to offer every facility for the extension of trade and commerce between the two countries".[19] This continentalist orientation has been checked at times by nationalist forces, to which we shall turn in a later chapter, but has never ceased to occupy an important place in Canadian liberal (and Liberal) thinking.

The Liberal rejection of any comprehensive economic programme (save free trade) for the province was closely connected with rising Liberal sentiment for sectional or local rights, and an increasing aversion to the existing union of the Canadas, which subjected them to the rule of a French-dominated Conservative majority. The initial reaction of the English Reformers to the union had been that of Lord Durham, to assimilate the *Canadiens* and cement the union with cultural and ideological uniformity. Twenty years of experience had taught the Reformers tolerance, or at least convinced them that the French were too tough to swallow, and with this realization, the Liberals abandoned simple political unification[20] as a solution by itself.

Instead, the Liberals sought to dissolve the union of 1841, and replace it with a looser, federal union which would grant its constituent parts autonomy over the local matters. The exact nature of the new union was a matter of some contention in Liberal ranks. There was a strong sectional desire to achieve a maximum amount of provincial independence, particularly to allow the farmers and businessmen of Canada West to exploit the resources of the Hudson's Bay Company's vast landholdings in the Northwest, and the Reform Party was quick to advocate expansion which would enhance the opportunities for individual enterprise and profit. At the same time though, there was a strand of nationalism among Reformers like Brown that provoked the vision of a new continental nation and moderated the demand for decentralization. Thus original Reform demands for only the loosest sort of connection, an amorphous "joint authority"[21] to deal with the matters common to two virtually autonomous states, were modified by the pressure of nationalist and centralist feeling to the point where Brown, at the Quebec Conference in 1864, was virtually in agreement with Macdonald that the provincial governments were to be merely quasi-municipal bodies. The intervention of nationalism, which we shall examine in Chapter VI, and its mixture with Brown's liberalism is but another example of the way in which practical politics tend to be, not unideological, but ideologically fuzzy. The second important point to note in connection with this mixture of liberalism and nationalism, is that the tension between the two has never disappeared from the Liberal Party and potential conflict between them has remained a permanent feature of Liberal politics in Canada.

Thus the actual form of Confederation owed a good deal to the force of Ontario separatism and its political expression in the Liberal Party, which doomed any plans for a centralized legislative union. Indeed, the desires of Quebec for more autonomy, so often cited as an important factor in the making of the Confederation settlement, were as much or more an effect rather than a cause of the British North America Act. As long as most powers were vested in the central government (as in the union of 1841), the French-Canadians had a compelling interest in maintaining their influence in it. This in turn required political accommodation with at least some of the English-speaking, and an effort to moderate, or at least compromise, more extreme sectional demands. When this system broke down, due to the refusal of Western liberals to accept the limitations it imposed on certain of their individual liberties; and separate provincial governments with significant powers were established, the loyalties of the French were given a compelling new focus.

These nationalist or centralist impulses in Canadian Liberalism weakened markedly after 1867, particularly when the party split into Dominion and Provincial wings. The latter were often a powerful stimulus to separatist leanings, as when Oliver Mowat, Liberal Premier of Ontario from 1872 to 1896, led a provincial assault on the Dominion power that substantially changed the intent if not the letter of the original plan of Confederation.

This reassertion of an older Liberal goal after Confederation was, moreover, not an isolated example for federation made remarkably little difference to the goals pursued by Canadian liberalism or the policies of the Liberal Party. Until Laurier's day the party itself remained the same loose grouping of Ontario Grits, and *Rouges,* with only a leaven of Maritime Reformers and anti-Confederates. Its policies retained the same bias towards an individualistic organization of society, and the removal of restraint or restriction on individual liberty. Mackenzie and Blake alike maintained an unyielding opposition to the use of the tariff for any other than revenue purposes, rejecting protection as an unjust restriction on individual liberty. As Blake put it in the 1882 election campaign, "I do not approve of needless restrictions on our liberty of exchanging what we have for what we want, and do not see that any substantial application of the restrictive principle has been or can be, made in favour of the great interests of the mechanic, the laborer, the farmer, the lumberman, the ship-builder, or the fisherman".[22]

This led the Liberals to oppose not only that part of the National Policy dealing with tariffs, but also Macdonald's railway policy. The CPR contract was, to Blake, "improper", "indefensible", and "premature". The political functions and aims of the Canadian Pacific as a means of tying East to West, and securing British Columbia for Canada, were, for the Liberals, subordinate to the economics of the line. The "true policy", said Blake, was to build only the cheaper and more profitable Prairie section at first, "to give value to our lands and a traffic for the road before contracting for the completion of the eastern and western ends".[23]

The growth of large-scale manufacturing in Canada, which the protective policy of the Conservatives both recognized and encouraged, was also disturbing in certain respects for Liberals for it introduced a relatively collectivist from of social organization, the factory and its attendant system of factory discipline, which ran counter to liberal individualism and tended to widen the gap between employer and employed, encouraging class distinctions and conflict. Mackenzie blamed the growth of the "Communistic movement" in certain American centres on protection which he thought tended to impoverish the working classes, while enriching a few manufacturers, thus driving the workers to the conclusion "that the only remedy was an equal distribution of property".[24] Thus, Mackenzie reasoned, interference with the individual's freedom of action through protection eventually produced an equally nonliberal demand to curtail individual freedom by equalizing wealth. This new world of collective action was an unfamiliar one for liberals and eventually required a minor revolution in liberal thinking in the aftermath of the Great War. All this however lay in the future. For the moment, liberals contented themselves with damning protection, and, like Brown and Mackenzie, bitterly opposing collectivist strike action taken by nascent trade unions as limitations on individual liberty. Brown's death at the hands of a disaffected employee was in a sense symbolic.

The early years of Confederation also witnessed one of the periodic eruptions of the Liberal left, neither the first nor the last of its kind. Radical liberalism was not new in Canada — both William Lyon Mackenzie's reform followers in 1837, and the Clear Grits of Canada West in the 1850's had pushed liberal ideas to extremes when they pressed for the complete separation of church and state, for greater colonial freedom and for political reforms designed to make government more fully representative and democratic: "rep. by pop.", the secret ballot and more elective offices. Individual issues such as the church-state question disappeared as time passed, but the underlying attachment to a radical reading of liberal ideas remained, to issue forth in new forms over the years. The great Progressive revolt after the First War was one such; the Canada First movement of the 1870's incorporated significant radical liberal elements. All of them have had important repercussions for Canadian Liberalism, either by swinging the more conservative mainstream of the Liberal Party to the left, or in the formation of new liberal political groups outside the Liberal Party, such as the Progressive Party of the 1920's. This only existed independently for a relatively short time before it was re-absorbed into the Liberal mainstream, but other radical liberal elements have found a permanent political home outside the Liberal Party by allying with labour and socialist groups in the CCF and NDP.

The Canada Firsters never became more than an intellectual pressure group on the fringes of Canadian party politics. Their ideas and policies had no sectional appeal or roots, and Canada by the 1870's was too settled a society to allow any disruption of the party system as it was emerging. The combination of the new society of the Prairies, and the turmoil of war which blessed the Progressives had no parallel for their predecessors in 1874. Nevertheless the movement is of interest for two reasons. In the first place, the Canada Firsters, as their name implied, were nationalists, and made an important contribution to the development of Canadian nationalism. They felt that Canada was ready to have a greater say in its affairs, and resented the restrictions imposed on Canadian liberty by the imperial relationship as it stood at the time. As Edward Blake, close to Canada First in sentiment if not an actual member, put it, Canadians were "four millions of Britons who were not free".[25] The Canada Firsters were by no means agreed ideologically though and the remedies they proposed varied a good deal. The more conservative favoured imperial federation, aiming to raise Canada's status in the world by increasing its influence and autonomy within the empire. These conservative nationalists, seeking greater Canadian participation in imperial affairs, soon parted company with their initial allies of a more liberal disposition, who distrusted imperialism in any form, and sought instead to increase Canadian autonomy by reducing to a minimum Canadian ties or participation in the Empire. Their calls for "independence" for Canada were greeted with open hostility from more conservative, pro-British Liberals like Brown and Mackenzie who feared that Canada was in no position at its current stage of development to stand alone against the United States. In so doing they exposed a significant contradiction in the ideas of the liberal anti-imperialists in Canada First; for it was by no means clear that they had any compelling and genuinely nationalist alternative to the existing situation they criticized.

This contradiction was revealed clearly in the chief intellectual mentor of the anti-imperialists in Canada First, Goldwin Smith. Smith, an expatriate Oxford don living in Toronto, was a thorough-going liberal in all his social, political and economic views. A convinced individualist, he was bitterly opposed to collectivism in any form, whether the remaining vestiges of toryism in Britain, or the rising forces of socialism, sounding the "trumpet of industrial war".[26]

Smith's dogmatic liberalism led him to advocate complete continentalism. He saw Canada as an irrational and unwise creation, because it was founded only on sentiment. The "primary forces", "geography, commerce, identity of race, language, and institutions" were bound to triumph over the meagre forces buttressing a separate Canadian identity.[27] Canada was in his eyes an integral part of the North American liberal and democratic society; it was an "American community",[28] despite the attempts to import feudal institutions like the monarchy from Europe. Only by integrating with the United States could Canada attain "the glorious era of perfect order and civilization".[29] This continentalist outlook was even more strongly expressed in Smith's economic views. Trade ought, and in the long run was bound, to flow without any political interference, and protective tariffs were a "desperate war against nature".[30] Smith supported his *laissez-faire* economic arguments by noting the degree to which Canadian voluntary organizations, businesses, magazines and sports were integrated with their American counterparts, or were under their control and influence. English Canada and the United States were "in a state of economic, intellectual, and social fusion".[31]

Smith doubted that "the four blocks of territory constituting the Dominion can for ever be kept by political agencies united among themselves and separate from their Continent".[32] The problem, which Smith called the Canadian Question, revealed the glaring inadequacies of Smith's liberalism. He had contempt for politics, especially in an ideologically diverse country like Canada in which a number of rival ideological understandings intermingled. He revealed the intolerance that subsequent majority Liberal governments in Canada have displayed to rival ideological voices. His desire was to crush the diversity that Cartier lauded. This hope comes out clearly in his attitude to Quebec. Annexation, as he knew, would speed the elimination of the nonliberal and ideologically unwelcome conservative society of Quebec. Smith understood well the powerful homogenizing capacity of the dynamic, liberal society of the United States: "Nationalities are not so easily ground down in a small community as they are when thrown into the hopper of the mighty American mill."[33]

Smith's importance lay in his ability to carry liberal individualism to its logical end-point untrammelled by the exigencies of practical politics or by nationalist sentiment. While he was able to move from liberal anti-imperialism to continentalism his contemporaries in the Liberal Party were inhibited by sentiment or calculation from going more than part way down the road. The demand for the primacy of economics over politics, seen clearly in Smith's highly pejorative use of "political", and his contrast of the artificiality of political decisions to the naturalness of economic or geographic ones, has remained very important in Liberal thinking. Similarly the demand for greater Canadian autonomy, in terms of separation from Britain and withdrawal from European affairs rather than participation on a basis of greater equality, became a constant theme in Liberal policy, reinforced by isolationist sentiment in Quebec. The line runs unbroken from Smith to Laurier, King and Trudeau.

We have seen how the desire to pursue economic rationality animated Brown and Mackenzie in the 1870's in their efforts to increase trade ties to the south and to sink the National Policy. The goal of greater economic integration with the United States has since been pursued by Laurier in the reciprocity campaigns of 1891 and 1911, by King in the 1938 trade agreement with the United States, by St. Laurent and Howe in the resource export boom of the 1950's, by Pearson in the *Automobile Pact* of 1965, and by the Trudeau government in its original inclination to continental sharing of energy resources. The logical end of such policies, which Smith saw clearly, has either been obscure to, or obscured by, many Liberal politicians. The connection between political unification and continental integration in other areas has never been fully resolved in the Liberal Party, witness the present conflict between the main body of the party and its nationalist wing.

When Laurier came to the Liberal leadership in 1887 the party was still a sectional rather than a national force, based largely in Ontario. Perhaps his greatest political achievement was to broaden the party's support in Quebec, and give it a genuinely national basis. The winning to the Liberal Party of a province which had in no way abandoned its social and religious conservatism at first sight presents difficulties for any account which purports to see certain ideological positions running through Canadian politics. However, it was precisely the liberalism of the party which enabled it to accommodate Quebec until habit and circumstance hardened the mould.

In particular, the Liberal Party had espoused the cause of provincial rights, largely as a result of the liberal demands of Ontarians to be free from the restrictions of a French-dominated government. Initially this stand had no attraction for Quebec; her interests had been well served through her influence in the central government of the united Canadas, and Confederation was in some ways a less satisfactory arrangement than the union of 1841. However, with Confederation, Quebecers were given a choice between a provincial government which they controlled, and a dominion government dominated by the English. When the latter acted against the interests of the French minority, the attraction of the provincial government became irresistible. Such a situation occurred in the aftermath of Riel's rebellions and subsequent execution.

The understandable reaction of Quebec towards the Opposition Liberals was cemented by their ideological commitment to provincial rights. Had not the Liberal platform of 1882 declared that "Our provincial rights are amongst the chief jewels of our constitution; and on their preservation rest the prosperity and the permanence of the Confederation";[34] and that of 1887, called for "full recognition of provincial rights".[35] Even before Laurier became leader, Liberal representation in Quebec had doubled, and the attraction of a French Catholic leader gave the Liberals a majority of seats in the province by the election of 1891.

Liberal success in Quebec was further aided by Laurier's skilful repudiation of the electorally damaging anticlericalism of the old *Rouges*: "They are not Liberals; they are revolutionaries; ... With these men we have nothing in common". Laurier's model was the "great English Liberal party", which was neutral in matters of religion and had indeed championed the cause of Irish Roman Catholics. The anticlerical *Rouges* of the Guibord affair were gone, and with them their programme; "only the principles of the English Liberals"[36] remained. The sins of the *Rouges* were expunged, in the eyes of the average voter, if not of the hierarchy.

Laurier's attachment to provincial rights received its greatest test before he attained the prime ministership, in the Manitoba schools crisis which came to a head in 1896. Despite intense conservative pressure from Quebec, and in particular the Catholic hierarchy, to sanction dominion government intervention to protect the separate schools, Laurier refused. The government, he argued, had "outrageously misinterpreted"[37] the constitution in introducing remedial legislation in disregard of provincial rights. Laurier's victory in 1896, based on a Liberal sweep in Quebec, vindicated his stand, and further lessened the faith of French Canadians in the readiness of the dominion government to protect their rights.

Although Laurier came into conflict with a series of provincial governments seeking to limit or extinguish French language and religious rights, he did not seek to employ the dominion powers of disallowance or intervention to halt such actions. Thus, in 1905, when the new provinces of Alberta and Saskatchewan were being set up, he attempted to provide for separate schools, but backed down in the face of strong territorial disapproval. Even more explosive was the controversy over the infamous Regulation 17[38] in Ontario, particularly as it reached its height in the shadow of the 1917 conscription crisis. Despite this direct attack by Premier Ferguson on French language rights, Laurier refused to counsel dominion intervention: in a speech in Toronto in 1916 he declared himself to be "of the old school of Mowat and Blake, the parent school of Provincial Rights. By that doctrine I stand. The province of Ontario, and the province of Ontario alone, will and shall determine for herself the decision".[39]

The Liberal Party's successful wooing of Quebec was not without its ideological price to the party. Quebec had never shown any sympathy with the free trade principles of liberalism, and the growth of manufacturing in the province under the wing of the National Policy had confirmed the traditional position. Such however was the personal commitment of Laurier and the English section of the party to economic liberalism that this functioned only as a sort of sea-anchor on Liberal economic policy. Neither it, nor the growing importance of protected manufacturing in Ontario brought about any fundamental change in Liberal policy in Laurier's time. He came to the leadership of a party which in 1882 had disapproved of "needless restrictions on our liberty of exchanging what we have for what we want", had rejected the proposition that "any substantial application of the restrictive principle has been, or can be, made in favor of the great interests of the mechanic, the laborer, the farmer, the lumberman ...",[40] and in 1887 had called for "an earnest effort to promote reciprocal trade with the South".[41]

Trade depression in the late 1880's brought forth fresh Liberal demands for freer trade, this time in the form of a continental common market or "commercial union". Sir Richard Cartwright, Laurier's chief lieutenant in Ontario at the time, indicated the lengths to which some Liberals were willing to take their belief in the primacy of economics:

> I have no hesitation in saying frankly that if the United States are willing to deal with us on equitable terms the advantages to both countries, and especially to us, are so great that scarcely any sacrifice is too severe to secure them. I am as averse as any man can be to annexation or to resign our political independence, but I cannot shut my eyes to the facts.[42]

Laurier would not go so far and refused to commit himself to commercial union, preferring the simple elimination of tariff barriers with the United States. The time had come to "show the American people that we are brothers, and to hold out our hands to them",[43] and as Laurier pointed out, to profit from this new attitude: "the hositility which now stains our long frontier will disappear, the barriers which now obstruct trade will be burst open, and trade will pour in along all the avenues from the north to the south and from the south to the north, free, untrammelled and no longer stained by the hues of hostility".[44] The 1891 election was fought and lost by the Liberals on the issue of "unrestricted reciprocity" or all-out free trade short of a common market. The defeat killed the idea of commercial union, but reciprocity persisted, and the party again promised a "fair and liberal reciprocity treaty" in the 1896 elections.

Victory for the Liberals did not bring free trade. The Americans were cool, protectionist elements within the party were opposed, and a growing wave of prosperity blunted criticism of the National Policy. For the time being Laurier maintained the existing protective system but the idea of free trade was not so easily disposed of, and when, in 1910, the American government expressed its sympathy for a new reciprocity scheme, Laurier jumped at it. An agreement was made and put before Parliament where it became the subject of a long and bitter debate, and finally of the 1911 election.

This final attempt of Laurier to realize freer trade with the United States precipitated not only his defeat at the polls and resignation as prime minister, but an ideological split within the Liberal Party. A group of Toronto Liberals, led by Clifford Sifton, a former minister, broke with the party and repudiated reciprocity. This "Revolt of the Eighteen", together with the crushing defeat suffered by the Liberals in Ontario, brought home the degree to which central Canada was bound to protection; a lesson which was not lost on Mackenzie King. The reciprocity campaign of 1911 was the last appearance of simple free trade under Liberal colours. The economic liberalism of the party was to be recast in a rather different form in the future, although the old free trade doctrine itself reappeared for a time in the 1920's with the more radically liberal Progressives.

Laurier's approach to the issue of Canadian autonomy however proved to be more durable than his advocacy of reciprocity. As we have seen, there were two quite different ways of dealing with Canada's status in the world. The negative or isolationist response was to use the increasing strength of Canada to reduce the ties which bound it to the outside world and in particular to Britain.

This was designed to maximize Canadian freedom of action or in-action. Others advocated a more positive use of Canadian power to ensure that Canadian participation in the affairs of the Empire or the world was carried out on a basis of greater equality. This was designed to maximize Canadian influence and promote a different sort of national freedom.

Borden's Conservatives adopted the latter course; Laurier and the Liberal Party chose the former. Canadian Liberals had inherited from English liberalism a hostility to imperialism and colonial sub-ordination and saw imperial ties as an unjustified restriction of their liberty. This alone was not sufficient to produce the attitude of Laurier (and King), for it did not bar a voluntary decision, freely taken by self-governing dominions, for continued close co-operation or even integration within the Empire on a basis of greater equality. Canadian Liberals had also developed a typically North American distrust and sometimes hostility for Europe, which resulted in pressure not only for independence, but isolation. Many liberals, like Goldwin Smith, saw Europe as the home of an old and disreput-able class-ridden society, in sharp contrast to the liberty and egali-tarian promise of the New World.[45] In particular, Europe was seen as a hive of militarism and the worst sort of power politics, a mael-strom which wise colonials did well to avoid.

This attitude was both encouraged and restrained by ethnic loy-alties within the party. French Canadians had few emotional ties to Europe, France included, and tended to be isolationist; but English Canadians, many born in Britain, had strong personal ties which could outweigh the strictly liberal view. This created continuous tension within the party, and split it entirely in 1917; but in the long run the declining power and prestige of Britain, and the trau-matic experience of the Great War tipped the scales in favour of isolation.

In the early years of his regime, Laurier faced strong pressure both in Canada and from Britain for "Imperial Federation", closer association with Britain and the Empire on some unspecified basis of greater colonial participation. For a brief period in 1897 Laurier showed some sympathy for the idea[46] but when the question of Canadian participation in the Boer War arose Laurier was at pains to disavow any commitment to a common imperial policy: "I claim for Canada this, that in future she shall be at liberty to act or not act, to interfere or not interfere, to do just as she pleases".[47] At the Colonial Conference of 1902, he put his objections to a com-mon or co-ordinated imperial foreign and defence policy in terms of the frequent liberal aversion to Europe's ills: "There is a school in England and in Canada ... which wants to bring Canada into the vortex of militarism which is the curse and blight of Europe. I am not prepared to endorse any such policy".[48]

As the possibility of a general European war increased, the question of the nature of Canadian participation arose. Laurier's autonomist position was demonstrated in the *Naval Service Bill* of 1910 which provided for the establishment over several years of a separate Canadian naval force rather than an immediate contribution to the Royal Navy balanced by a larger share in imperial decision-making. The isolationism which underlay Laurier's stand was off-set during the war, among English Liberals by a wave of patriotic fervour. While for Laurier, and some English Liberals, the contribution that conscription might make to Canada's overseas commitments and interests was simply not worth the price in terms of domestic unity, many English Liberals thought otherwise, and the party temporarily split in 1917. Thus Laurier entered politics in a predominantly English Liberal Party, and left at the head of a largely French parliamentary faction.

When Mackenzie King succeeded to the Liberal leadership in 1919, he inherited a party divided not only by race and language, but also by a revolt of liberal radicalism in the period after 1918 which the Liberal Party was unable to contain. The election of 1921 brought sixty-four Progressive members to parliament, from all provinces except Quebec, Prince Edward Island and Nova Scotia, and revealed the seriousness of the ideological fragmentation. Party splits were not a new thing; Henri Bourassa had led a nationalist secession from the Liberals twenty years before, but it had not survived 1921, for nationalism by itself is not a sufficiently comprehensive ideology to sustain a continuing political party. Liberalism is more comprehensive however, and those Progressives who rejected King's blandishments to return to the Liberal fold later carried elements of their radical ideology into both the CCF and Social Credit parties.

Progressivism was an agrarian movement, and strongest in the West, though it enjoyed a good deal of support in the old Clear Grit areas of Western Ontario. Its roots can be traced to an American farmer organization, the Grange, which began to organize in Canada in the 1870's, at much the same time as trade unions were beginning to organize the workers. Much of the sentiment in favour of these farmers' movements was of a radically liberal sort. J. W. Dafoe expressed this attitude when he wrote in 1911:

> I should be very well content to see the Liberal party
> remain in opposition for the next fifteen or twenty years,
> if it will devote itself to advocating real Liberal views
> and building up a party which, when it again takes of-

fice, will be able to carry out a programme without regard to the desires and feelings of the privileged classes.[49]

W. L. Morton spoke in terms of the "search for such a purged and
radical Liberal party", though curiously he goes on to argue that
such a party would be a "sectional third party"[50] rather than an
explicitly ideological one. There were three main elements in the
thought of these forerunners of the Progressive movement: "faith in
democracy, hatred of corporate wealth, and distrust of the political
system".[51] Each of these elements was significant, but the ideology
as a whole contained contradictory elements.

First, their faith in democracy entailed a collectivist view of the
people. They viewed men primarily as co-operators, not as competitors. It was for the people as a whole to speak with a single voice
through such techniques as the initiative, the referendum and the
recall. The political system as a whole could not be trusted because
the members of Parliament spoke as individuals, and were susceptible to the corruption of the Eastern financiers and corporations.

On the other hand, their hatred of corporate wealth was not
based on envy; nor was it an expression of a dislike for privilege in
itself. The privilege of the Eastern interests was objected to, not
because it was inherently wrong, but rather because it oppressed
the farmers, because it imposed limitations on their freedom. As
R. C. Henders, president of the Manitoba Grain Growers Association put it in 1912:

> We are governed by an elective aristocracy, which in its
> turn is largely governed by an aristocracy of wealth. Be-
> hind the government and the legislators are the corpora-
> tions and trusts . . . behind the political monopolists are
> the industrial monopolists.[52]

Therefore, if the wishes of the people could be directly expressed
by the use of certain electoral devices, the people would be able
to "break the hold of the 'bosses' ".[53] What the Progressives sought
to do was use their collective political power, made effective
through political reforms, to further their welfare and position as
independent individual producers. Their radicalism was a mixture
of collectivism and egalitarian individualism, a half-way house to
socialism, which eventually was to find a foothold in all the parties,
and more than a foothold in the Western Conservatives, and in the
CCF/NDP.

Economically, their main hostility was to the protective tariff.
Although the Liberal Party had, in 1891 and 1911, contemplated

schemes of freer trade, they had both times been rebuffed by the electorate, in spite of almost solid support from Saskatchewan and Alberta in 1911. In 1921 under the leadership of T. A. Crerar, the Progressives ran as an independent political party, bent on achieving free trade in foodstuffs and agricultural equipment, and "an immediate and substantial all-round reduction of the customs tariff".[54] They vigorously opposed the protective tariff on the grounds that it "fostered combines, trusts and 'gentlemen's agreements' in almost every line of Canadian industrial enterprise", that it made "the rich richer and the poor poorer", and it "has been and is a chief corrupting influence in our national life because the protected interests, in order to maintain their unjust privileges, have contributed lavishly to political and campaign funds, thus encouraging both political parties to look to them for support, thereby lowering the standard of public morality".[55]

Although Mackenzie King attempted to form a government composed of Liberals and Progressives,[56] the negotiations between the two sides broke down, and the Progressives refused even to form the official Opposition, confident that they would retain their ideological purity, and serve best the interests of their constituents by taking an independent stand on such important matters as the tariff. King himself was ideologically close enough to the Progressives on this important matter that generally he could count on their support in parliament.

During the parliament of 1921, the party was riven by internal ideological disputes. Suporters of Henry Wise Wood, mainly from Alberta, distrusted the party system generally, and were "in concept revolutionaries".[57] Supporters of Crerar from Manitoba were less hostile to traditional party and parliamentary tactics, and wanted to see the Progressive movement continue as a reformist political party. The ascendancy of this group was demonstrated by the election of Robert Forke as leader in 1922.

The strength of this Manitoba faction proved to be its great electoral weakness. These men were the first "Liberals in a hurry". There was no significant ideological difference between them and King's Liberals, and as a consequence there was little excuse for them to continue as a separate political party. In the 1925 election, their numbers in Parliament were reduced to 24. In that campaign, Forke continued to attack the protective tariff, and to hold out the Progressive Party as a "promise of salvation".[58] But even in that year, the Progressives were on the defensive, and Forke felt called upon to defend the necessity of "maintaining our independence as a group and freedom of judgment and action in the parliamentary arena".[59]

By the 1926 election, the absorption of most Progressives into the Liberal Party had almost been completed. Nine members were elected as Liberal-Progressives, and there were only thirteen Progressives who found seats in the House of Commons. The more radical Albertans had broken with the main body of the Progressives, and founded their own party, the United Farmers of Alberta. While the rump of the Progressives continued to press lamely for such policies as "reciprocity with the United States in natural products",[60] the UFA demanded much more vigorous political reforms to break the hold of the Eastern financial interests and to re-affirm their desire to have a Parliament directly responsive to the wishes of the constituents. It was not until the founding of the CCF in 1932 that the ideological confusion was temporarily to resolve itself, with the more collectivist elements finding a home in the new party, and the reformist liberals relatively content back in the mainstream of Canadian Liberalism with King.

The challenge to King in 1919 then was to reunite the shattered forces of the Liberal Party, a process which employed not only King's very considerable talents of political conciliation and accommodation, but also involved an important recasting of the party's inherited ideology. This was not necessary in all areas — King's policy on Canadian autonomy and foreign relations simply took up where Laurier had left off, though adjusted to changed conditions. The problem area was social and economic policy, for the postwar depression in world markets, the strains and problems of rapid industrial and urban growth, and the general social malaise following the war combined to produce a high degree of unrest and dissatisfaction, evidenced by the Progressive revolt on the farms, and considerable labour unrest (of which the Winnipeg general strike was only the most spectacular example) in the cities. The traditional Liberal policy of *laissez-faire,* of economic liberty as the ultimate solution, was simply not acceptable to unemployed and exploited workers, and farmers facing ruinously low prices for agricultural products.

In the face of this situation, King proposed two major changes in Liberal ideas. In the first place, he tempered the *laissez-faire* view that economic liberty was essentially negative in nature, the absence of restraints (and particularly government interference) on economic activity, with the new ideas of "positive" liberalism of English liberals such as L. T. Hobhouse. Hobhouse argued, in his *Liberalism,* that individual liberty was restricted as much by the lack of certain things (adequate food, housing, or medical care) as by the presence of onerous restrictions. Hence positive government action to fill these needs was quite consistent with liberalism.

King accepted this repudiation of all-out *laissez-faire* without qualms, and at the 1919 leadership convention committed himself and the Liberal Party to the eventual achievement of a welfare state, including medicare, pension and insurance schemes. The ease with which this was done, and the importance of King's new ideas to his convention victory were partly due to the general dissatisfaction of the times and readiness to seek new solutions; but no less to the fact that these ideas were within the canon of the Liberal ideology, and were seen as a creative adaptation of the Liberal tradition rather than a leap in the dark.

For positive liberalism still saw society in individualistic terms, and only approved collective action as a means of maximizing individual initiative and opportunity. King himself clearly recognized the difference between this and genuine socialism. In supporting legislation against sweatshops and cartels he argued that "it is the business of the state to play the same part in the supervision of industry as is played by the Umpire in sports to see the mean man does not profit in virtue of his meanness, and on the other hand that nothing should be done which will destroy individual effort and skill. Some may term this legislation Socialism, but to my mind it is individualism".[61] The ultimate justification of such measures was that they produced a larger amount of liberty in the end. "Most effort to promote human welfare necessitates some interference with individual liberty. Where wisely applied and enforced, it is an immediate restriction, that a wider liberty in the end may be secured".[62] To this end, the convention of 1919 resolved that, "in so far as may be practicable, having regard for Canada's financial position, an adequate system of insurance against unemployment, sickness, dependence in old age, and other disability, which would include old age pensions, widows' pensions, and maternity benefits, should be instituted by the Federal Government".[63] King did not rush to fulfil the promise made; it was only fully redeemed by the Pearson government. Nevertheless, the commitment was made, and the seal was set upon a permanent change of direction in Liberal thinking.

King's other major contribution was in recasting the Liberal view of class and industrial strife. Again, his success was due to the degree of continuity he preserved with traditional Liberal thinking. Liberals had always viewed society as primarily a collection of individuals, and the common interest of society as the sum of the interests of the individuals who composed it. Subordinate groups were likely enemies of the overall good, and many liberals had found trade unions a plausible candidate for this anti-social role. King accepted the basic analysis: economic conflicts were not based on the objective group or class interests of the parties but on individual failings, selfishness or stubbornness, which blinded them to their more important common interests.[64]

Thus King rejected socialism to the extent that it involved a theory of class conflict: the Progressives may have been "Liberals in a hurry"; but the CCF in the 1930's could not "be regarded in any sense as allies".[65] However, like the Progressives, he realized that individual interests in an industrial society could often best be realized through joint action, and accepted unions as the workers' representatives, ending the old liberal hostility. Government was to be the conciliator mediating between the two parties, unions and employers, inducing each to moderate its own position, and leading them towards the common good. King's early political career in the Labour Department and his service as labour relations manager for the Rockefellers exhibited this concern for compromise and conciliation. The 1919 convention endorsed the *Labour Convention* of the League of Nations, and called for the, "introduction into the government of industry of principles of representation whereby labour and the community as well as capital, may be represented in industrial control, and their interests safeguarded and promoted in the shaping of industrial policies".[66]

King's position was in no sense revolutionary. He wanted no fundamental changes in the distribution of economic power in society of the sort which socialists sought by nationalization or worker control; no basic change in the capitalist, private enterprise economy. His aim was to improve the lot of the worst off within the existing system, through the welfare state and reforms in industrial relations. This served to make the Liberal Party more attractive to those, particularly in Progressive or Labour groups, who after 1918 had forsaken it. King's ideas thus had an immediate political relevance in 1919, a fact which was not lost on the delegates to the convention, and which was demonstrated by the ingathering of most of the errant Progressives through the 1920's. King's reinterpretation of liberalism for an urban, industrial society was a major achievement, and perhaps his greatest legacy to the Liberal Party.

However, King's skilful development of the notion that the Liberal Party was somehow the party of "national unity" ranks a close second. The idea originated with Laurier, when the party had with apparent success combined an English majority and French minority in a government possessing broad support across the country. This was in ruins by 1919, but King assiduously set out to rebuild. He began from his support in Quebec as an anticonscriptionist, and because, like Stalin five years later, he had put it about that his deceased predecessor had favoured his succession. This Quebec support was the basis for the Liberal claim to be *the* national party. In the fight to retain it King had an important ideological advantage in the growing Liberal commitment to Canadian independence along isolationist lines. Isolationism accorded with the absence of any emotional attachments for Europe among the French-Canadians; even more important, it allowed the Liberals to place the accommodation of French Canadian interests, in the name of national unity, ahead of wider Canadian commitments and interests. Thus, in the Great War, the Laurier Liberals placed Quebec's opposition to conscription ahead of Canadian military commitments. During the elections of the 1920's and 1930's, French Canadian voters did not (and were not allowed) to forget that the Conservatives had taken their sons in 1917; in 1940, King specifically repudiated conscription. When circumstances and mismanagement forced the gradual abandonment of this policy, King took every possible opportunity to delay the event and reduce the effects of conscription.

Other aspects of King's foreign policy showed a similar bias. He equated any close imperial connection with the sort of colonial subordination against which his grandfather had rebelled, and avoided any international commitments or entanglements. The differing attitude of Meighen and King to the Chanak crisis in 1922 was a case in point. Through the 1930's he avoided any Canadian involvement in the collective security plans of the League of Nations. The repudiation of Dr. Riddell's commitment (as Canadian Ambassador to the League) to resist Italian aggression in Ethiopia in 1935 marked the zenith of King's retreat into the "fireproof house" of North America. Indeed, the Liberal Party in its platform for the 1940 elections boasted of King's avoidance of any prior national commitments: "The King Government — wisely interpreting the wishes of the Canadian people — refused to commit this country, in advance, to a policy of fighting wars at unpredictable times, at unknown places and for undetermined causes".[67]

Closely connected with King's isolationism was his inclination to see Canada in a North American, or continental perspective, rather than in a European context. This was a common Liberal view, derived from the liberal tendency to give economic factors free play. King had modified this belief in *laissez-faire* by endorsing, for example, the welfare state, but had by no means entirely abandoned it. He remained committed to freer trade, particularly with the United States; the platform for the 1921 election supported tariff reductions and commended the ill-fated *Reciprocity Agreement* of 1911.[68] In office, King had to step gingerly in order to maintain his support among Quebec protectionists, but was able to satisfy the

Progressives sufficently well on the tariff question to induce them to return to the fold. In any event, King never lost his faith in the virtues of free trade. In 1935, despite the advent of Keynesian economics and the example of Roosevelt's New Deal, King clung to what he termed the "Liberation of External Trade" as the primary solution to the economic problems posed by the Depression:

> I cannot stress too strongly the importance the Liberal party attaches to getting rid of prohibitory tariffs, and other restrictions which have been strangling Canada's trade. It believes that upon the development and expansion of our domestic and foreign trade depends the only ultimate solution of the problems of unemployment, railways, debt and taxation, and the establishment of substantial measures of social reform.[69]

On resuming office in 1935, the Liberal government was content to allow the Bennett New Deal legislation to fall undefended and unwelcomed before the onslaught of the courts. In 1938 important tariff reductions were agreed with the United States.

Not surprisingly, King was willing to allow economic forces to take their course in integrating Canada with the United States, and he failed to pursue the National Policy's aim of a high degree of Canadian economic independence. He did maintain the form of the National Policy, but the policies of 1879 were no longer relevant to the situation after 1920. New resource-based industries serving American markets had grown up outside the National Policy and were weakening the national, east-west orientation of the Canadian economy. At the same time American ownership of Canadian business began to rise sharply. At no time did King interfere with either of these trends. This process of economic integration went along with an increasingly continentalist defence policy. King's decision in 1940 to accept extensive Canadian collaboration with the Americans in a common continental defence scheme (the direct ancestor of NORAD) was of a piece with the tariff agreements of 1938, and the continued drift to continental economic integration.

It should be clear that this continentalist orientation was by no means a mere personal choice of King's, but a position inherent in the Liberal commitment to a high degree of economic liberalism, and the consequent tendency to place the demands of economics before those of politics. It had been a constant factor in the liberal ideology since at least the 1850's, though sometimes offset by strong national or imperial loyalties held by liberals, and often rejected by the voters. It also accorded with Liberal sympathy for provincial rights, for the new resource industries fell largely under provincial jurisdiction, and any attempt to alter their course would have involved an extension of central government control. King's position then was perfectly consistent with the Liberal past, and indeed, was to be carried on by his successors.

King's later years in office witnessed only one break in the pattern established after 1919. The Second World War, while restoring prosperity and providing fresh impetus for the welfare state, forced King to abandon his attachment to provincial rights, for prosecution of the war required a high degree of central control of the economy and the belated arrival of Keynesian ideas in Ottawa made the federal authorities loath to surrender their new-found powers. This swing to centralization was not to prove permanent, for Lester Pearson was to make a major retreat in the face of the resurgent provinces in the 1960's.

Neither was it entirely at variance with the party's ideological tradition, for Liberalism had always approved of Canadian capitalism (if deploring some of its excesses) and during the years in power had developed a close relationship with the Canadian business community. Business in turn, while deploring certain types of government intervention, was always sympathetic to government action which favoured its interest. In the interwar period, most of the demands of business on government fell at the provincial level, for the growth industries, like pulp and paper and mining, required specifically provincial assistance, for example, in developing hydroelectric power. After the war, as corporate integration on a nation-wide basis increased, business often came to depend on dominion assistance, for example, in pipeline construction or regulation on an interprovincial basis. The tendency of the Liberal Party to accommodate itself to business interests eased the transition from the traditional provincial rights position. Businessmen, with the exception of the more old-fashioned and less perceptive, reconciled themselves to a more active central government on two grounds. First, they realized that some government interference, such as welfare measures or steps to control unemployment, was necessary to secure public acceptance of the continued existence of capitalism. In short, they were a form of innoculation against the far more serious threat of socialism. Second, many of these government measures were distinctly congenial to business interests, (the construction of the fateful gas pipeline for instance) and to the continuing process of economic integration with the United States, whence so many Canadian businesses were now controlled.

The identification of the Liberal Party and the Canadian corporate world reached its highest point under Louis St. Laurent, and was personified in C. D. Howe, his aggressive, American-born, (and self-made millionaire) Minister of Trade and Commerce. However, though Howe, and other Cabinet colleagues such as Robert Winters and Walter Harris dramatized this aspect of Liberal policy, there was no real ideological change in the transition from King to St. Laurent, and the latter contributed little to Liberal thinking, though he seems to have stimulated the Liberal Party to restate its fundamental belief in liberty and individualism in fuller terms than at any time since 1919. Thus the 1948 convention which ratified St. Laurent's succession declared that:

> Liberal policies are those which protect, sustain and enlarge the freedom of the individual. The Liberal . . . believes in freedom because he believes the resources of human personality and endeavour to be rich and varied beyond calculation or prediction. Liberalism rejects the unreasoning preservation, in the name of freedom, of outworn existing arrangements and measures. It rejects the maintenance of privilege however historic. Liberalism equally rejects the theory that state ownership of the instruments of production in itself constitutes progress and a solution of social problems.[70]

In office, St. Laurent continued King's mixture of cautious positive liberalism in social welfare policies and antinationalist *laissez-faire* economic policies. Such nationalist feeling as did exist in the Liberal Party was expressed in policies which were largely the loose-ends of King's anti-imperialism. The institution of a fully separate Canadian citizenship in 1947, the abolition of remaining judicial appeals to the Privy Council in 1949 and the promise of "an exclusively Canadian flag",[71] whittled away at the few remaining formal ties with Britain; but the problem of increasing dependence on the United States in other areas was ignored entirely. The military alliance with the United States was strengthened, and the government's reaction to the Suez crisis in 1956 marked the final passage of Canada from the diplomatic orbit of Britain into that of the United States.

St. Laurent also maintained King's approach to centralization although it involved a continuous and bitter confrontation with Quebec. For the moment he could sustain this position politically; as a French Canadian he enjoyed an attraction for his compatriots that temporarily offset their attachment to provincial rights.

The outward calm, if not torpor, of the party was rudely shattered by the Conservative victories of 1957 and 1958, and the questioning which subsequently took place opened up an ideological division that persisted after the Liberals returned to office in 1963. The critics were largely on the party's left, and were part of a general upsurge of radical liberalism which was finding expression both in Diefenbaker-style populism in the Conservative Party, and in the growth of the New Party movement.

The Liberal critics, chief of whom was Walter Gordon, Pearson's first Finance Minister, had two targets: the organization of the party and its policies. The party organization, it was argued, was not democratic enough, and did not allow for rank-and-file participation in party decision-making. Its policies were too business-oriented, and required more emphasis on extending the welfare state. At the same time, a growing body of nationalists questioned the traditional Liberal commitment to continentalism, and pressed for policies of economic and cultural nationalism. Nor was this the end of Pearson's problems for the postwar policy of centralization was being challenged both by the resurgent Quebec wing of the party, and many of the provincial governments.

Pearson met this situation with much the same ideological stance as his predecessors, though the emphasis he placed upon the various elements in it differed. Liberalism's primary concern remained with the individual: "The fundamental principle of Liberalism ... is belief in the dignity and worth of the individual. The state is the creation of man, to protect and serve him; and not the reverse"; and particularly, with individual liberty: "the first purpose of goverment [is] to legislate for the liberation ... of human personality".[72] Furthermore, Pearson restated the distinction between positive and negative liberty, between merely removing restraints on individual action, and providing men with the wherewithal to exercise to the full their opportunities:

> Liberalism includes the negative requirement of removing anything that stands in the way of individual and collective progress.
> The negative requirement is important. It involves removal and reform: clearing away and opening up, so that man can move forward and societies expand. The removal of restrictions that block the access to achievement: this is the very essence of Liberalism.
> The Liberal Party, however, must also promote the positive purpose of ensuring that all citizens, without any discrimination, will be in a position to take advantage of the opportunities opened up; of the freedoms that have been won ....[73]

Pearson made it clear, however, that positive freedom was not to be confused with socialism; its purpose was only to provide equality of opportunity — a common starting point in the race — not to guarantee equality at the finishing-post.[74]

In office, Pearson remained well within the limits of liberalism though shifting the emphasis somewhat towards positive liberty by adding the Canada Pension Plan and Medicare to existing welfare measures. He was distinctly cool to nationalism: his liberalism and his diplomatic experience had made him a convinced internationalist and led him to downgrade national differences which might impede international integration. His government placed a high priority on restoring the closest possible trade and diplomatic relations with the United States after 1963, and pursued vigorously the traditional Liberal policy of continentalism. Defence production-sharing agreements with the United States opened the profitable war-time market to Canada, and encouraged continental integration in the aircraft and electronics industries. The *Automobile Trade Pact* of 1965 effectively ended any hope of a separate Canadian automobile industry. When American exchange difficulties threatened to disrupt the free flow of capital within North America, the Pearson government hastened to Washington to seek exemption.

Nevertheless, Pearson's habit of acting as a sort of mediator between the different factions in the government allowed him to accept certain nationalist measures (restricting foreign ownership of financial and communications industries) pressed on him. When, however, Walter Gordon precipitated a major debate on economic nationalism in the party during 1966, Pearson stood on the sidelines while Mitchell Sharp led the majority of the party into a decisive rejection of nationalist policy.

Pearson retreated substantially from the the policy of centralization by bowing to pressure from the provinces, particularly Quebec, for more independence in taxation and welfare policy and reverted to the older Liberal ideas about provincial rights, to the position taken by Laurier, or by King in the interwar period. Pearson also attempted to conciliate French Canada by the Liberal expedient of extending their individual rights as Francophones through policies designed to encourage bilingualism in the civil service and in the longer term, by the appointment of the Dunton-Laurendeau Royal Commission on Bilingualism and Biculturalism in Canada. The "Bi and Bi" Commission was intended to assess the overall status of the French culture and language and to make concrete recommendations for its improvement. This was a massive undertaking and was still unfinished when Pearson retired in 1968, having done little on the face of things to reduce separatist pressures. This apparent failure increased the feeling of concern for national unity which provided such a receptive welcome for the ideas of Pierre Trudeau.

The Liberal convention of 1968 which brought Trudeau to the party leadership displayed in microcosm the spectrum of thinking in Canadian Liberalism. Although the notion of positive liberalism and consequent state intervention had become a permanent part of the party ideology with King, enthusiasm for its extension varied a good deal within the party. In particular, Liberals differed on the desirability of reducing the negative liberties of some men, through interference with their property rights, to further the positive liberties of others. The right wing, or property rights liberals were represented by Paul Hellyer, Robert Winters and Mitchell Sharp; the left wing by Paul Martin, his credentials a trifle tarnished by time, and Allan MacEachen. Trudeau confounded both with a skillfully conceived and executed flanking movement: through his engaging style of life his leadership campaign succeeded in convincing a great many delegates (and voters two months later) that he was on an entirely different plane from the other candidates. The categories of right and left were a remnant of the old style politics of ideology and emotion: Trudeau, the New Man of Canadian politics was beyond all this.

In retrospect, Trudeau has proved to be firmly in the traditional Liberal mould; not above his rivals of 1968, but in the middle of them; like King, a representative of the Liberal centre, with leanings to the right. The relatively conservative nature of Trudeau's political thinking can be seen clearly in his reaction to growing separatist pressures in Quebec; the issue which was, on Trudeau's own admission, the reason for his entry into federal politics: "It was because of the federal government's weakness that I allowed myself to be catapulted into it".[75] Trudeau's solicitude for the federal status quo and the maintenance of national unity played a major part in the victory of 1968 as he proclaimed his support for "one Canada" in the face of the Conservatives' confused courtship of the "two nations" theory. Ironically, Trudeau's position was more reminiscent of John Diefenbaker's cry for "unhyphenated Canadianism" than Lester Pearson's policy of diplomatic retreats in the face of provincial pressure.

In asserting that Trudeau is a conservative Liberal we wish to make two points: first, that it is important to distinguish between the apparent radicalism of the Trudeau rhetoric and style, and the actual ideas and policies put forward; and second, that in substantive terms, this conservatism is not to be confused with the toryism of the Conservative Party; it indicates Trudeau's adherence to a traditional body of liberal thought, and to the Canadian liberal tradition. We are arguing that Trudeau approaches politics with a stock of ideas drawn from the Canadian Liberal armoury, albeit expressed with an elegance and style all too frequently absent from political discourse in this country.

Foremost among these ideas is the familiar liberal concern with liberty, and in particular, with the liberty of the individual. The commitment to individualism is prominent in Trudeau's thinking, and comes from long-standing personal inclination: "I have never been able to accept any discipline except that which I imposed upon myself. ... I found it unacceptable that others should claim to know better than I what was good for me."[76] From this basic premise, Trudeau draws several conclusions. One is the value of the rights of individuals, and the consequent necessity for tolerance.[77] Another is that the "primordial responsibility" of the liberal to foster individual freedom entails an open-ended commitment to change:

> The first visible effect of freedom is change. A free man exercises his freedom by altering himself and — inevitably — his surroundings. It follows that no liberal can be other than receptive to change and highly positive and active in his response to it, for change is the very expression of freedom.[78]

The notion that freedom means change or movement is in turn connected with the view that the human essence is found in activity or movement — to be human is to be active, competitive, in motion. This has been implicit in liberal thinking at least since Thomas Hobbes but has rarely in Canada been expressed as explicity. Indeed, Trudeau put it in terms strikingly reminiscent of the author of *Leviathan:* "Life is confrontation, and vigilance, and a fierce struggle against any threat of intrusion or death".[79] Interestingly enough, this statement was made within a few weeks of the invocation of the Leviathan-esque powers of the *War Measures Act,* and exposes an aspect of liberalism rather different from the "bleeding heart" variety he repudiated at that time.

This individualist premise necessarily implies a somewhat restricted view of the power of society and the state in relation to the individual, though it is important to note that Trudeau is no Spencerian individualist. In the Throne Speech debate in January 1973, Trudeau was careful to restate the Liberal commitment to positive liberty, talking of the

> ... liberal philosophy according to which, in an orderly society, we are each other's co-insurers, all required

to come to the aid of other members of the society who are in need, who are less favored. We are co-insurers, by way of taxation or otherwise, of certain fundamental rights that we want to make available to all individuals in our society. Without getting into details, Mr. Speaker, I think it would be fair to state that one of the most fundamental rights is the entitlement to hospital and health care, and in this field, projects and programs have already been well outlined in the past, mostly by Liberal governments.[80]

Nevertheless this question of positive liberty, of giving individuals assistance to enable them to exercise their freedom, has never been prominent in Trudeau's thinking, and this has been translated into a governmental approach which is perhaps best described as a holding action. Inherited programmes (like health care) have been maintained and sometimes improved, but new initiatives have been few. This change of emphasis (though not of absolute beliefs, for other things aside it is doubtful that any government could exist in Canada without a degree of positive liberty thinking) away from the more activist position which Pearson took is a noticeable feature of Trudeau's leadership. On the other hand this concern for the negative form of individual liberty has been exhibited in the removal of certain restrictions on personal freedom, the liberalization of the law of divorce and abortion, the amendment of the Criminal Code to remove the state, in Trudeau's memorable phrase, from the bedrooms of the nation; and in the reform of parole and bail arrangements.

It can be seen most clearly however, in the way he deals with the problem of Confederation and the French Canadians. There are essentially two theoretical approaches to the problem of the place of French Canadians in Confederation, one more individualist, the other more collectivist in nature. In the former, French Canadians, as individuals, are considered to have certain individual rights to the use of the French language, denial of which is both wrong in principle and a threat to the future of Confederation. The solution from this standpoint is to safeguard these *individual* rights, and the Trudeau government has proceeded in this direction, chiefly through the *Official Languages Act,* which extends bilingualism across much of the country; and through administrative action to increase the use of French in the civil service. The Trudeau bilingualism policy then has a distinct individualist bias.

On the other hand, it is argued that the real question is not the rights of French-speaking individuals, but the rights of the French Canadian *collectivity,* the *nation;* and that the solution lies in extending and safeguarding the rights of that collectivity. This collectivist, or group-oriented argument is based on a perception of the primarily emotional or nonrational group loyalties of French Canadians, their deep attachment to their own collectivity, and on the assertion that the transmission (and hence the safeguarding) of a culture can only be successfully accomplished within a sympathetic social *milieu*.[81] Thus it is argued that the preservation and extension of French culture depends not on the legal rights of individuals, but on the strength of the collectivity, the *nation*, and for obvious reasons, the province of Quebec has generally been identified as the political embodiment of that *nation*. Hence demands are made for particular rights and powers to be granted to Quebec to enable it to fulfil its role as the protector of French Canada.

The gist of this position then is that Quebec *n'est pas une province comme les autres*, because of its special relationship to the French Canadian *nation*, and deserves "special status" with respect to the central government and the other provinces. Demands of this sort have been made by a series of provincial governments in Quebec, both Liberal and Union Nationale, as well as the Parti Québecois (which carries the argument to its extreme conclusion) and the federal Conservative and New Democratic parties have briefly flirted with similar ideas. For a time it seemed that the federal Liberals, under Pearson, would move in this direction, following the retreat before pressure from Quebec on the Canada Pension Plan and passage of opting-out legislation in 1964-1965.

Trudeau's reasoning is in part that of a conventional constitutional lawyer — concern over the problems involved with special status, the anomalous position of French Canadian representatives in a Canadian Parliament which had less jurisdiction over Quebec than the other provinces, or the position of non-French minorities in Quebec. Underlying this is a deep hostility to the notion that the state should be organized on any primarily collective or group principle, whether class or nationalist. For Trudeau, the state exists to serve primarily individual ends; "Men do not exist for states; states are created to make it easier for men to attain some of their common objectives".[82] Thus, while agreeing that Quebec could rightfully take steps to promote the French language and culture above others, he insists that this is based solely on the state's obligation to serve the individual interests of its citizens, who in this case happen to be largely French speaking: "It is inevitable that its policies will serve the interests of ethnic groups, and especially of the majority group in proportion to its numbers; but this will happen as a natural consequence of the equality of all citizens, not as a special privilege of the largest group".[83]

Trudeau's long-standing hostility to nationalism of all sorts is based partly on the familiar case against nationalist excesses. Nationalism is blamed for the creation of modern total warfare by imparting a quasi-religious fervour to it:

> [T]he tiny portion of history marked by the emergence of the nation-states is also the scene of the most devastating wars, the worst atrocities, and the most degrading collective hatred the world has ever seen . . . . the nation-state idea has caused wars to become more and more total over the last two centuries; and that is the idea I take issue with so vehemently. . . . In days gone by religion had to be displaced as the basis of the state before the frightful religious wars came to an end. And there will be no end to wars between nations until in some similar fashion the nation ceases to be the basis of the state.[84]

Furthermore, Trudeau points out that many, if not most states, contain various ethnic, or national minorities; and that in consequence, attainment of the nationalist ideal of each nationality embodied in its separate nation-state would mean intolerable disruption. Thus, "the very idea of the nation-state is absurd".[85]

He goes beyond this however, and argues that the basic nationalist attitudes or ideas must be ultimately rejected, even if they are not taken to these extremes in actual practice. The element of collectivism in nationalism, that is, the attachment it demands to the national or ethnic group, is repugnant to the liberal preoccupation with individuality; national loyalties are incompatible with the liberal assertion that the lone individual is the ultimate moral unit. In making this point, Trudeau approvingly quotes Renan's assertion that "man is bound neither to his language nor to his race; he is bound only to himself because he is a free agent, or in other words a moral being".[86] Thus, even while recognizing the desirable qualities fostered by the nation and sustained by national feeling — "a cultural heritage, common traditions, a community awareness, historical continuity, a set of mores, all of which . . . go to make a man what he is" — he insists on their purely temporary value — they are only valid "at this juncture of history" — and ought to be superseded in the long run:

> Certainly, these qualities are more private than public, more introverted than extroverted, more instinctive and primitive than intelligent and civilized, more self-centred and impulsive than generous and reasonable. They belong to a transitional period in world history.[87]

The presence, particularly in French Canada, of such dangerous and undesirable nationalist sentiment explains in turn Trudeau's enthusiasm for federalism, for he, like his mentor the nineteenth century English liberal Lord Acton, sees in federalism the ideal means to tame, and eventually eliminate nationalism. By dividing sovereignty between different levels of government in one state, federalism allows the accommodation of different nationalities within one political framework. This not only gives nationalist feelings an outlet at a level where the harm they can do is minimized, but in the long run teaches toleration, and works toward the end of nationalism.

One of the important corollaries for Trudeau of this notion that federalism is essentially anti-nationalist is that attempts by federal governments to hold together federations by encouraging nationalist sentiment at the federal level are ultimately self-defeating. Trudeau's description of the nature of such policies is an almost exact description of the sort of programme advocated by contemporary Canadian nationalists:

> Resources must be diverted into such things as national flags, anthems, education, arts councils, broadcasting corporations, film boards; the territory must be bound together by a network of railways, highways, airlines; the national culture and the national economy must be protected by taxes and tariffs; ownership of resources and industry by nationals must be made a matter of policy.[88]

Trudeau objects that national feeling fostered in this way may often not reflect equally the aspirations of all the groups within the state and thus simply exacerbate separatist feelings; and more important, the ultimate basis of a federal state is not any emotional loyalty to the country, but a rational and calculated compromise of a number of regional interests. A federal state is maintained by the gradual and prosaic alteration of the "terms of the federative pact", "by administrative practice, by judicial decision, and by constitutional amendment".[89] Indeed, such appeals to nationalist or patriotic emotions create an "inner contradiction" in a federal state for "in *the last resort* the mainspring of federalism cannot be emotion but must be reason".[90] In the light of this, it is not surprising that Trudeau has been distinctly cool to demands for nationalist responses to issues like the foreign ownership of Canadian resources and industry, and his government has done remarkably little in this whole area, even when pressed by electoral reverses. Indeed, Trudeau, looks to the complete displacement of nationalism and nationalist emotion:

Thus there is some hope that in advanced societies, the glue of nationalism will become as obsolete as the divine right of kings; the title of the state to govern and the extent of its authority will be conditional upon rational justification; a people's consensus based on reason will supply the cohesive force that societies require; and politics both within and without the state will follow a much more functional approach to the problems of government. If politicians must bring emotions into the act, let them get emotional about functionalism.[91]

Trudeau's use of "reason" and "rationality" in this connection is important, for it illustrates the liberal tendency to see men as essentially homogenous beings, despite differences of nation, culture of history; a tendency which arises from the atomistic individualism of liberalism. If what is really important for man is that which pertains solely to him as an individual, differences among men which are the result of collective influences — linguistic or cultural for instance — are only secondary. For Trudeau, this common core in every individual is his "reason" or "rationality". This explains Trudeau's hostility to nationalism, and ultimately to national differences, for the basis of national differentiation is thus emotional and irrational; and hence, hopefully transitional and temporary. Indeed, Trudeau equates any sort of "emotional" response to political questions to superstition, and leaves no doubt that such sentiment, nationalist, patriotic, or whatever, must be discarded in the future:

No doubt, at the level of individual action, emotions and dreams will still play a part; even in modern man, superstition remains a powerful motivation. But magic, no less than totems and taboos, has long since ceased to play an important role in the normal governing of states. And likewise, nationalism will eventually have to be rejected as a principle of sound government.[92]

This liberal bias against cultural differentiation has allied itself with the liberal inclination in favour of technology, and rapid technological innoculation. Technology is a natural companion for liberalism, for, as liberals seek to maximize human freedom, technology, by extending man's natural powers, works to the same end. Furthermore, technologies, whether of production or of business organization, operate best with the maximum of standardization, and the greatest possible economies of scale. The combination of liberal attitudes and a highly developed technology thus produces a dynamic set of social forces, for liberalism demands the maximization of freedom or liberty and technology promises this in direct proportion to the degree of its employment. There is thus a constant pressure or impulse to extend the scope and speed of technological progress and innovation. At the same time, as we have noted, technology tends to standardize and simplify, much like a production line, so that a liberal technological society has a powerful dissolvent effect on pre-existing cultural or national differences. The constant impetus to standardization across national boundaries given by multinational corporations, the marketing of identical products on a continental basis, and the integration of the production of those goods on a continental or inter-continental scale are all examples of this process at work.

Trudeau recognizes this homogenizing force: "... if technology is free to enter, the country must irrevocably step into the era of great communities, of continental economies", [93] and it is clear that he is highly sympathetic to this sort of dynamic, dissolvent technological society. For Trudeau, the mastery of technology is the key to the future; the "banana republic" of tomorrow is the state which has not mastered the "cybernetic revolution". Technology is the key to political progress:

> [T]he state — if it is not to be outdistanced by its rivals — will need political instruments which are sharper, stronger, and more finely controlled than anything based on mere emotionalism: such tools will be made up of advanced technology and scientific investigation, as applied to the fields of law, economics, social psychology, international affairs, and other areas of human relations; in short, if not a pure product of reason, the political tools of the future will be designed and appraised by more rational standards than anything we are currently using in Canada today.[94]

Reason no longer seeks, as in the classical view, to know the ultimate ends or purposes of the state and of man, but merely to master the techniques or tools necessary to the infinite and purposeless expansion of human freedom.

Once Trudeau's secular, calculating rationality had led him to espouse technology, he readily accepted the corollary that barriers should not be placed in its path and he argues that cultural values, like technologies, should be exposed to a maximum degree of competition. A special, protected position for Quebec within Confederation "can only tend to weaken values protected in this way against competition. *Even more than technology,* a culture makes progress through the exchange of ideas and through challenge".[95]

In "advanced societies", "cultural differentiation is submitted to ruthless competition", and, "the road to progress lies in the direction of international integration".[96] The message is clear: technological forces ought to be given full play, and cultural or national values which succumb to their dissolvent effects are not worth having anyway.

It is obvious then, that Trudeau's political ideas provide no theoretical basis for any programme of cultural or economic nationalism. This explains the absence or weakness of nationalist measures in the plans of the Trudeau government, and suggests that what measures have been taken are more likely to be a result of pressure from the nationalist elements in the Liberal Party or electoral difficulties. Indeed, the continuity of Liberal theory from King to Trudeau is marked by a consistent policy of either encouraging, or acquiescing in, the continued integration of Canada into the dynamic liberal society of the United States.

Finally, it is worth noting Trudeau's restatement of the common liberal argument that liberalism is the enemy of ideology rather than one of its examples. Liberals have tended to think of ideologies as collections of abstract and complicated systems of ideas, and consequently have placed them in opposition to their own rather simplistic view of society as a collection of atomistic individuals governed by a calculating rationality which they dignify by calling pragmatism, empiricism, or, in a phrase Trudeau uses, common sense. Hence Trudeau's boast that he is not tied down or restricted by any ideological superstructure; indeed, his reason is free to scurry among them at will, nibbling away as he goes: "The only constant factor to be found in my thinking over the years has been opposition to accepted opinions".[97] Indeed, such "ideological systems are the true enemies of freedom".[98]

This attitude may well deliver liberals from the clutches of some ideological ways of thinking, with the liberal mind trained on the low but solid ground of furthering individual interests by the use of a reason limited to discovering techniques rather than ends. Not only can it not help but miss the lure of more speculative or less popular systems; it does not even, except when forced by electoral considerations, pay them the compliment of listening to what they have to say. However, it is this very simplicity, or commonsensical aspect of liberalism which justifies our calling it an ideology, for, as such, it presents a very partial or limited view of the world. The liberal preoccupation with the individual and the consequent shallow analysis of the social and collective aspects of man's existence is an excellent example of this limited nature, and in itself a sufficient refutation of the argument that liberalism heralds

Political Parties and Ideologies

the "end of ideology" and the reign of "reason". Indeed, the partialness and incompleteness of this Liberal account of the nature of political and social life goes a long way to account for the continued strength of the other ideologies to which we now turn.

[1] *The Report and Despatches of the Earl of Durham.* (London: Ridgways, 1839). Reprinted London, Methuen Publications, 1902, p.8

[2] *Ibid.,* p.12

[3] *Ibid.,* p.12

[4] *Ibid.,* p.16

[5] *Ibid.,* p.16

[6] *Ibid.,* p.22

[7] The popular misconception that economic individualism meant an automatic decrease in governmental activity is belied by this. In fact, individuals who wished to exercise their economic liberties more fully, were quickly led, on both sides of the Atlantic, to demand certain kinds of government action to support this provision of transportation facilities and enforcement of common standards, for example. They also required, to match the new technological advances, a greater degree of technical sophistication in such government actions. The result was, in real terms, a net growth in governmental activities and expertise, despite its retreat from other areas.

[8] *Ibid,* p.31

[9] *Ibid.,* p.31

[10] *Ibid.,* p.30

[11] *Ibid.,* p.33

[12] *Ibid.,* p.105

[13] *Ibid.,* p.117

[14] *Ibid.,* p.111

[15] Samuel Thompson, *Reminiscences of a Canadian Pioneer,* Vol. 1. (Toronto: Hunter Rose: 1884) p. 215. Reprinted by McClelland and Stewart, Toronto, 1968.

[16] Although the anticlericalism they acquired from continental European liberalism was a good deal more secularist than the voluntarism of the Clear Grits, which derived more from a concern for the vitality of religion, than any coolness or scepticism about it.

[17] Sir Allan MacNab, an arch-Tory, was known to have declared, on his appointment to the presidency of the Grand Trunk, that "my politics are railroads".

[18] See J. M. S. Careless, *Brown of the Globe,* (Toronto: MacMillan), I. p.295

[19] "Resolutions of Reform Convention, Toronto June 27,1867", Toronto *Globe* June 28, 1867 in D. O. Carrigan. *Canadian Party Platforms 1867-1968.* (Toronto: Copp Clark, 1968) p.6.

[20] Their reasoning was put succinctly by Alexander Mackenzie in a speech of 1865: "The French people ... felt it necessary to maintain a strong national spirit, and to resist all attempts to procure justice by the people of the west, lest that national existence should be broken down .... mere representation by population, under which such circumstances, would perhaps scarcely meet the expectations formed of it, because although Upper Canada would have seventeen more members than Lower Canada (in the proposed Dominion House), it would be an easy thing for the fifty or fifty-five members representing French constituencies to unite with a minority from Upper Canada, and thus secure an Administration subservient to their views". p. 423. *Parliamentary Debates on the Subject of the Confederation of the British North American Provinces,* (Quebec: 1865).

[21] J. M. S. Careless, *Brown of the Globe,* Vol. II, *Statesman of Confederation* (Toronto: MacMillan, 1963) p.19.
1963) p.19.

[22] *The Address of the Liberal Leader* (Toronto: 1882), in Carrigan, *Canadian Party Platforms,* p.19.

[23] *Ibid.,* pp.18-19

[24] Parliamentary Debates: Vol. VI, No. 1. 14 March 1879, p. 468, 473, revised.

[25] *A National Sentiment* (Ottawa, 1497), in Careless. Vol. II. *Statesman of Confederation,* (Toronto: Macmillan, 1963) p.325.

[26] Goldwin Smith, *Canada and the Canadian Question* (London: Macmillan, 1891) p.45. Reprinted Toronto © University of Toronto Press 1971.

[27] *Ibid.,* p.278, 279

[28] *Ibid.,* p.157

[29] *Ibid.,* p.30

[30] *Ibid.,* p.284

[31] *Ibid.,* p.56

[32] *Ibid.,* pp.2, 3

[33] *Ibid.,* p.39

[34] *The Address of the Liberal Leader,* in Carrigan, *Canadian Party Platforms,* p.20.

[35] *Ibid.,* p.24, Toronto *Mail,* Feb. 1, 1887, Campaign Speech by Edward Blake.

[36] O. D. Skelton, *Life and Letters of Sir Wilfred Laurier.* Vol. I, (Toronto: Oxford University Press, 1921) p.149.

[37] *Ibid.,* p.472.

[38] Regulation 17 was intended to forbid French-language schools in Ontario.

[39] Skelton, Vol. II, p.479.

[40] Carrigan, *The Address of the Liberal Leader* in *Canadian Party Platforms,* p.19.

[41] Campaign Speech by Blake, in *ibid.,* p.24.

[42] Skelton, Vol. I, 376-377.

[43] *Ibid.,* p.376

[44] *Ibid.,* pp.380-81

[45] The reluctance or outright refusal of Liberals like Brown, Mackenzie, and Laurier to take titles or knighthoods was but one manifestation of this.

[46] In 1897, he apparently approved the seating of colonial representatives in the Imperial Parliament, saying "it would be the proudest moment of my life if I could see a Canadian of French descent affirming the principles of freedom in the parliament of Great Britain." This, however, seems to have been an aberration produced by the intoxicating display of imperial might in the Diamond Jubilee celebrations. Skelton, II, p.72.

[47] *Ibid.,* p.105

[48] *Ibid.,* p.293

[49] W. L. Morton, Dafoe to George Iles, 27 September 1911. Dafoe Papers in *The Progressive Party in Canada.* Copyright, Canada, 1950 by University of Toronto Press, Toronto, p. 26.

[50] Morton, *ibid.,* p.26

[51] *Ibid.,* p.15

[52] *The Grain Growers' Guide,* 7 February 1912, in Morton, p.25.

[53] Morton, p.16

[54] The United Farmer's Platform, 1919, *The National Liberal and Conservative Handbook,* I, pp.74-77, in *Canadian Party Platforms 1867-1968,* p.91.

[55] *Ibid.,* p.91

[56] See Morton, *The Progressive Party in Canada,* p.130.

[57] Morton, p.164.

[58] Statement on Progressive Policies, Issued by Robert Forke, Progressive Leader, *The Grain Growers' Guide* in *Canadian Party Platforms 1867-1968,* p.99.

[59] *Ibid.,* p.102

[60] *Ibid.,* p.105, Toronto *Globe,* July 24, 1926.

Political Parties and Ideologies

[61] Quoted in H. B. Neatby, "The Political Ideas of William Lyon Mackenzie King" in *The Political Ideas of the Prime Ministers of Canada*, (Ottawa: University of Ottawa, 1968) p.125.

[62] William Lyon Mackenzie King, *Industry and Humanity* (New York: Houghton Mifflin, 1918) p.336.

[63] National Liberal and Conservative Handbook, I, pp.55-62 (Ottawa: 1921) in *Canadian Party Platforms*, p.82.

[64] "Every dispute and every controvsery of which I have had any intimate knowledge has owed its origin, and the difficulties pertaining to its settlement, not so much to the economic questions involved as to 'this certain blindness in human beings' to matters of real significance to other lives, and to an unwillingness to approach an issue with any attempt at appreciation of the fundamental sameness of feelings and aspirations in human beings." King, *Industry and Humanity*, p.7.

[65] Mackenzie King to Charles Dunlop, 8 July 1933, in Neatby, p.128.

[66] *National Liberal and Conservative Handbook*, in Carrigan, p.82.

[67] A Campaign Statement of the Liberal Party, Sydney *Post-Record*, March 8, 1940, in *ibid.*, 140.

[68] We as "Liberals again place on record our appreciation of the object of the said Agreement and our faith in the principles of friendly international relations underlying it, and we express our earnest hope that in both countries such principles will be upheld, and that a favourable moment may come when there will be a renewed manifestation by the two Governments of a desire to make some similar arrangements." *National Liberal and Conservative Handbook* in Carrigan, p.81.

[69] Mackenzie King, *The Liberal Party's Position* (Ottawa: 1935), in *ibid.*, p.128. Reprinted by permission of The National Liberal Federation of Canada.

[70] "Resolution Adopted by the Third National Liberal Convention," Ottawa, 1948. *The Liberal Party of Canada* (Ottawa: 1957) in *ibid.*, p.181. Reprinted by permission of the National Liberal Federation of Canada.

[71] *Ibid.*, p.182

[72] From "Introduction" by Lester B. Pearson to *The Liberal Party* by J. W. Pickersgill (1962, p. ix) reprinted by permission of The Canadian Publishers, McClelland and Stewart Limited, Toronto.

[73] *Ibid.*, p. ix

[74] "Liberalism, also, while insisting on equality of opportunity, rejects any imposed equality which would discourage and destroy a man's initiative and enterprise. It sees no value in the equality, or conformity, which comes from lopping off the tallest ears of corn.... Liberalism accepts social security, but rejects socialism; it accepts free enterprise but rejects economic anarchy."

[75] P. E. Trudeau, *Federalism and the French Canadians* (Toronto: Macmillan, 1968) p. xxiii.

[76] *Ibid.*, p. xxi

[77] See P. E. Trudeau: *Conversations with Canadians*, p.86 © this selection University of Toronto Press 1972, Toronto.

[78] *Ibid.*

[79] *Ibid.*, p.87

[80] House of Commons Debates, 8 January 1973, Vol. 117, no. 3, p.55 unrevised.

[81] See R. Joy, *Languages in Conflict*, (Toronto: McCelland and Stewart, 1972).

[82] Trudeau, *Federalism and the French Canadians*, p.18.

[83] *Ibid.*, p.4

[84] *Ibid.*, pp.157-8

[85] *Ibid.*, p.158

[86] *Ibid.*, p.159

[87] *Ibid.*, p.177

[88] P. E. Trudeau, "Federalism, Nationalism and Reason" in P. A. Crépeau and C. B. Macpherson, eds. *The Future of Canadian Federalism*, p.26, © University of Toronto Press, 1965.

[89] *Ibid.*, p.26.

[90] *Ibid.,* p.27.
[91] *Ibid.,* p.28
[92] *Ibid.,* p.34
[93] Trudeau, *Federalism and the French Canadians,* p.13.
[94] Trudeau, "Federalism, Nationalism and Reason", p.34.
[95] Trudeau, *Federalism and the French Canadians,* p.33.
[96] Trudeau, "Federalism, Nationalism and Reason", p.34.
[97] Trudeau, *Federalism and the French Canadians,* p. xix.
[98] *Ibid.,* p. xxi.

Chapter IV

Canadian Conservatism

Canadian Conservatism, unlike Liberalism, is not a pure doctrine. Horowitz argued that there was a Tory strain in Canada, collectivist and hierarchical, brought by both Loyalists and emigrants direct from the United Kingdom. This toryism is one important strand of Canadian Conservatism, and is the most important element which distinguishes it from Liberalism. To the Liberal belief in individualism and freedom, the Conservative adds a belief in collectivism and privilege. It does not require deep pentration to appreciate that these two sets of ideas are not easily reconciled into a coherent doctrine, and part of the history of Canadian Conservatism has consisted in the shifting balance of the mix of liberalism and toryism.

Conservatism, however, is the most procrustean of doctrines. The word is often used promiscuously to describe all those who are hostile to change, or who prefer things as they are. Such men with their preference for the familiar can easily fall into nostalgia for the immediate or distant past. If social or political conditions have been rapidly changing, it is not unlikely that some men will look with longing on the world they have lost, and will seek to re-impose the old order rather than engage in the difficult task of re-ordering their ideological understanding of the world. So all parties, but especially the Conservatives, have at times in their history become the preserve of men whose ideas lived in the past. Such a state of affairs existed in the Conservative party under Meighen's leadership in relation to imperial affairs. The substance of the nostalgia can run from preference for one particular flag such as the Red Ensign, to a belief in a particular set of remedies against economic depression, to the belief in a completely different social order which prevailed, or was imagined to have prevailed, in the past.

Finally, when people talk of conservatism, sometimes they mean little more than a disposition. This disposition is one which dislikes rapid changes in identity; which prefers change to be slow and cautious; which regrets any alteration in the state of affairs that destroys whatever is known and loved, regardless of the advantages to be gained by the change. Like nostalgia, this disposition is by no means the prerogative of any one political party in Canada. Almost all men, at certain times, are suceptible to its charm. Yet throughout its history, the party that Macdonald created has attracted on the whole more men of this character than the Liberal Party or the CCF/NDP.

These three constituents of Canadian Conservatism — toryism, nostalgia, and hostility to rapid change — have been a source of much confusion to discussions of the ideas of Canadian political parties. The party's tory ideas, and its nostalgia, have sometimes placed these aspects of the ideology outside of the mainstream of Canadian political life. Because the tory strain in Canada, like the socialist strain, is indigenous but not pervasive, the party's doctrines have always been mixed with a healthy dose of liberalism. We will argue later that there are good grounds for this, stemming primarily from the predominant importance of liberalism in Victorian British North America; but for the time being it will suffice to not that leading Conservative apologists such as Heath Macquarrie and George Hogan denied that there were "deep philosophical differences" between their party and the Liberals.[1] More recently the Conservative Party's research director repudiated, in the strongest possible language, the notion that either party had a consistent ideology in the twentieth century: "The names Liberal and Conservative do not have ideological meanings vis-à-vis their parties".[2]

All these writers have made a common mistake. They have been preoccupied with the indisputable fact that their party shares an obvious concern with the Liberals for individualism and for enhanced liberty. Indeed there have been members of the Conservative Party whose ideology was unalloyed liberalism, and who found a haven in the Conservative Party only by dint of an accident of history, such as family connection, electoral opportunity or even a wearied indifference to what they considered insubstantial ideas. Men who accepted what we called earlier the "ideology of actual operating institutions" could be easily content to join whichever party offered to provide the roads, schools, hospitals, railways or canals which would best service their local constituencies. The guidance to practical political action provided by this low level ideology has often proven adequate especially to men of conservative temperament, who are incapable of imagining any dramatic alteration in the world as they know it. To such men the liberal aspects of the Conservative Party's doctrine are sufficiently famil-

Political Parties and Ideologies

iar to be reassuring; to them the tory and nostalgic aspects are little more than weapons with which to attack a partisan enemy.

The carelessness in the use of the description "conservative" especially by journalists, has added one more dimension to the problem which has to be sorted out before we can proceed with our analysis. In the 1950's and early 1960's in the United States a political movement arose, centring finally around the Republican presidential candidate in 1964, Senator Barry Goldwater, that decribed itself as conservative. Because the United States was fundamentally a liberal country, as Hartz has argued, conservatism in that country took on the guise of nostalgia for a return of the days of unrestricted business activity which had been challenged and defeated finally by the New Deal of Franklin Delano Roosevelt in the 1930's. Since this style of political thought had its admirers in this country, such as the former Social Credit premier of Alberta, Senator E. C. Manning, it was deceptively simple for commentators to assume that ideologies which bore the same names in two closely related countries were in truth the same ideology with only local peculiarities. This was the error of Hartz' follower, Macrae, as well as of the recent critics of Canadian ideologies whom we cited in our first chapter. Yet when Senator Manning proposed to "rationalize federal party politics", and selected the Conservative Party as the agency to polarize Canadian politics "over fundamental values and principles of life, government, and nationhood" he was seeking to create a novelty unlike any party described in the studies of Hogan, Macquarrie or by any Canadian historian. In substance, Senator Manning sought to import an exogenous ideology from another country to serve him, and he hoped others, as a guide for the reconstruction of Canadian political life.[3]

There is then something curious at the very heart of Canadian Conservatism. There can be little doubt that Senator Manning believed himself to be a man of sound conservative principles and that he was widely acknowledged to be one. Yet there also seems to be something which links Macdonald, Meighen, Borden, Bennett, Bracken, Diefenbaker and Stanfield, something which gives more than merely a nominal unity to their claims to be Conservatives. This riddle is not a particularly difficult one to unravel, nor is the problem itself new. Lord Durham in his famous *Report* drew to the attention of his readers what he took to be a perplexing feature of Canadian politics.

> Thus the French have been viewed as a democratic party, contending for reform; and the English as a conservative minority, protecting the menaced connexion

with the British Crown, and the supreme authority of the Empire .... But when we look to the objects of each party, the analogy to our own politics seems to be lost, if not actually reversed; the French appear to have used their democratic aims for conservative purposes, rather than those of liberal and enlightened movement; and the sympathies of the friends of reform are naturally enlisted on the side of sound amelioration which the English minority in vain attempted to introduce into the anticipated laws of the Province....[4]

Durham's observations are important for two reasons. First, they lend credence to the Horowitz thesis that there has long been in Canada an indigenous conservative tradition with strong local roots, more pervasive in French Canada than English Canada, though at the time Durham wrote still dominant in English Canada, through the political control of the Family Compact. Second, he highlights the difficult nature of conservatism, for he notes that the word could correctly be used to refer either to the substance of a particular political position which at that particular time involved the continuation of Canada as a monarchy within the Empire; or it could more generally refer to a disposition. The French Canadians wanted to preserve a particular state of affairs to which they were, for various reasons, attached. Now this disposition is most often found in those who are, in the words of Professor Michael Oakeshott, "acutely aware of having something to lose".[5] As a consequence, it is more often the businessman or the farmer than the property-poor wage earner who is disposed to be hostile to change, since he has a stake in the status quo which an alteration might imperil. As nations become richer, however, even the labourer begins to have a consideration in things as they are, and he in his turn begins to resist change.

Material goods are only one, albeit an important, type of possession, and the conservative disposition can appear in any class of society and in any age group. It is in this sense, as Durham understood, that the *Canadiens* were profoundly conservative. They had been threatened, first by the Conquest, and then by the concurrent drying up of immigration from France. The flood of immigration initially by the United Empire Loyalists and then from Britain placed their language, their customs, their culture and their faith in jeopardy; indeed, everything was put to risk, and *la survivance* became the rallying cry for those with a consciousness that they had something valuable to lose. Again, in Oakeshott's words: "With some people this is itself a choice; in others its is a disposition which appears, frequently or less frequently, in their prefer-

ences and aversions, and is not itself chosen or specifically culti-
vated."[6] It was in both these senses that Lord Durham believed that
the French Canadians were conservative: "They clung to ancient
prejudices, ancient customs and ancient laws, not from any strong
sense of their beneficial effects, but with the unreasoning tenacity of
an uneducated and unprogressive people."[7]

Conservatism began to take its shape as a powerful political belief in Canada under the influence of John A. Macdonald, who
sought, he said, to "enlarge the bounds of our party so as to embrace every person desirous of being counted a progressive Conservative. . . ."[8] He was however anxious to claim that "while I have
always been a member of what is called the Conservative party,
I could never have been called a Tory."[9] Macdonald's desire to
disembarrass himself of this description and the connotations it
bore in the Canada of his day is understandable. What we might
describe as the High Tory ideology consisted of a doctrine centered
exclusively around collectivism and privilege; but as Durham had
argued in his *Report* those beliefs were becoming increasingly less
adequate as an explanation of contemporary political and social
realities.

Macdonald cast his net more widely and developed a party with
a doctrine of wider appeal to the increasingly liberally minded
populace of the Canadas. The historian W. L. Morton distinguished
three important strains in this ideological coalition that Macdonald
was attempting to construct: the French Canadian tradition of the
Bleus, the United Empire Loyalists, influenced by the principles of
the Whig Settlement in England in 1688, and the second Tory party
in the United Kingdom, whose desire it was to give Canada "the
British Constitution in all its balanced perfection, confident that the
liberty it conferred would ensure the loyalty of those who enjoyed
that liberty".[10] The consequent melding of these different traditions,
Morton believed, led to the significant conclusion that although
Canadian Conservatism took its intellectual source from England, it
developed in Canada a unique national character of its own.[11]

Although historians normally date the origin of the party with
the MacNab ministry of 1854, it was not until the Confederation
controversy of 1864-67 that Macdonald's group in the legislature
had an issue of sufficient importance to transform its organization
from an electoral faction to a party. It was at this time that many
of the ideas that were to become important in Canadian Conservative thought were first given expression in an institutional setting.
Confederation itself, as a scheme, was scarcely a novelty in the
politics of British North America. The idea had first been mooted
as early as 1754, as a system of defence against the French and

Indians; by 1858, when Alexander Galt moved the last of his three resolutions, the possibility of a union of all British North America, little interest was shown "in the grandiose scheme of a young man; they had heard it all before. Theirs was not the indifference of hostility but of over-familiarity."[12]

It would be contentious, however, to suggest that merely because an idea has a long history, it thereby acquires a conservative character when it comes to implementing it. At least one anticonfederate took his stand on such grounds. Luther Houlton suggested in the Canadian Confederation debates that Macdonald's faction had not established the need for this measure. "They are proposing revolution, and it was incumbent upon them to establish a necessity for revolution. . . ."[13]

In spite of opposition of this sort, which could be characterized as Tory in the terms Macdonald used, it can be seen on inspection that the Confederation package contained certain key elements which were to become central features of the Conservative ideology in Canada. First, there was the question of loyalty to the Crown and membership in the Empire. In Taché's words: ". . . if [we] were anxious to continue our connection with the British Empire, and to preserve intact our institutions, our laws, and even our remembrances of things past, we must sustain the measure."[14] The alternative to preserving the distinct British identity in North America was absorption by the United States: "We would be forced into the American Union by violence, and if not by violence, would be placed upon an inclined plane which would carry us there insensibly."[15] Macdonald shared this attitude. In the words of an historian, "his dominant concern was to keep the British connection unbroken, to follow British institutions, to preserve the spirit of the British constitution, and to save Canada for a British civilization. . . . Canadians must be either English or American, said Macdonald, and he was determined to be English."[16] Cartier also shared a love for British institutions, and even more than Macdonald, a dislike and distrust of the Republic to the south. "To Cartier the United States was a menace or, at best, an example of what not to do. . . ."[17] Nor was Cartier untypical of French Canadian sentiment at the time.[18]

This attitude can be understood if we examine the fundamental premise upon which it was based. The assumption was that a shared loyalty to a common Crown was a bond between diverse subjects. Considered together with economic interests and potential future development, as well as geographic proximity, this shared allegiance made enough to constitute a nation. Thus Cartier: "Now, when we were united together, if union were attained, we would form a political nationality with which neither the national origin, nor the religion of any individual would interfere."[19] The desire to form such a union and the belief that it was possible to do so evidenced an attitude to the whole which we will call collectivism.

To some extent, of course, it is not possible to look on any state in other than collectivist terms; so a word of caution concerning this description might be in order. What is at issue here is really a question of perspective, of what first catches the attention of the observer. It is possible to draw attention first to the constituents of the nation — for example, individuals — and it is this approach, we have argued, that liberalism adopts. Or, it is possible to draw attention in the first place to the whole nation, to the confederation, and to move from there to a consideration of the constituent parts. To some, this would seem merely a difference in emphasis; to others it appears a more significant and fundamental divergence in approach. Nonetheless, important consequences flow from this distinction.

Liberalism, taking the fundamental diversity of individuals into account, has to devise an explanation for the coherence which is to be found in society. How is it that these individuals hold together, in spite of their cultural, educational, linguistic, religious, and economic differences? One conclusion which it can draw is that it is difficult for them to do so, and that policy should attempt to minimize these differences. A greater similarity between the constituent units in the state makes the development of a consensus easier and the difficulties of governing fewer. For the conservative, this problem is less pressing, since he is more willing than the liberal to assume that the unity is already present, and indeed is disturbed by disruptions which indicate anomalies in the presumed order. Hence Cartier observed: "It was lamented by some that we had this diversity of races. . . . Distinctions of this kind would always exist. Dissimilarity, in fact, appeared to be the order of the physical and of the moral world, as well as of the political world."[20] And Taché, also thinking in the context of an ordered social and political system was convinced that "the French Canadians would do all in their power to render justice to their fellow-subjects of English origin, and it should not be forgotten that if the former were in a majority in Lower Canada, the English would be in a majority in the General Government. . . ."[21]

A second important feature of Canadian Conservatism as it developed at this time was a belief in the importance of privilege, an element we have isolated in our more general discussions in the two introductory chapters. It has been noted about Macdonald, and this observation doubtless would hold about most of Victorian British North America, that he "accepted and approved of class, rank, and distinctions."[22] This same attitude comes out strongly in Cartier. He described some of the opponents of Confederation as the "extreme men, the socialists, democrats and annexationists",[23] and went on to say that he "was opposed, he might as well state most distinctly, to the democratic system which obtained in the United States".[24]

A similar cast of thought was revealed in Macdonald's analysis of the composition of the proposed Senate. The appropriateness of an hereditary upper chamber in Canada was not a new issue. It is worth recalling that a major disagreement between Burke and Fox developed during the course of the debate over the *Quebec Act* in the imperial Parliament. One of the important issues at stake there was the question of a local aristocracy in Canada. Burke favoured one on the grounds that it was giving to the colonies a faithful model of the British original. Fox, on the other hand, objected that it was unnecessary and undesirable to attempt to export marks of hereditary distinction to a new country which did not know them, and in which they would be alien elements, not of native growth.

Macdonald took an intermediate position, influenced probably by the local experience with the select Executive Councils which had tended to oligarchy. That fight had only recently been won, and Macdonald was not willing to yield anything on those grounds. The position he took was not dogmatic; he did not contend that there was anything *prima facie* wrong about such institutions. Rather he suggested that such a scheme would be "impractical in this young country". His analysis was one in sympathy with the main lines of the position Burke took on key issues: namely, that the test of the appropriateness of constitutional arrangements was whether they were in harmony with the social structure of the country. What worried Macdonald was that there was no large landed interest which composed a distinct and identifiable social class — therefore no class of natural and stable leaders in the community from whom this hereditary aristocracy could reliably be chosen. "An hereditary body is altogether unsuited to our state of society, and would soon dwindle into nothing. . . ."[25]

Macdonald, then, accepted privilege as a possible guide in the construction of the new country's government. He did not reject it out of hand, and this willingness to use such a principle is surely part of the tory inheritance which forms part of the Canadian ideological structure. But Macdonald could not escape the influence of liberal ideas,[26] even if he had wanted to do so. Part of the ideological coalition from which he fashioned his Liberal-Conservative party consisted of the United Empire Loyalists, who, although they had too much of the tory in them to accept the doctrinaire liberal society of the United States, were also strongly influenced by the Whig Settlement in England consequent on the Revolution of 1688. The ideas of Locke, who was the foremost propagandist for the winners in that controversy, were in the air in the eighteenth century; so much so that they were a pervasive influence throughout Anglo-American political thought from which few if any of the major thinkers of the eighteenth or nineteenth century escaped.

This Lockean liberalism, with its concern for the rights of property had been raised by subsequent thinkers in Britain, especially Jeremy Bentham, to the status of a doctrinal orthodoxy. No political thinker in the mid-nineteenth century Canada could have hoped to strike a responsive chord in the vast majority of those who heard him, without incorporating substantial liberal elements into his message.[27]

Although Macdonald was undoubtedly concerned to enhance liberty and promote individualism, his toryism kept him from pursuing these ideas to the conclusions reached by men such as Mackenzie and Goldwin Smith. He was not convinced by the arguments of such men as John Simpson who objected to the construction of the Intercolonial Railway on the grounds that it would be a political interference which would "divert trade and commerce from their natural channels [i.e. New York and Boston]".[28] In fact, he seems to have indicated a belief in the primacy of politics over economics, which entailed among other things a repudiation of continentalism.

The tradition of economic liberalism in Britain, from Adam Smith through the Manchester School and Herbert Spencer, was to curb the power of the state over the organization and conduct of both industrial and commercial enterprises. It enthusiastically canvassed the possibility that the demands of the economy should, in most instances, predominate over merely political problems and arrangements. Macdonald clearly did not accept this approach. It is a commonplace that the *British North America Act* did not make provision for the extensive range of social services which the state is now expected to provide for its citizens. But it is also an accepted interpretation that Macdonald, whatever some of the other Fathers of Confederation might have envisaged, preferred a strong central government, if possible, a legislative union, in order both to avoid what he had analyzed to be major weaknesses in the American federal system, and to endow the Canadian general government with sufficient powers to engage in the important task of building a transcontinental political unit in British North America.

Macdonald set out on this task by acquiring the lands of the Hudson Bay Company. To prevent the Americans from annexing the land by settlement and to entice British Columbia into Confederation, he sought to construct the railway that eventually became known as the CPR. The brunt of the Liberal criticism of the railway was that it was too expensive for the young country and that it was unnecessary since a more economical system could be devised which would utilize the existing American rail lines.[29] In 1874 Macdonald had objected to the proposed Liberal scheme on two grounds. First, such a proposal as Mackenzie had made would violate the terms of the agreement made with both British Columbia and with the Imperial Government. Second, "[w]e would build no railway for the United States as Mr. Mackenzie wanted, and we would have no hermaphrodite system of transport, carrying away the great products of the West from Canada."[30]

As Macdonald saw it, the choice of a tariff strategy was one which should be made politically, as a conscious attempt to control economic forces, which would otherwise operate to the detriment of the people of the country:

> The time has come, gentlemen, when the people of this Dominion have to declare whether Canada is for the Canadians, or whether it is to be a pasture for cows to be sent to England. It is for the electors to say whether every appliance of civilization shall be manufactured within her bounds for our own use, or whether we shall remain hewers of wood and drawers of water to the United States.[31]

The same issue was joined again in 1891 when the Liberals put forth the suggestion of Unrestricted Reciprocity with the United States as an alternative to the National Policy of the Conservatives. Macdonald was quick to note what he feared were the political consequences of this economic suggestion: "I have of course pointed out that U.R. meant annexation. . . ."[32]

Intimately connected with this approach to the relationship between politics and economics was an aspect of nationalism. Conservatism, concerned as it is with a desire to preserve what is "our own", and with a disposition to maintain the existing state of affairs in most essentials, is necessarily more sensitive to new foreign infusions of ideas or capital than are either liberalism or socialism. This hostility, though, expressed a gruff and irritated annoyance at being disturbed, and a suspicion of the foreigner, rather than a systematic doctrine. Macdonald, for example, in the letter mentioned above, went on to say "the movements of Cartwright, Farrer & Wiman enabled us to raise the loyalty cry, which had considerable effect". This sounds cynical, but there can be little doubt that Macdonald had a dislike and distrust of Americans which ran deep:

> If left to ourselves, I have no doubt of a decision in our favour, but I have serious apprehensions which are shared by all our friends here, that a large amount of Yankee money will be expended to corrupt our people. ... Sir C. Tupper will tell you that every American statesman (and he saw them all in 88), covets Canada. The greed for its acquisition is still on the increase, and God knows where it will end.[33]

This fear of American invasion or annexation had, whether true or not, been one of the lodestars of Macdonald's political conduct; and it is therefore not at all surprising in a man who was one of the founders of a political approach with a distinctively national character. What is more curious is the observation Macdonald makes in the sentence which follows on directly from the passage quoted above. "If Gladstone succeeds, he will sacrifice Canada without scruple."

Here then is no blind and dogmatic devotion to Britain, no willingness to be subordinate to the imperial design for its own sake. Was the man who spoke about raising "the loyalty cry" merely a cynic, willing to use whatever rhetoric would prove effective, within the limiting constraints imposed by the established traditions of his party's doctrine? We think not. Macdonald's attitude to Britain here has all the hallmarks of ideological politics. He was undoubtedly committed to a belief in the importance of the Empire and the value of the British example. Because he could not follow every twist and turn of imperial policy, he adopted a simplified image of what Britain stood for. Britishness was an ideal, to be imposed not only on Canada, but on Britain itself; and Canada was justified in charting an independent course whenever Britain deviated from the true British policy. To approach the point from a slightly different point of view, one could suggest that Britain, from a Canadian viewpoint, had a divided self. On the one hand, she was the centre of the Empire, seat of the Imperial Parliament, presiding over a colonial assembly of free men. On the other hand, she was the home of traditional European intrigues, pursuing a national interest at the expense of the Empire. It was only the former to which Macdonald thought Canadians owed strong allegiance.

Macdonald's Conservative ideology was a skilful blend of toryism and liberalism. It was never thoroughly consistent, but Macdonald succeeded well in keeping the different elements in an harmonious balance which allowed him to win every election he fought from Confederation to his death, with the exception of his defeat in 1872 when the American railway interests handed his Liberal opponents a major scandal to embarrass his ministry. Macdonald's success should not be surprising since his ideological appeal was diverse compared to the more limited ideological range of the Liberals in the early years of Confederation. Even the execution of Louis Riel might not have hurt the Conservative predominance in Canadian politics were it not for the rise of Laurier to the leadership of the Liberal Party. We traced in the last chapter Laurier's modification of Canadian Liberalism, and his truce with the nationalist and collectivist sentiments in Quebec through the doctrine of provincial rights. Canadian Conservatism had to await John Diefenbaker before it was again to have as wide an appeal as it had under Macdonald's tutelage.

When Laurier deprived the Conservatives of their Quebec support, he cut them off from the collectivism and heirarchy of the *bleu* tradition. The tory elements within the Conservative party were thereby isolated from precisely that society for which their ideology had the greatest appeal and the greatest explanatory power. Under Borden and Meighen the liberal elements in the party took on an increased prominence, implied in a reminiscence of Borden, written in 1935. When Lord Curzon of Kedleston asked him, in the Imperial War Cabinet during the Great War what he thought of the English social system, Borden replied: "If you wish me to speak frankly, we regard your social order as little more than a glorified feudal system."[34] This liberal hostility to privilege was also reflected in Borden's unwillingness to allow Canadians to receive peerages or other British marks of social distinction.[35] Arthur Meighen showed the same resentment of privilege in 1911 when he attacked the Liberals for becoming "the slaves of those who helped them into power and who now maintain them there behind ramparts of gold".[36]

Borden had not become the captive of a pure liberal ideology. The Conservative doctrine his party inherited from Macdonald still contained powerful collectivist elements, which came out most clearly in his hostility to Liberal proposals for a reciprocity treaty with the United States. The Conservative belief in the primacy of politics over economics was a derivation from the principles of collectivism — the nation had a right and a responsibility to ensure that the interests of the whole took precedence over the liberty of the business interests to pursue their economic advantage unchecked. It is therefore worth looking at Borden's objections to Laurier's proposed reciprocity treaty with the United States for the light it sheds on the post-Macdonald nature of Canadian Conservatism.

Reciprocity was a policy which was incompatible with Canadian Conservatism. It flew in the face of Macdonald's National Policy by segregating "the provinces which confederation aimed to unite". It stood in the way of improving cooperation within the Empire: "The President of the United States had avowed that the main purpose with which he sought the treaty was to prevent consolidation of the British Empire." Finally, it abandoned the attempt on the part of the Canadian nation to control economic forces: it "virtually surrenders control of [Canada's] destinies". Although this would have been sufficient reason in itself to lead Canadian Conservatives to oppose the measure, they also continued to worry about the same fear that had haunted Macdonald and Taché, that without firm control over economic forces the nation's political sovereignty would be eroded: "if Canada places itself under the commercial control of the United States its political independence, if retained, will be a shadow and not a substantial reality."[37]

Although Borden did not get much sympathy from "certain leading British statesmen", whom he claimed did not understand the basis upon which the Canadian economy, and especially the protected industries in this country, stood, he did get assistance from American politicians:

> President Taft's indiscreet reference to Canada as being "at the parting of the ways" was . . . useful to us during the campaign. Mr. Champ Clark was even more indiscreet in his declaration that he favoured Reciprocity because: *I hope to see the day when the American flag will float over every square foot of the British North American possessions, clear to the North Pole. . . .*[38]

As far as Borden was concerned the very survival of Canada as an independent political unit in North America was at stake in this election; and here the Conservative Party's collectivism triumphed over the free trade doctrines of Laurier's Liberals. It would be perverse in the extreme to try to fit the events of 1911 into a brokerage theory of politics. If there ever was a difference between the parties over an issue fundamental to the nature of the Canadian polity, this was it; and Borden was consciously aware of the fact.

His successor, Arthur Meighen, was a different type of conservative. The rural, socially stratified and unindustrialized Maritimes from which Borden hailed had an ideological composition different from the West in which Arthur Meighen lived during the early days of his adult life. This difference draws attention to a weakness in Horowitz' thesis similar to that to which we drew attention in Chapter II relating to French Canada. On the whole Horowitz treats the social and ideological composition of Canada as if it were relatively uniform. Clearly this is not the case. In the Maritimes the liberal fragments were much weaker, and a more tory attitude was implanted by the predominately loyalist settlement. The settlement in the West was much later and of a much more strongly liberal bent. The frontier spirit, the rough equality of the settlers and the absence of an indigenous local history all gave ample opportunity for the development of an increasingly powerful liberal strain in the political thought of that area. Meighen reflected this disposition.

He was, of course, one of the major architects of the Canadian National Railways system, a policy which earned him the implacable hatred of the Montreal business community and especially the Canadian Pacific interests, who would have preferred to be given control of their bankrupt competitors. Moreover, Meighen did not follow the course of nationalizing the railways out of mere expediency, for he believed in the state control of certain important natural resources. As he said in London in 1918: "Dictates of wise policy have suggested that our invaluable water-powers — an asset of a clearly distinctive character — should be to the utmost possible extent not only state-owned and controlled, but state developed and operated. All arguments that go anywhere to support Government monopoly apply with peculiar force to water-power."[39] This was, after all, traditional Conservative policy. But it was nothing more than that.

The tory strains in Meighen's thought did not involve a belief in equality. Meighen, in the year after this speech, in 1919, took firm and vigorous action to repress what he considered to be the dangerous sedition of the Winnipeg General Strike. State ownership was as far as he was willing to do. In his 1918 speech, he was quick to point out to his listeners that, although the Conservative government was willing to undertake the regulation and operation of what economists know as natural monopolies, "there is no spirit of rampant or headlong socialism in possession of the Canadian mind." And he assured his audience that: "Capital is as safe as in any country on earth."[40] This defence of business and capital, as we will see later when we come to consider Meighen's position in the 1940's, was a preoccupation with him. But it is not this aspect of Meighen's political approach to which we wish to draw immediate attention. We noted earlier that conservatism stands in constant danger of being overtaken by events, and that it easily becomes transformed into what we called nostalgia.

The Great War and the peace negotiations which led, among other things, to full Canadian membership in the League of Nations had effectively raised Canada to the status of a fully independent nation. This and the declining position of Britain in the world had changed the entire nature of the imperial tie and the implications of this would have profound implications on Canadian development. In Borden's address to the caucus in 1920 on his retirement, he mentioned "our relations with the Mother Country and the other nations of the Empire" first in the list of "the most immediate and urgent problems" which the new government faced.[41] Of what was this new bond to consist?

This question was to arise for Meighen in an unexpected way, in the famous King-Byng constitutional controversy of 1926. For reasons we have touched on more fully in the last chapter, Canadian Liberalism was prone to identify the cause of Canadian independence with a breaking of ties with Britain and the Empire, and the Crown as the central link in the chain which bound Canada to a colonial dependence. There can be little doubt, especially after the analysis of the crisis by both Forsey[42] and Graham[43] that Meighen and Lord Byng acted on correct constitutional principles, as they were then understood. King's attempt to escape from the vote of censure on corruption in the Customs Department had been an audacious manoeuvre, which, thanks to Meighen's actions, led to King's victory in the 1926 election.

Meighen took the fateful step of assuming office with a very thin majority in a confused constitutional situation because he felt that he owed a debt of honour to the Governor General, and because he thought that it was constitutionally proper for him to do so. Clearly this was an ideologically motivated move, and not one induced by consideration of electoral advantage, although some of the latter could reasonably be expected to accrue to an incumbent prime minister. Canada's changing relationship within the Empire was at stake here. A Conservative apologist such as Heath MacQuarrie might call the whole issue fallacious,[44] but Mackenzie King was probably closer to the truth when he described it as "a constitutional issue greater than any that has been raised in Canada since the founding of this Dominion".[45]

The Imperial Conference of 1926 and the *Statute of Westminster* in 1931 clarified the situation. A constitutional revolution, however peaceful, had taken place on the matter of the imperial relationship which was even to have an important, though transitory effect on the federal-provincial distribution of power through the Radio Reference and the Aeronautics Reference cases decided by the Privy Council in the early 1930's. Meighen's attachment to the Crown, real as it was, and expressive of traditional Conservative policy, blinded him, as we argued in Chapter I as ideologies sometimes do, to the important changes that were taking place in both Empire and nation. King's anti-imperial ideology was a handier instrument in this crisis for understanding the changing nature of this relationship, and this greater clarity partly accounts for King's electoral success in the succeeding election.

Meighen, for all his intellectual penetration and brilliance, spoke more truly than he knew when he titled his collection of speeches, *Unrevised and Unrepented*. His greatest weakness was that he knew too well what were the traditional policies of his party, and his disposition was to hold fast to them. His nostalgia for the Empire came out in the "Ready, aye, ready" of the Chanak crisis, and his belief in the tariff and in class stability made him unsuited for dealing with the turmoil of the West. He could, and did, write powerfully and evocatively in defence of this conservative disposition of his character. During the debate over Church Union in 1924 he said that his "inclinations lead me naturally to cling to the Church with which my family for many generations has been associated".[46] In an address in the next year, 1925, in commemoration of D'Arcy McGee, he expressed the belief that it "will be a good thing for the national personality when we can all join in veneration of the great deeds of the fathers of our country".[47] And in 1927, when he addressed the convention that chose R. B. Bennett his successor, he gave a powerful and moving address in defence of his controversial Hamilton speech, but the mode he chose here was also retrospective:

> The chords of memory unite us with the past, and this is the time and this is the place when all of us ... should catch the spirit and hear the voice of the noble founders of our political faith. . . . They would urge us to be conscious of our mighty heritage, proud of the Imperial Fountain of our freedom and the flag that floats above us, worthy of those British liberty and justice which have sent their light forth and their truth among all races of men. To our history, our principles, our traditions let us be faithful to the end.[48]

This aspect of Meighen's conservatism has not passed without notice. George Hogan described Meighen's economic policies as almost "a reversion to the mercantilist theories of colonial Toryism",[49] and accused Meighen and Bennett of letting the Conservative Party drift "away from the positive nation-building concepts upon which its earlier greatness was based".[50] Hogan's description is not fair. Meighen could not be called a reactionary in the way that Hogan's argument implies. His nostalgia was for continuation of the traditional policies of the party, not for a return to a state of affairs which had long since been outmoded. Meighen's politics were ideological, and probably outdated, but they did not represent an attempt to turn back the clock. Neither were they a repudiation of the nation-building principles of Canadian Conservatism. As we have just seen, Meighen was not a man to make such a repudiation. His guilt, if any, was one of omission, rather than of commission; his treason was a failure to adapt.

The Depression, on the other hand, presented the two leading ideologies with a set of problems that Conservatism was better suited to handle than Liberalism. The advantages of hindsight, aided by Keynes' modifications of macroeconomic theory allow us to understand that more extensive and more vigorous state action was required to alleviate or moderate the ravages of the economic decline of the 1930's. The Conservatives were in possession of ideological equipment which would have allowed them to make the move to Keynesian economics. The central issue here was their belief in the importance of using the state to control the outcome of economic events.[51] Bennett's ill-fated tariff policy of 1930 is a case in point. Bennett spoke in his Winnipeg speech of how he would use tariffs to sell Western agricultural products.

> You have been taught to mock at tariff and applaud free trade. Tell me, when did free trade fight for you? You say our tariffs are only for the manufacturers; I will make them fight for you as well. *I will use them to blast a way into the markets that have been closed to you.*[52]

This policy of protection was not the only instance of this cast of mind that Bennett evidenced in 1930. He also spoke vigorously in favour of the Canadian National Railway: "I love my country and what it has done, and one of its greatest achievements, has been the development of this great national transportation system of which I believe every Canadian is proud. Amalgamation? Never! Competition? Ever! That is the policy for which I stand."[53] This short passage reveals the inconsistent mix of liberal and conservative principles to which we have drawn attention to several times before. Although Bennett here showed a strong belief in the importance of continuing this state activity ("And more, I say, that if you see any attempt on my part at any time to violate that pledge I give you here and now, then ask for my resignation —

insist upon it. . . ."),[54] and indignantly refused, as Meighen had done before him, to hand the CNR over to CPR interests, he justified his stand by appeals to patriotism ("I love my country") and to the capitalist aspects of liberalism (Competition? Ever!')'.

These liberal aspects of Bennett's Conservatism impeded his adoption of a more vigorous programme of state action in the early days of the Depression. Herridge, Bennett's brother-in-law and then Canadian Ambassador to Washington, had been early impressed by the success of Franklin Roosevelt's New Deal. In September 1933 he wrote a secret memorandum to Bennett, counselling him to abandon *laissez-faire,* at least for the duration of the Depression.[55] By June 1934 Herridge was pressing the idea on Bennett with much increased vigour. He argued that the time had come to rid the party's ideology of the increasingly burdensome legacy of the past, a task, we have argued, for which Meighen was unsuited, although the events of the 1920's necessitated it in imperial relations as much as those of the 1930's did in economics.[56] As long as the party held to its old ideological vision, it would encounter difficulties because it would prove unable to devise any effective solutions to the problem. It had to be willing to repudiate those aspects of its thought which we have called nostalgic.[57]

To this end Herridge put forward two initial suggestions. First, it was critical for Bennett to understand the importance of ideological thought and to guide his actions by an underlying philosophy.[58] Second, the ideology that Bennett adopted should be as free as possible from liberal elements. In Herridge's view liberalism was an outmoded doctrine that had to be superseded.[59]

So far, Herridge was proposing nothing more than an ideological purification of Canadian Conservatism, ridding it of liberal elements, and adding to its traditional policy of state action and political control over economic forces. But Herridge went dangerously beyond this; he advanced a dramatically exaggerated notion derived from another constituent element in Canadian Conservatism: the belief in inequality or privilege. In April 1934 he wrote of the American New Deal as a Pandora's box, and argued that the American President had been successful precisely because he had mystified the American people. The important thing was that Roosevelt had created an illusion that he was a saviour of the American people. Whether he had any practical solutions was of less immediate importance.[60]

Canada too needed a Pandora's box, a programme or slogan to persuade the people that a better life was in the offing for them as well.[61] To achieve what he called a new order of prosperity[62] Herridge went wildly beyond anything that the Conservative Party had contemplated before this time. Herridge was influenced by the American New Deal; but his eyes were on Europe as well. He drew Bennett's attention to the success of Stalin, Mussolini and Hitler and urged him to imitate their success by imitating the motor spring of their greatness — a new and coherent ideological vision.[63]

Herridge's analysis of the problems which Canada faced bore an affinity to some of the doctrines of European fascism. In an important letter to Bennett in June 1934 he argued that the Depression had led to a serious crisis of confidence. Worse, the people of the country had begun to despair that prosperity would not return under the old regime. Herridge urged Bennett to harness the discontent that had been created and seize the opportunity which events afforded him to take a commanding control of the situation.

The Liberals might suggest, as they did in 1935, that the choice was between King and chaos, but they did not have the inherent disposition in favour of privilege to take them as far as Herridge. Herridge here showed no confidence in the judgment of the democratic process or in the people of the country. He argued that they were incapable of judging their own best interests. This was not the time to consider the "present whims of the electors", the "noncombatants in this battle".[64]

It is impossible, in the light of this analysis to agree with Horowitz that Bennett was a "red tory", a man who might prefer the CCF-NDP to the Liberals. In no way can we accept the argument that the Bennett New Deal was, as Horowitz claims, a manifestation of "leftism" derived from tory democracy. From Herridge's appeal to Bennett ("you alone can save the day") the conclusion is inescapable that the Bennett New Deal, under Herridge's influence was not socialist at all, but rather closer in spirit to fascism than to Roosevelt.

Herridge and Bennett were locked into an ideological understanding of Canadian society which placed great emphasis on privilege. Bennett's late programme certainly contained collectivist elements, but these were enduring features of Canadian Conservatism. Although it was this which he shared with the socialists, we will see in the next chapter that one of the abiding concerns of Canadian socialism was precisely the elimination of that privilege for which the Conservatives stood. The traditional picture has painted Bennett as a man who was an autocrat when it came to dealing with his cabinet colleagues. Neither did he have great faith in democracy. "It is almost incomprehensible that the vital issues of life and death to nations, peace or war, bankruptcy or solvency, should be determined by the counting of heads and knowing as we do that the majority under modern conditions — happily the majority becoming smaller — are untrained and unskilled in dealing with the problems which they have to determine".[65]

Bennett announced his New Deal in a series of surprise radio addresses, which look in retrospect like a mild *coup de main* against his cabinet. Borden noted at the time that they were undertaken "without previous consultation with any of his colleagues" and went on to observe, perhaps with some understatement that several "were extremely disturbed by his course".[66] More significantly, though, Borden realized that a change of some significance was in the air. "Undoubtedly, the Prime Minister has entirely changed the current of political thought in Canada by his enunciation of these policies."[67]

Bennett was, however, no Canadian Mussolini or Hitler. He did not wish, nor did he intend, to subvert the democratic basis of the Canadian government, however sceptical he may have been about certain of its features. He had no wish to work a revolution; in his own words, "I am for reform".[68] What Bennett was attempting to achieve in the five radio broadcasts that he made was to reassess and modify Conservative thought in Canada, a body of doctrine which we have argued, had become increasing rigidified and nostalgic. Bennett's very language signals an awareness of the need for an ideological alteration of perspective, a change at least in emphasis among the conceptual categories in which Canadian Conservatism thought. "In the last five years, great changes have taken place in the world. The old order is gone. It will not return."[69]

The question which Bennett had squarely to face was, in what direction would Canadian Conservatism move? Would it emphasize the liberal, *laissez-faire* aspects which Meighen seemed to favour, and would it look back to the past? Meighen himself seemed to think it should. In 1935, he confessed that he did not "believe the thinking of today is nearly as careful or as well-informed or as thoroughly guided by moral principles as the thinking of forty years ago".[70] Or, would he pursue the exaggerated elitism that Herridge was pressing on him from Washington?

Bennett took neither of these courses. The strains of the party's past on which he tried to build the new Conservatism were its collectivism, especially the belief in the value of political action to control economic forces. Conservative unwillingness to participate in a class war, to set one section of the country against another finds its intellectual ancestry in England, in Burke and in the doctrines of Disraeli's second Tory party. In the second address, Bennett announced this choice: "I hold the view that if we are to have equality of social and political conditions throughout this land, we must have equality in economic conditions as well."[71] It is only on the assumption that Canadian Conservatism is nothing but a business doctrine that this position sounds implausible or hypocritical. But within the collectivist assumptions of Canadian Conservatism — sometimes very misleadingly described as organicism — the belief that the government should attempt to serve the interests of all is an entirely possible one, once we grant the assumption, which we have previously argued that Canadian Conservatism makes, that there is a fundamental unity of the whole which neither needs to be explained or justified.

Second, Bennett did as Herridge urged; he repudiated *laissez-faire*. "Reform heralds certain recovery. There can be no permanent recovery without reform. Reform or no reform! I raise that issue squarely. I nail the flag of progress to the masthead. *I summon the power of the State to its support.*"[72] This was brave, but it could not be expected to work an ideological miracle overnight. After all, the majority of Canadians still held liberal notions; and they were all the less liable to be persuaded to what they would have taken to be socialism. Although some of Herridge's dangerous rhetoric found its way into the speeches (Bennett spoke of "the corporate strength of the State" in the third address), the legislation which followed on these addresses was considerably less radical. As Meighen said, in a curiously ambivalent farewell to Bennett in 1939: "Our guest will not be offended when I say that what a lot of people have still in their minds like a nightmare is not the legislation, which was enlightened, but the speeches, which frightened."[73]

The election of 1935 returned Mackenzie King to power, and by putting Bennett into opposition ended his chance of transforming Canadian Conservatism along the lines set out in the New Deal addresses. Bennett's successor, R. J. "Fighting Bob" Manion, was not a man for the times. He does not appear to have had a wide ideological vision; and when the war intervened, he attempted to stand against King's administration in the election of 1940, exclusively on a modified version of Conservative collectivism — National Government. The National Government policy, like the Union Government before it in 1917, can be explained partly, of course, by the dictates of electoral expediency. But the reasons why the Conservatives, both in and out of office proposed it, and the Liberals, both in opposition and government, refused it, must include a reference to this ideological difference between the two parties in Canada.

Disregarding Manion, Canadian Conservatism had three clear choices, though none would guarantee success. First, Herridge, like H. H. Stevens before him in the 1935 election, left the Conservative Party and led his antifinancialist New Democracy Party to ten seats in Social Credit Alberta. But Herridge, as we have suggested before, was too extreme in the implications he drew from certain intimations of Canadian Conservatism, and it is not surprising that he met with little electoral success, except where Social Crediters supported him. Second, Canadian Conservatism could have attempted to return to its more rigidified, nostalgic beliefs. It indicated that it might move in this direction when it again chose the redoubtable Meighen as leader.

Like the Bourbons it could be said that Meighen forgot nothing and learned nothing. His ideas had changed very little since he had given up the leadership of the party. The question of the imperial relationship was not the pressing issue that it had been in the 1920's, though Meighen still was as much an Anglophile as ever.[74] In the early 1940's Meighen was faced with another challenge to his ideological presuppositions: the rise of Canadian socialism through the CCF. Meighen objected to this ideology on two grounds. First, it conflicted with his tory ideas of collectivism, to the extent that he believed that the CCF demanded that "the nation be split in twain on a class basis".[75] Second, it also contradicted his individualist assumptions. Meighen rejected the ideal of the co-operative commonwealth. We argued in Chapter I that one important function of ideology was to settle the question of the nature of the relations between those who compose society. Meighen's clear choice was that men were competitors: "Rivalry and struggle under equitable laws are the glory of living."[76]

Meighen's 1942 by-election defeat at the hands of a CCF candidate settled his fate politically; but it also probably settled the fate of the conservative blend of nostalgia and liberalism for which he stood. He was succeeded as leader in 1942 by John Bracken, the former Progressive Premier of Manitoba. Prior to that convention influential Conservatives had met at Port Hope in Ontario to reassess the political principles of the party. The choice of Bracken, and the addition of "Progressive" to the name of the party, were indications that, for the time being, they were attempting to chart a course different from that over which Meighen would have guided them. The important choice made at this time, however, was not in favour of a more distinctive style of Canadian Conservatism, as Bennett, Herridge and Meighen had unsuccessfully attempted. The party decided to minimize the differences between the two parties. Here is ample testimony, if proof of this really be needed, of the power at this time of Mackenzie King's ideological vision.

The post — Port Hope party reversed a number of historic stands. First, they adopted the Progressive hostility to tariffs, and proposed that "... as far as may be practicable, those barriers to trade must be taken away".[77] This was a momentous step, because, as we have argued, time and again, Canadian Conservatism had affirmed the importance of state intervention and control over economic forces in the interests of the nation. But now, Bracken was repudiating this position. A corollary of this new emphasis was the diminished importance of state initiatives. Previously, Conservatives had sought to harness the state's power in the national interest; Bracken, on the other hand, believed that "government must be decentralized". And more, in place of the traditional assumptions of privilege displayed by the party's leaders, Bracken was a more thoroughgoing democrat: "All organized elements in the community should be given an opportunity to paricipate in the determination of policy."[78]

Perhaps the most significant change, however, that Bracken introduced in the party's ideology was on the issue mentioned above in connection with Meighen, the nature of social relationships. Meighen had favoured a policy of individualism, of competition in business matters, but that individualism had been little more than economic. His views did not trench on a doctrine which had been fundamental in Canadian Conservatism from the time of Cartier — a belief in the importance of diversity. The liberal elements in Bracken's thought denied this value; Bracken believed, not only in the advantages of economic individualism, but also in social individualism; but his was an individualism which led in the direction of greater conformity. "Let us have less of hyphenated Canadianism."[79] To solve the problem which this new emphasis created — how does a society of competitors hold together — Bracken was driven to assume away major divisions and differences. This done, it was possible to take the next step, and affirm that it "is a most ironical paradox that the Party which I lead is striving to *create* a co-operative Commonwealth, while most of those who parade under the banner of the Co-operative Commonwealth Federation are advocating state socialism."[80] Since the men he observed in his contemporary society were manifestly not co-operators, Bracken had to make one final move.

Canadian Conservatism before Bracken had consistently displayed what we have called the conservative disposition. For example, in 1933, Bennett had mused (and his reflections were in no way untypical of a widespread spirit among Canadian Conservatives) "I begin to realize how slow indeed has been the progress of mankind...."[81] This scepticism about the possibility of making radical and dramatic improvements in the condition of mankind is perhaps the feature most commonly meant when a man or attitude is referred to as conservative. Bracken's new Conservatism would have none of that. More satisfactory, Bracken preached, was the liberal ideal of progress. His party, he said, believed "that our economy is man-made — and, therefore, not necessarily perfect, and that our duty is to work toward its perfection".[82]

In the last chapter we argued that the Progressive Party to which Bracken belonged advocated a more radical form of liberalism than found a home in the mainstream of the Liberal Party. Therefore, the change in the Conservative Party's name in 1942 was significant. From the time of Macdonald, with a few deviations, it had been known officially as the Liberal-Conservative Party. This name, as our discussions to date indicate, was singularly appropriate. The substitution of Progressive for Liberal signalled the infusion of a more powerful and more radical strain of liberalism into the party, almost, in Bracken's pronouncements, inundating the Conservative touches.

Although Bracken proved to be an electorally more satisfying leader than Manion, the Progressive Conservatism he confidently offered the party and the country did not appeal to the voters as strongly as King's Liberalism. Bracken's successor, the former Conservative Premier of Ontario, George Drew, also had little to offer in the way of ideological differences between the parties. Under Drew, the party continued on in the new paths charted by Bracken, repudiating many of the historic principles which had comprised Canadian Conservatism before that time. Drew signalled this by quoting, in the 1949 election campaign from the party's Declaration of Policy: "Economic freedom is the essence of competitive enterprise, and competitive enterprise is the foundation of our democratic system."[83] Although he spoke of the "vast areas of the North [which] challenge our vision and our courage",[84] he did not pursue the plan in a thorough or systematic fashion. It was left for John Diefenbaker to recapture the historic Conservative attitude to the use of government for nation-building purposes. Drew's preoccupation in the legal sphere were individualist in orientation as well. He was concerned about what he considered were the infringements on liberty under the Liberals and pledged his party to end them: "We believe in the widest possible measure of personal liberty consistent with law, order and the general national welfare."[85] Beyond any doubt, then, Drew narrowed the ideological breadth of Canadian Conservatism. It is not surprising that lacking even the sense of transformation and novelty that Bracken enjoyed, Drew collected fewer seats in both 1949 and 1953 than had his predecessor.

The convention which met in 1956 on the resignation of the ailing George Drew was presented with an intriguing ideological choice.

John Diefenbaker, Donald Fleming and Davie Fulton were the candidates for the leadership of the party, and each can be seen as representing distinctly different mixes of conservative principles. The weakest candidate, securing less than 10 per cent of the votes, was the one who represented the clearest, and in some ways, the most radical ideological choice — Davie Fulton.

Fulton relied on only one indigenous strand of traditional Canadian Conservatism, the tory element of British inspiration. Early in 1957 he contributed an introduction to John Farthing's book with the revealing title *Freedom Wears a Crown*. Farthing was a man of strong attachment to the British monarchical tradition in Canada, one which he emphasized to the exclusion of all others.

Fulton subscribed completely to Farthing's argument that the Crown in Parliament was the considered choice of the "two main elements of the population of Canada".[86] On this proposition hangs the Farthing-Fulton defence of the British tradition in Canada. By "British", it must be pointed out, Fulton is referring to an ideal, one which "must be given local habitation".[87] He does not mean the anglicization of the Canadian nation. Rather, he believed that this tradition was of value to French as well as English. "I have never found any thoughtful French Canadian who did not agree that the British tradition on which our constitutional processes are based, and particularly the preservation of the proper position of the Crown, is, by its protection of the rights of Parliament, in itself the surest protection of those rights — personal, cultural and religious freedom — which they hold dear."[88] Here Fulton is on firm ground, expressing a line of thought which stretched back to Cartier, Taché and Macdonald. There can be no doubt that most, if not all, leading Canadian Conservative thinkers have been firmly convinced that the Crown and the British connection is a thing of value to all Canadians, English, French and others, as well as to the Canadian polity as a whole.

However, Fulton was also in agreement with "the belief of the author that all life, in its fullest sense, and certainly all political conduct, must be conducive to the realization of, as well as answerable to, some higher moral concept. . . ."[89] This emphasis puts both Fulton and Farthing in a very small group of English Canadian political thinkers, of whom the most notable is George Grant, who have attempted to introduce an element of natural law philosophy into a consideration of Canadian political life. In Canada, this is a strictly exogenous ideological element derived, at least in Fulton's case, most likely from Catholic doctrine and the works of the eighteenth-century Anglo-Irish philosopher and statesman, Edmund Burke. Such providential and religious assumptions were unpalatable in the market place of secular Canadian Conservatism.

To these principles, Fulton added others, borrowed from the writings of Burke and Disraeli: "The reverence of our ancestors, the soundness of those past institutions and laws suitable to changing conditions, and the proposition that conservatism is not a class position, but an attitude of mind which aims at the general benefit of all classes and occupations in society."[90] However, Fulton did not pursue the implications of his doctrines rigorously to their conclusions. The fact that he too was captivated by the importance of "private property and a system of free enterprise" and that strongly affirmed that individualism was "so much a part of Conservative philosophy" is dramatic evidence of the power of the liberal element in Canadian political thought.[91] Underlying Fulton's ideas, however, was the basic caution which we have called a conservative disposition. This preference for slow, incremental change, this preference for the familiar rather than the novel, has usually been justified by reference to the utilitarian standards represented by fears of palpable harm if not observed. Fulton preferred other grounds. He suggested that the disposition was one of "humility, because he [the Conservative] is conscious of the degree to which his conduct falls short of the ideal, and indeed of the limitations of his very horizion as compared to the concept of the Universe that is there if we had the capacity to grasp the vision."[92]

Donald Fleming, who attracted the support of about 30 per cent of the delegates, was a man whose ideas were different from Fulton's in a number of important ways. He was the candidate most closely in the style of thought which had prevailed in the party during Drew's leadership. Fleming shared with Fulton the belief that the Conservative Party stood for the continuation of the Monarchy in Canada,[93] and feared the influence of the United States[94] perhaps even more than Fulton. But the important difference between the two men can be seen in their attitudes to the past and to change. Fulton was sceptical about the future, and emphasized the importance of preserving traditions and opposing inroads on the cherished institutions of the past. Fleming had much more a forward looking approach: "We always advance. Like Abraham Lincoln, we never take a step backwards."[95] Since Fleming offered little in addition to the ideas which Drew already had put forward, his appeal was limited to those with a strong commitment to Drew's liberal, business-oriented Conservatism.

The convention's choice turned out to be a man who had twice before contested the leadership of the party, John Diefenbaker. Their decision gave them and the country perhaps the most enigmatic and controversial prime minister since Confederation. Diefenbaker has perplexed such serious writers on Canadian affairs as Peter Newman and George Grant. The latter wrote in 1965 that in "studying his government, one becomes aware of a series of mutually conflicting conceptions",[96] of which populism, nationalism and small-town free enterprise were the most prominent. That these conceptions were ideological in Grant's understanding is not in doubt. Peter Newman, in the other hand, whose lengthy contemporary sketch was a valuable source of propaganda to the anti-Diefenbaker forces in the party and the country, denied that he was ideological at all: ".... Diefenbaker seemed bent on destroying whatever ideo-The disagreement between these two commentators must be super-logical boundaries remained between Canada's political parties."[97] ficial, however, differing only to the extent that Newman is using a personal definition of ideology which he does not explain to his readers. Newman agrees that Diefenbaker had an understanding which guided his way through politics. He observed that Diefenbaker "behaved as if he were the sacrosanct head of a people's government and tended to view events at home and abroad in black and white terms, depending on their appropriateness to his scheme of things".[98] And further, he "tried to reduce complicated national issues to memorable slogans — the Vision, the National Development Policy, Unhyphenated Canadianism, the Confederation Platform, the Five-Year Plan, the Bill of Rights, pro-Canadianism...."[99]

Now, both of these facts noted by Newman are manifestations of ideological behaviour. More exactly, they are what ideological behaviour is all about. In the first instance, Diefenbaker's "scheme of things" is another way of noting that Diefenbaker operated through a set of conceptual categories, which allowed him to make choices; or more simply, to favour the white over the black. Second, we have made the point earlier that one of the hallmarks, as well as one of the major weaknesses, of the ideological mode of understanding politics, is its inherent tendency to distort by simplification. This is precisely the role played by the "memorable slogans". Indeed, so useful an indicator of ideological position are such catchphrases, that it is worth looking at the ones contained in Newman's list in some detail, for the light they throw on the interesting contradictions in Diefenbaker's position.

Like Meighen, Diefenbaker was a man who lived his early manhood in the egalitarian and liberal Canadian West; and to some extent, especially on matters such as the monarchy and the British connection, Diefenbaker was Meighen's as well as Drew's heir. But to understand the overall mix of his ideological package, he is more fruitfully compared with the man against whom he stood in 1942 for the leadership of the Conservative Party: namely, John Bracken.

The strong liberal strains that Bracken attempted to make the dominant partner in Canadian Conservatism permeated most aspects of Diefenbaker's political understanding. However, Diefenbaker was a much more complex figure than Bracken, and his general stance brought to fruition, for the first time since Bennett, a comprehensive balance between the two main strains in the party's ideology.

The first slogan, the Vision, is the vaguest. To some extent, the notion of the Vision is a corruption of the higher law in which Fulton believed. It is an affirmation of the claim that the leader of the party sees further and more truly than the followers, who should give their obedience on faith alone. As such it is essentially an undemocratic idea, and merits comparison with the suggestions and observations that Herridge was making to Bennett in the days of the Depression. Because only the leader or leaders can possess the Vision, the concept cannot be associated with an egalitarian society. It is fundamentally incompatible with the classical liberal notion of a commonwealth of free, reasonable, deliberating individuals.

However, like Bennett, Diefenbaker was no ruthless demagogue. His Vision was closely associated with the next slogan, the National Development Policy. The platform of 1957 was called "A New National Policy" and the title was revealing. First, like Meighen, Diefenbaker was deeply conscious of his party's and his nation's heritage. In itself, this is neither good nor bad. The danger lay in a failing to which both men succumbed, the enervating lure of nostalgia. The recurrent references to the maintenance "as a sacred trust [of] the vision of Macdonald and Cartier. . . ."[100] was an indication more of Diefenbaker's awareness of the extent to which the country had deviated from that original conception, than it was a guide to creative policy for present circumstances. However the National Development Policy revealed a return to the traditions of Conservative collectivist control over economics. The Five Year Plan was evidence of this. There can be little doubt that Diefenbaker saw the national government as a powerful agent that could be used, in the northern development programme for example, to create a sense of national urgency and importance by expanding and exploring a vast, undeveloped area of the country. This development was to take place for political, more than economic, reasons.

Diefenbaker was too strongly under the influence of the competing liberal strains in his ideology to pursue this policy uncompromisingly. He was committed, as Grant has noted, to free enterprise, and more particularly, to a model of free enterprise which was in itself nostalgic, or at least inappropriate. It was the model of wheat farmers, on relatively equal lots of land, producing a homogenous product for a diverse market. But it was not even a model which recognized the significance of Grain Pools and international wheat agreements. This economic understanding, as Grant notes throughout his study[101] undercut the only important ideological structure of sufficient importance to maintain the integrity of the Canadian nation — the idea that there are political considerations of more importance than the most convenient and least expensive way of producing the material means of existence.

Associated with this economic individualism was, just as in Bracken, a strong feeling of social individualism. Unhyphenated Canadianism was an idea which Bracken himself had advanced as early as the 1940's. It expressed a preference for the melting pot over the mosaic, for the American ideal of assimilation rather than Cartier's theory of diversity. It is small wonder that Diefenbaker had difficulty in recognizing the cultural aspirations of French Canadians as a unit, because the terms in which he thought were individualist. Although he had no conscious desire to undermine the basis of French culture, his refusal to acknowledge the role that the collective French Canadian group played in maintaining a distinctive identity led in that direction. His decision, in 1968, to contest the leadership of a party that had obviously repudiated him, in the hope of persuading it to abandon the *deux nations* concept, is a significant example both of an ideological conflict, and an indication of the strength with which Diefenbaker held to his social individualism.

A second feature of Unhyphenated Canadianism merits attention, and that is the assumption upon which it is based. We have argued throughout this chapter that Canadian Conservatism had a consciousness of privilege which it was willing, from time to time, to defend against encroachments. Ideologies draw attention to important features of the political life of the community, but they do not always indicate the same solutions, and this fact is one of the more fruitful sources of ideological cleavages and bitterness. Unhyphenated Canadianism is a case in point. It rests on the assumption that there are privileged groups in the country which either appear to, or actually do, dominate. English Canadian Protestants and French Canadians would be the two most likely candidates. The tactic for undermining their power, then, lies in removing their distinctiveness. Conservatism, and Canadian socialism as well, possess the conceptual apparatus which allows them to isolate and identify this feature in Canadian social and political life, more clearly than do other ideologies, such as liberalism. Diefenbaker recognized the importance of privilege, but aligned himself with those whom he thought would benefit by its destruction. The distinction he made between Main Street and Bay Street is a related notion. Bay Street was the possessor of economic and social privileges which the people on Main Street did not enjoy, and Diefenbaker exhorted the people of the country to ally themselves with him in the interests of greater equality.

The *Bill of Rights* was another related idea. If Diefenbaker believed, as we have argued, that Canadians were oppressed by being subordinated to a privileged class, it was important that they be given means of redress. A Bill of Rights, which minimized the importance of the differences between individuals by endowing them all with equal rights, appeared a handy instrument for this end. Because of the political and legal problems of Canadian federalism, Diefenbaker could not go as far as he had wished in establishing an entrenched and justiciable document. The course he chose is still an interesting one. The easiest thing for Parliament to do was to pass a bill declaratory of the common law rights which Canadians already enjoyed. This tack had the advantage of being consonant both in spirit and in substance with the accepted British approach to the subject. Its major importance, though, lay in the extent to which it was a defiant assertion on behalf of Main Street Canadians of fundamental equality; and, conversely, of an articulate rejection of the principle of privilege.

Finally, we come to pro-Canadianism. In George Grant's view this was the area in which Diefenbaker's greatest and most tragic failure lay. His attempts to preserve Canadian independence, or to prevent an increasing dependence on the United States, by, among other things, diverting trade from that country to the Commonwealth met with failure. That he made the attempt at all is an important indication of the continuing hold of the pro-British element in Canadian Conservatism. Pro-Canadianism is an appropriate Conservative phrase; it is neither aggressively internationalist nor nationalist in approach. It expresses most acutely exactly what it is that the Canadian Conservative is interested in: namely, the preservation of an identity distinct from all others. To the extent that it concerns itself with identity, and indulges itself in merely a suspicious hositility of foreign elements, it is probably the mildest and safest form of nationalism. Grant's charge was that it was insufficient; lamentably, it probably was.

There can be no doubt at all, if our argument is correct, that Diefenbaker expressed a complex ideological vision of Canada. His appeal, so widely successful in 1958, was dissipated by 1962. The reasons for this are not as difficult to understand as some commentators have made out. In the campaigns of 1957 and 1958, Diefenbaker's ideological appeal, containing as it did such powerful liberal and conservative elements could not help but attract wide support. The liberal elements in the doctrine add a reassuring ring to a basically liberal population; yet there were sufficient traditional conservative elements to preserve the support of the smaller conservative section of the country. Diefenbaker's failure arose from the very success he originally enjoyed. He had evoked a heightened awareness of the divergent strains in Canadian Conservatism; he had used the different elements to appeal to different segments of the community. But he never succeeded in reconciling them, of resolving them into a new synthesis which would preserve him from mere inconsistency on the ideological level, and confused directions when fundamental policy choices had to be made. It is one of the merits of Grant's argument in *Lament for a Nation* that he realized that Diefenbaker's problem was not that he promised things that he could not provide, but that he promised things which no man could provide. His personal appeal had succeeded, for a brief period, in masking the ideological divisions in the nation, but when it came to the task of governing, it was no longer possible to avoid the choice. Had he made a choice, or had he, more significantly, succeeded in achieving a new synthesis of Canadian Conservatism, he might easily have become the national hero he aspired to be. His tragedy is that there is no evidence he even tried.

In the early 1960's, Canadian Conservatism was threatened by another danger, the growing influence of a doctrine in the United States propounded by Senator Barry Goldwater, which also called itself conservatism. Because there is a primitive magic in names, and because Canadian Conservatism was visibly decaying under Diefenbaker, whereas American conservatism appeared on the ascendant under Goldwater, some Canadian Conservatives found the new doctrine appealing. It is especially clear in retrospect that Goldwater's conservatism, in the Canadian context, was an exogenous doctrine which could only have succeeded in Canada if there had been a dramatic loss of confidence in the older parties. Its only appeal to Canadians could have come because it was an intellectualized form of liberalism. As such, it provoked mild response in the residual *laissez-faire* liberal strains of Canadian Conservatism. But liberalism in Canada had been modified, as we argued in Chapter II, by the existence of other ideological strains in a way that American liberalism had not, and as a consequence, the two liberalisms were fundamentally incompatible.

What is interesting is the response made by two Canadian Conservatives, Heath Macquarrie and George Hogan. With the intention of displaying the difference between the two doctrines, both wrote books in which they sought to demonstrate, by historical exposition, that the doctrines of Canadian Conservatism were different from those being urged on the party by admirers of the American variety. By marshalling the evidence of the past, they sought to show that Canadian Conservatism had an identity which distinguished it in most fundamentals. Hogan came closer than Macquarrie to an attempt to identify and defend the principles of the party, but both lapsed fairly quickly into a narrative of events rather than of ideas. Their books showed that Canadian Conservatism possessed an identifiable past; Goldwater's conservatism had temporarily placed that past in doubt. To that extent they were successful. But no more than Diefenbaker did they know whether it had a future; and more, what that future should be. At the same time, George Grant added his opinion that it did not much matter anyway, since the possibility of an independent Canadian nation had been eroded.

Grant had made this point as early as 1959 when he wrote: "To express conservatism in Canada means *de facto* to justify the continuing rule of the businessman and the right of the greedy to turn all activities into sources of personal gain."[102] He followed this argument up more systematically in *Lament for a Nation*. There he spoke of:

> . . . the impossibility of conservatism as a viable political ideology in our era. The practical men who call themselves conservatives must commit themselves to a science that leads to the conquest of nature. This science produces such a dynamic society that it is impossible to conserve anything for long. In such an environment, all institutions and standards are constantly changing. Conservatives who attempt to be practical face a dilemma. If they are not committed to a dynamic technology, they cannot hope to make any popular appeal. If they are so committeed, they cannot hope to be conservatives.[103]

Grant's pessimistic conclusion is open to two major objections: that he has overestimated the force and power of the technological society, or underestimated the strength of substantive conservatism in Canada, or both. Grant himself admitted in the introduction to the Carleton Library edition of *Lament for a Nation* (1970) that the situation was not one of unrelieved gloom, noting the resurgence of nationalism in the young, and even "traces of care about Canada" in the Trudeau government.

Grant's estimation of the dissolvent effects of technology is based on a powerful and compelling argument which cannot be discounted.

Nevertheless, the survival of non-liberal values in the public realm, which we have examined in this chapter and shall consider further with respect to socialism and nationalism in Canada, and their resurgence in the present time clearly blunts the full force of Grant's argument. This conclusion is only strengthened if we examine more closely the rather misleading way in which Grant treats Canadian conservatism.

He tends to reduce conservatism to a mere disposition against change, a nostalgic longing for the past. He speaks of de Gaulle as "the most brilliant conservative of our era" and makes it clear that he considers de Gaulle conservative because he wished to "preserve what he loves".[104] It is this unnecessary restriction of "conservatism" to a mere inclination against change which leads Grant to undervalue its persistence. For the conservative disposition alone is a poor weapon to pit against the technological leviathan. It has rarely held exclusive sway, except in decaying societies; almost always coexisting with the disposition to change, sometimes stronger and sometimes weaker. Similarly the appeal of nostalgia is retrospective like Meighen's regret that the world forty years earlier was happier and more moral.

We have argued, on the contrary, that Canadian Conservatism is based on a central structure of substantive political beliefs, clustering around the notions of collectivism and privilege, to which the disposition against change and nostalgia are merely peripheral. It is these substantive ideas which make Canadian Conservatism not only a doctrine which has enjoyed an effect in the past, but give it an appeal to the present and to the future. It also endows it with a much more powerful set of defences against the incursions of technological liberalism than Grant recognizes. It is this misunderstanding about the nature of Canadian Conservatism which led Grant to write its obituary and to lament its passing.

Whether or not Canadian Conservatives have the courage to vitiate Grant's despair is not yet clear. The 1968 leadership convention revealed the extent to which Diefenbaker had splintered the ideological compromise of the party by his clarification of the diverse strains. No fewer than eleven candidates presented themselves, of whom nine were men of substance, including the former prime minister, six of his cabinet ministers and two provincial premiers. The result of the balloting further revealed the extent to which the party was split. No candidate secured more than 25 per cent of the votes on the first ballot, and five received the support of at least 10 per cent of the delegates. The successive ballots eliminated the more extreme or ideologically limited candidates — Fulton, Hees, McCutcheon, Hamilton and Fleming — as well as

Diefenbaker himself. On the fifth ballot, the choice was between the two provincial premiers, Roblin and Stanfield, and the victory went to the East. The Western forces which had predominated in the leadership of the party from Manion to Diefenbaker, with the exception of the Drew period, still remained a significant influence within the party, as Roblin's 969 votes out of a total of 2119 indicated. But if Stanfield's supporters expected a distinctively new ideological perspective, they were bound to be disappointed. In his major address to the convention Stanfield had rejected the idea that he would work for a cohesive ideological vision. As he put it: "The Progressive Conservative Party is big enough, and great enough, to accommodate all of us. . . ."[105]

Nonetheless, important changes in party doctrine could be seen in the leader's subsequent pronouncements and in the party's platform. Perhaps the most significant of these is a decline in the importance of the individualist element which the western members of the party had encouraged. The 1968 Platform, while acknowledging that "Canada is, and should be, one country" took pains to emphasize the bi-national nature of the country: "Canada is composed of the original [sic] inhabitants of this land and the two founding peoples with historic rights to maintain their language and culture, who have been joined and continue to be joined by people from many lands who have a right to play a full part in Canadian life."[106] Stanfield returned to this theme in a speech delivered in April 1972 in Toronto. There he rejected the beliefs which the slogan of Unhyphenated Canadianism implied. "[T]his is not a country that believes in the philosophy of the melting pot. This is not a country where it is necessary to submerge your national or ethnic origins, nor forget the language of the country of your birth in order to function as a good citizen."[107] In rejecting rigorous indvidualism, Stanfield went even further. He affirmed that the "kind of society I am talking about involves a number of groups, each of which has a rich and cohesive interior life, but each of which also has a desire to reach outward to others."[108] This style of pluralism, whether applied to the French Canadian *nation,* or to the immigrant communities which have been much more recently formed in Canada, is a return to Cartier's enunciation of the value of diversity. It is also renewed belief in the importance of Conservative collectivism, and a willingness to assume that unity rather than division is present: "What we feel for Canada is our common bond. What we do about it is our common purpose."[109]

It was therefore a significant choice when Stanfield selected Marcel Faribault as his Quebec lieutenant in 1968. Such a move did more than indicate an appreciation of the electoral importance of the province of Quebec. It also was a manifestation of this new direction in Canadian Conservatism. The party seemed in danger of splitting over the *deux nations* concept in the convention which chose Stanfield leader of the party. Yet his Quebec lieutenant was a man who affirmed that this idea was "a good notion"[110] and who believed that: "When one speaks . . . of the two founding peoples, their differences in approach and the actual clash of their national traits should always be remembered, the more so for being so often ignored in the past."[111]

The corollary of this larger concept was a rejection of one of the strong liberal strains in Canadian Conservatism — unhyphenated Canadianism. "For we are, after all, all hyphenated to a certain degree. . . . Has not your own Conservative party been called for many decades Liberal-Conservative or Progressive Conservative?"[112]

Secondly, there are signs that Canadian Conservatism may recapture in a serviceable form, the spirit of the primacy of politics over economics which was perhaps its greatest contribution to Canadian political thought. In another speech in April 1972, delivered in Winnipeg, Stanfield declared that: "Canada must have and must have quickly a national development strategy that will enable us to decide our industrial, environmental, social and human priorities for the years and decades to come." He went on to say that "such a plan involves a close look at our economic and trading regulations with other countries, and especially the United States. It involves planning for our industrial and agricultural future. . . . It involves the quality of life and environment and it *involves a choice of the way in which we want to organize our economy and our whole society.*"[113] The Conservative position paper on the Canadian identity speaks in the same vein: "The threats to the survival of Canada as a nation can be met only by a comprehensive policy embracing all aspects of the question — cultural, economic, and political."[114] Stanfield's persistent demands for price and wage controls in 1973 is a further example of this attitude.

Finally, there is an indication that Stanfield is willing to discard some of the more nostalgic aspects of the party's ideology. One example of this will have to suffice, but it is one of major importance. The 1968 platform refers only in passing to the United Kingdom, and that in a way to indicate that Canadian Conservatism may now be confident of its own identity. "Canada's need to look for trading partners other than our traditional ones, particularly in view of the eventual entry of Great Britain into the European Common Market, is another reason for a comprehensive review of our relations with other countries."[115] It would have been inconceivable, during Diefenbaker's time at the head of the party, for a Conservative platform to contain such a casual reference to the United Kingdom.

In spite of these hopeful signs, though there are few grounds for real confidence that Canadian Conservatism is developing a fresh and distinctive approach to Canadian problems. In the 1972 election campaign Stanfield concentrated on issues like unemployment and the cost of living which fall into the area of ideological agreement between all of the major parties in Canada. He appeared to accept that the voters did not want a genuine ideological choice offered them in clear terms. His selection of the former Liberal, Claude Wagner, as his Quebec lieutenant and spokesman was a further indication that, for the time being at least, he was relying on his party's liberalism to bring him electoral victory.

This tactic was partly successful; the Liberals were reduced to a minority government. At the same time, though, by accentuating to such an extent the liberal elements in the Conservative ideology, Stanfield made it easier for the Liberal minority government to construct a Throne Speech in January 1973 that included a number of the more prominent suggestions that the Conservatives made during the campaign. The Leader of the Opposition was reduced at one point early in the session to the charge that "we have a lame duck Liberal government, bargaining with the New Democratic Party to keep it in office so that it may attempt to implement some Progressive Conservative policy."[116]

Stanfield is in the quandary that all Conservative leaders since Macdonald have faced. Pure toryism commands neither majority support in the country, nor even within the party as Fulton's unsuccessful attempts at the leadership have shown. Further, the conservative disposition, as Grant's analysis reveals, is neither strong enough in itself to check the harmful effects of modern technology, nor electorally sufficiently appealing to displace that technology's present political ally, the Liberal Party. Yet to transform the Conservative Party into a liberal one is to make it redundant in a political setting which already has a party which espouses a relatively pure liberalism. Further, to attempt this last possibility would be effectively to deprive Conservatives in Canada of any genuine expression of their ideological understanding of the country. The continued popularity of John Diefenbaker within the party and the country is partly a reflection of the uncertainty that these Conservatives feel about the directions that Stanfield intends to chart for the party. The only satisfactory choice for the Conservative Party under Stanfield is to give more weight to the collectivist, hierarchical and dispositional elements in Canadian Conservatism, at the expense of the liberal features which are already adequately represented by the Liberal Party. Only such a reordering of ideological priorities offers the Conservative Party any real hope in the long term to continue as a valuable alternative to the Liberals.

[1] H. Macquarrie, *The Conservative Party* (Toronto: McClelland and Stewart, 1965), p. 1.
See also, George Hogan, *The Conservative in Canada* (Toronto: McClelland and Stewart, 1963), p. xi.
[2] P. L. McCreath, *The Canadian Party System,* (Ottawa n.p. 1969) p. 2.
[3] E. C. Manning, *Political Realignment,* (Toronto: McClelland and Stewart, 1967), pp. 11, 21, 72.
[4] *The Report and Despatches of the Earl of Durham* (London: Ridgways, 1839) p. 12. Reprinted by Methuen and Co. Ltd., London, 1902.
[5] Michael Oakeshott, "On Being Conservative" in *Rationalism in Politics* (London: Methuen Press, 1962) p. 169, (New York: Basic Books, Inc., 1962).
[6] *Ibid.*, p. 169.
[7] *Durham Report*, p. 17.
[8] Quoted in D. Creighton, *John A. Macdonald*, (Toronto: Macmillan, 1966) Vol. I, p. 199.
[9] Quoted in L. J. Ladner, *The Progressive Conservative Party*, (n.p., n.d.) p. 1.
[10] W. L. Morton, *Canadian Conservatism Now,* (Winnipeg: The Progressive Conservative Party, 1959) p. 104.
[11] *Ibid.*, p. 9.
[12] L. F. S. Upton, "The Idea of Confederation: 1754-1858" in *The Shield of Achilles*, W. L. Morton, ed. (Toronto: McClelland and Stewart, 1968) p. 202.
[13] Luther Hamilton Holton, *Parliamentary Debates on the Subject of the Confederation of the British North American Provinces* (Quebec: 1865) p. 147.
[14] Taché, *ibid.*, p. 6.
[15] *Ibid.*
[16] T. W. L. MacDermot, "The Political Ideas of John A. Macdonald," *Canadian Historical Review*, XIV, No. 3, pp. 251-3.
[17] J. I. Cooper, "The Political Ideas of George Etienne Cartier," *Canadian Historical Review*, XXIII, No. 3, p. 293.
[18] Jacques Monet, "The Personal and Living Bond, 1839-1849" in *The Shield of Achilles*, p. 62.
[19] Cartier, *Confederation Debates*, p. 60.
[20] *Ibid.*, p. 60.
[21] Taché, *ibid.*, p. 10.
[22] Macdermot, p. 250.
[23] Cartier, *Confederation Debates*, p. 61.
[24] *Ibid.*, p. 62.
[25] Macdonald, *Confederation Debates*, p. 35.
[26] cf. the later statement,
"In each of us there is something of the liberal as well as something of the conservative — the desire for change struggling with the love of the familiar." Hon. L. MacAulay, "History and Aims of the Conservative Party" in *Canadian Problems as Seen by Twenty Outstanding Men of Canada* (Toronto: Oxford University Press, 1933) p.37.
[27] Macdermot, p. 251.
[28] Simpson, *Confederation Debates*, p. 234.
[29] See the "Liberal Platform of 1874" and the "Liberal Platform of 1882" in *Canadian Party Platforms, 1867-1968*, D. O. Carrigan, (Toronto: Copp Clark, 1968) pp. 12, 18, 19.

[30] "Liberal Platform of 1874," in Carrigan, p. 14.

[31] "Liberal Platform of 1878" in Carrigan, p. 16.

[32] Macdonald to Sir George Stephen, 31 March 1891. *Correspondence of Sir John Macdonald,* Pope, ed., (Toronto: n.d.) p. 485.

[33] Macdonald to Stephen, 10 November 1890, *Correspondence,* ibid, p. 477.

[34] Robert Laird Borden, *Letters to Limbo,* H. Borden, ed., p. 167, © University of Toronto Press 1971, Toronto and Buffalo.

[35] Borden, *Limbo,* pp. 166-7. *See also, R. L. Borden, His Memoirs,* H. Borden, ed., abridged and edited by H. Macquarrie, (Toronto: McClelland and Stewart, 1969) Vol. II, pp. 127-130.

[36] From *Unrevised and Unrepented: Debating Speeches and Others,* by the Rt. Hon. Arthur Meighen, Copyright by Clarke, Irwin and Company Limited, 1949, p. 5. Used by permission.

[37] R. L. Borden, "Manifesto to the People of Canada" in Carrigan, pp. 65-6.

[38] From *Robert Laird Borden: His Memoirs* (Toronto: McClelland and Stewart, 1969, Vol. I, p. 152) by R. L. Borden, abridged and edited by H. Macquarrie, reprinted by permission of The Canadian Publishers, McClelland and Stewart Limited, Toronto. Italics in original.

[39] Meighen, p. 98.

[40] *Ibid.,* p. 99.

[41] Borden, *Memoirs,* Vol. II, p. 245.

[42] E. Forsey, *The Royal Power of Dissolution,* (Toronto: Oxford University Press, 1968) passim.

[43] Roger Graham, *Arthur Meighen: A Biography* (Toronto: Clarke Irwin, 1963) Vol. II. and *The King-Byng Controversy,* (Toronto: Copp Clark, 1967), passim.

[44] Macquarrie, *The Conservative Party,* p. 97.

[45] Campaign speech of MacKenzie King, from Toronto *Globe,* in Carrigan, p. 104.

[46] Meighen, p. 114.

[47] *Ibid.,* p. 161.

[48] *Ibid.,* p. 206.

[49] George Hogan, *The Conservative in Canada* (Toronto: McClelland and Stewart, 1963) p. 10.

[50] *Ibid.,* p. 9.

[51] cf. Bennett. Q . . . The constitution of the Conservative Party as a Conservative Party is inconsistent with state interference to any extent with the individual right.
Mr. Bennett. "I would say that that is hardly the way you put it. With the development of public opinion state regulation of individual activities has been and will continue to be a part of the programme of any Conservative Government. It was so with respect to restriction of hours of labour as against laissez-faire opinions of their opponents. The Conservative Party has always taken the view that the order of regulation of individual activity may be of interest in the government of the whole." "Democracy on Trial" in *Canadian Problems, op.cit,* p. 30.

[52] R. B. Bennett's Winnipeg Speech, June 9, 1930, in Carrigan, p. 111. Our italics. Reprinted by permission of the Progressive Conservative Party of Canada.

[53] *Ibid.*

[54] *Ibid.*

[55] W. D. Herridge to R. B. Bennett, 13 September 1933. *Secret* reprinted in *The Bennett New Deal: Fraud or Portent,* J. H. R. Wilbur, ed., (Toronto: Copp Clark, 1968) p. 67.

[56] W. D. Herridge to R. B. Bennett, 22 June 1934, in Wilbur, p. 70.

[57] *Ibid.*

[58] W. D. Herridge to R. B. Bennett, 11 July, 1934, in Wilbur, p. 71.

[59] *See* note 56.

[60] W. D. Herridge to R. B. Bennett, 12 April, 1934, in Wilbur, p. 69.

[61] *Ibid.*

[62] *Ibid.*

[63] *See* note 58.

[64] *See* note 56.

[65] Bennett, "Democracy on Trial," p.13 cf Meighen, "Whither are we drifting?" (1935), ". . . whether or not the people in mass who now under universal suffrage determine the fate of many nations are really cognizant of their responsibility as well as their power. You will apprehend already that I am somewhat doubtful myself." *Unrevised*, pp.248-249.

[66] Borden, *Limbo*, p.163.

[67] *Ibid.*, p.164.

[68] R. B. Bennett, *The Premier Speaks to the People*, (Ottawa: Dominion Conservative Headquarters, 1935), reprinted in Wilbur, p.81.

[69] *Ibid.*, p.80.

[70] Meighen, p.253.

[71] Bennett, *The Premier Speaks*, in Wilbur, p.83.

[72] *Ibid.*, p.81 (our italics.)

[73] Meighen, p.317.

[74] *Ibid.*, p.320.

[75] *Ibid.*, p.437.

[76] *Ibid.*, p.443.

[77] John Bracken, *John Bracken Says*, (Toronto: Oxford University Press, 1944) p.8.

[78] *Ibid.*, p.66.

[79] *Ibid.*, p.17.

[80] *Ibid.*, p.67.

[81] Bennett, p.17.

[82] Bracken, p.92.

[83] George Drew, Sydney *Post Record*, June 9, 1949, in Carrigan, p.188.

[84] *Ibid.*

[85] *Ibid.*, p.192.

[86] E. D. Fulton, "Introduction" to John Farthing, *Freedom Wears a Crown*, (Toronto: Kingswood House, 1957) p.xvi. Leopold MacAulay in 1933, for instance, referred to Lord Hugh Cecil's study of English Conservatism, and observed that the "general characteristics of Conservatism in England are equally characteristic of the development of the Conservative Party in Canada." "History and Aims", *Canadian Problems*, p.189.

[87] *Ibid.*, p.xviii.

[88] *Ibid.*, p.xix-xx.

[89] *Ibid.*

[90] E. Davis Fulton, "The Basic Principles of Conservatism" (1964) in L. J. Ladner, *The Progressive Conservative Party*, p.6.

[91] *Ibid.*, p.7.

[92] Fulton, "Dynamic Conservatism", *Report of the Macdonald-Cartier Conference, 1959*, (Ottawa: 1959) p.24.

[93] Donald Fleming, "Distinctive Conservatism", (Ottawa: The Progressive Conservative Party of Canada, 1956) p.5.

[94] *Ibid.*, p.12.

[95] *Ibid.*, p.5.

[96] From *Lament for a Nation* (Toronto: McClelland and Stewart, 1965, p.12) by George Grant reprinted by permission of The Canadian Publishers, McClelland and Stewart Limited, Toronto, and the author.

[97] From *Renegade in Power* (1963, p.xiv) by Peter Newman reprinted by permission of The Canadian Publishers, McCelland and Stewart Limited, Toronto, and the author.

[98] *Ibid.*, p.xii.

[99] *Ibid.*, pp.xii.-xiv.

[100] *A New National Policy for Canada*, (Ottawa: The Progressive Conservative Party of Canada, 1957) in Carrigan, p.225.

[101] Grant, p.17.

[102] George Grant, *Philosophy in the Mass Age*, (Toronto: Copp Clark, 1959, 1966), p.109.

[103] Grant, *Lament*, pp.66-67.

[104] *Ibid.*, p.67.

[105] *Summary of Leadership Conventions*, (Ottawa: n.d.) p.11.

[106] Progressive Conservative Policy Handbook, (Ottawa: 1968) in Carrigan, p.349.

[107] Mimeo, p.11.

[108] *Ibid.*, p.4.

[109] *Ibid.*, p.11.

[110] From "The Relation of the Two Founding Peoples" in *Unfinished Business* (1967, p.174) by Marcel Faribault, reprinted by permission of The Canadian Publishers, McCelland and Stewart Limited, Toronto.

[111] *Ibid.*

[112] Faribault, "Conservatism and Confederation" in *Unfinished Business,* p.111.

[113] Mimeo, p.9 (our emphasis).

[114] Mimeo, December 1971, Section 1, p.2.

[115] *Progressive Conservative Policy Handbook;* in Carrigan, p.349.

[116] Robert Stanfield, *House of Commons Debates,* vol. 117, no. 3, p.47. Unrevised.

Chapter V

Canadian Socialism

Like conservatism, socialism has never enjoyed electoral success or widespread support in a pure form. The two successful socialist parties in this country, the Cooperative Commonwealth Federation (CCF) and its successor the New Democratic Party (NDP) have both tempered their socialism with strong doses of liberalism. Indeed at times the latter was so strong that it threatened to overwhelm the socialist strain in these parties, and reduce them to little more than exponents of positive or reformist liberalism, a variant of mainstream Canadian Liberalism, as the Progressive Party earlier had been.

The relative success of these two socialist parties offers a striking contrast to the situation in the United States, where socialist parties have on the whole presented doctrinaire ideologies to an indifferent, or more usually hostile, audience. Part of the reason for this indifference, as we argued in Chapter II, is that Canada contains, by dint of its toryism, an indigenous socialist tradition. The collectivist element in toryism, as Horowitz pointed out, meant that egalitarian protests against privilege could and did express themselves in a collectivist rather than an individualist form, producing in the combination of collectivism and egalitarianism, socialism. It also meant that Labour Party style socialist ideas brought by immigrants, especially from Britain in the late nineteenth and twentieth centuries, found a ready reference or entry point into the Canadian political tradition through shared collectivist values.

This collectivism was a feature almost coterminous with Canada. We have seen in the last chapter that the tory element in Canada contained a significant collectivist strain. In fact the desire to use the state to further collective ends dates back as far as the French colonial regime. The succeeding British regime with its policy of canal building and other public works made this an enduring feature of Canadian politics. After Confederation Macdonald continued to promote collectivist goals. The National Policy is perhaps as good as any overall description of Macdonald's plans which included the use of a tariff strategy to foster industrial development, a partnership with business interests to build the CPR and the settlement of the Northwest to prevent it from annexation by the Americans. Since Macdonald's time successive governments have been involved in extensive public enterprises, railways, broadcasting, banking, oil and gas pipelines and satellites, to name just a few.

All this is in sharp contrast to American individualism. In that country, from its eighteenth century founding as a state, there were *Bills of Rights* and Supreme Court decisions to enforce them which prevented the American state from joining in an active partnership to build the nation. It was not until the 1930's that Supreme Court decisions gave the central government power which Canadians had always expected their government to exercise. These rival traditions of government activity are important for understanding the different receptions that socialism received.

In both world and Canadian terms, socialism is the newest of the ideologies we have considered to date. G. D. H. Cole, looking on Canadian socialism from an international perspective, wrote that "there was very little significant development up to 1914." Paul Fox also notes that the early Canadian socialist parties were slow to develop ideas appropriate to a Canadian setting, and instead relied heavily on classical Marxism as interpreted by Americans like E. V. Debs and Daniel De Leon. The lack of any agreement among the scattered socialist groups concerning the nature or goals of socialism, and their failure to build a nationally successful party, lend credence to the belief that at least until the end of the Great War, Canadian socialism was not a major force.[1]

One important factor which deprived Canadian socialism of early success in this country was the preference of most early Canadian trade union leaders to ally with the previously existing parties rather than founding a political movement to promote their interests. It was only in 1871 that the first rudimentary alliance of trade unions, the Toronto Trades Assembly, had been formed. A year later that movement had its first major test in a strike against George Brown's *Globe* newspaper. Brown's liberal individualism rejected the essentially collectivist nature of trade unions, and Brown set out to break the strike of his newspaper by invoking the English *Combination Acts* of 1792 and 1800 which had been repealed in England but which were still law in Canada.

The consequence of this action, as with the later Taff Vale decision in England, was the opposite of what the employers hoped for. The working men's associations in Toronto organized public rallies, and the Conservatives, unwilling to let a golden opportunity slip from their hands, began to woo the workers. The egalitarian element in trade unions was intensely unpleasant to Victorian Canadian Conservatism; but collectivism was part of the tory inheritance, and Macdonald introduced legislation to "improve existing laws relating to Trades Combinations in Canada", following the lines of the British *Trade Union Act* of 1871.[2] The response of the working men was natural enough; they looked upon the Conservatives as their friends, and gave them their political support. The outcome had indicated a particularly important lesson: that labour could be politically influential, and more important, could secure significant gains for its members, by alliances with existing parties.

Macdonald's shrewd political move had both "dished" the Liberals and taken the steam, temporarily, out of the trade union movement as a political force. However, after a decade of inactivity, Canadian unionism was faced with a rapid series of imported American ideologies. The first Assemblies of the radical American organization, the Knights of Labor, entered Canada in 1881. This organization urged Canadian workers to take a broad view of their power, and to put an end to the "speculators, usurers, landgrabbers and other classes of idlers [who] live on the labour of other classes. . . ."[3] However this doctrine of class division and conflict had no roots in Canadian social reality, and after a brief spell of importance, was on the wane by 1887.

Its decay coincided with a second American onslaught, this time leading to the founding of the first socialist parties in Canada, the Workingman's Party of British Columbia in 1886 and the American Socialist Labour Party of Daniel De Leon, a branch of which was established in Ontario in 1894. "The S.L.P. was doctrinaire Marxist in ideology and exhibited from the outset an extreme sectarian and anti-trade union orientation."[4]

Other socialist organizations arose soon after, such as the Canadian Socialist League of George Wrigley which advocated a gentle Christian socialism.[5] However, it would be futile and redundant to trace the waxing and waning, the dividing and subdividing of these different socialist parties. Grace MacInnis, J. S. Woodsworth's daughter, describes the condition of the early socialist groups perceptively as follows:

> British Columbia's long tradition of Marxian socialism, European in origin, had been brought over by Britishers before the British Labour Party had become a major force. Labour parties rose and fell and rose again under other names. Each prairie city had its similar Labour

Party, autonomous and almost unaware of the existence of its neighbour. In two or three Ontario cities both Marxian and Labour Party traditions lived through a multiplicity of tiny parties, each the centre of a ring of deviationists. Quebec and the Maritimes had practically no organization.[6]

The failure of these socialist parties reflected the important choice that Canadian trade unionism had made in the early 1870's: to ally with existing parties. This doctrine became known as Gompersism, after the American trade union leader, Samuel Gompers, who succeeded in imposing it on the mainstream of the trade union movement in that country. On the whole Canadian unionists preferred this labourism to socialism; that is, they preferred that their trade union organizations pursue primarily economic goals, within the context of the existing society and economy. Just as the early unionists had welcomed the action taken by Macdonald's Conservative Government on their behalf, so later unionists were content to ally themselves with whatever political party seemed to be in a position to do them the greatest benefit.

It was neither accident nor corruption that led some of the pioneers of the Canadian labour movement into the government service. The Liberal Party of Laurier secured with the trade union movement a success similar to that which they achieved with the Province of Quebec. Liberalism used its concern for liberty to persuade the latter that it would be better able to defend its culture under the Liberal doctrine of provincial rights. The trade union movement also had much to gain from an increased liberty, hampered as it was by restrictive business practices and restrictive laws. Thus when Laurier's government established a Department of Labour in 1900, it sought to staff the new department with men who could command the respect and support of trade unionists in the country. Daniel O'Donoghue was invited to become a Fair Wage Officer and the young, prolabour Mackenzie King, whose positive liberalism was to become such a powerful force in Canadian politics, became editor of the *Labour Gazette,* and, in 1909, Minister of Labour. By accepting such government posts, labour supporters could be more certain that the working man's case would be given sympathetic consideration. From the socialists' point of view they were bolstering an oppressive system; but by their own lights, they were pursuing the only course that would lead to the bettering of the labouring man's condition.

For the rest there were indeed socialists in Canada, although they had to wait the founding of the NDP in 1961 for a formal union with labour. The socialists can be roughly classified as follows. There were the doctrinaires who imported the classical socialism of De Leon and Debs which Hartz argued was the type that had the largest following in the United States. Also there were European immigrants who brought socialist ideas of a Marxist variety from their homelands in, say, the Ukraine or Finland, where these ideas had served an anticzarist purpose. What distinguished these groups was their belief that socialism was a goal, something that could be finally attained; for example that socialism meant "the development of a society which would own and control the means of wealth production and distribution." In the terms we introduced earlier, this type of ideology was exogenous; it did not spring directly from the experience of Canadian workers or intellectuals, but was a system of ideas which they imported from other countries, and then used to explain Canadian problems, and to prescribe solutions for ills with the aid of their preconceived ideas. This type of doctrine is almost a classic case of an ideology.

But the other style of socialism was not less ideological for being less doctrinaire. This was the type of socialism which grew out of elements widespread throughout Canada, such as Christianity. Wrigley's Canadian Socialist League, mentioned above, believed that "Christ was the first socialist".[7] Such socialists normally emphasized that "socialism is a way of life" rather than a series of institutional arrangements. To explore the distinction between these two styles of socialism more fully, we will first turn our attention to the early ideas of the man who was the spiritual father of the mainstream of socialism in Canada, J. S. Woodsworth. Then, by way of contrast, we will consider a notable manifestation of the rival conception of socialism, the One Big Union (OBU) and the Winnipeg General Strike of 1919.

James Shaver Woodsworth was born in Ontario in 1874; his parents were Methodists, and interestingly from the point of view of our argument about the connection between toryism and socialism, his mother's ancestors were United Empire Loyalists. Even before birth, he was dedicated "to the service of the Lord"[8]; however, as a young man he decided that his vocation lay in teaching rather than in preaching.[9] When dissatisfaction within the Church led him to offer his resignation, he was offered a more secular position as Superintendent of All Peoples' Mission in Winnipeg in 1907. From his experience there came his first book, *Strangers within our Gates* (1909). It was not a socialist tract, but rather a compassionate look at the problems faced by the immigrants who had come to Canada. In spite of its predominantly factual character, there is clear evidence in it of certain strains which were to become important later in Woodsworth's ideological understanding of Canada, and which he was also to share with the others with whom he was associated, first in the Ginger Group in the House of Commons in the 1920's and then in the CCF in the 1930's.

In some ways the young Woodsworth's social understanding reflected a microcosm of Canada as a whole. There is a tory strain that manifests itself in places in the book, especially in Woodsworth's obvious preference for a British Canada. On a higher level, the collectivism that he expresses here also shows a strong tory influence, since it is more concerned with the collectivist aspects of the nation as a whole, rather than placing emphasis on collectivist elements such as trade unions within the nation. Such a tory collectivism is clearly present in his fear that the "presence of incompatible elements [as a result of immigration] changes the entire social and political life of a country; it is a fatal barrier to the highest national life."[10]

However, just as we identified a strong liberal strain associated with Canadian Conservatism, so also was it present in Woodsworth's thought. Here was an unwillingness to tolerate diversity. "There is an unfounded optimism that confidently asserts that all this mingling of the races is in the highest interest of the country."[11] His answer to the question "How are we to make them [immigrants] into good Canadian citizens?" was simple enough: "First of all, they must be in some way unified. Language, nationality, race, temperament, training, are all dividing walls that must be broken down." This doctrine, intolerant as it is, is surely the same individualism that is implicitly present in modern Canadian Liberalism.

Woodsworth came to this position by preferring to promote greater equality, in contrast to the liberal's emphasis on liberty. His analysis of the causes of immigration to Canada identified privilege as one of the most important forces: "the whole social system [in the immigrants' homeland] is iniquitous.... Privileged classes prey on the masses. The state exists not for the good of the people, but to gratify the ambition of a few leaders...."[12] His hostility to continued diversity in Canada stemmed largely from his belief that if immigrants retained their distinctive features, this might lead to the development of a class system in Canada:

> We can already perceive changes in Canada. The Westerner differs from the Easterner, not merely because East is East and West is West, but because of the mixed character of the population of the West. The character of Eastern cities, too, is changing. The people on the street differ in physique from those of a decade ago. Social distinctions, hitherto unknown, are being recognized. A hundred years from now who and what shall we be?[13]

This distaste for privilege and preference for an egalitarian society without class distinctions was the feature of Woodsworth's thought that prevented him from being either conservative or liberal, and which led him to develop a new social doctrine that contained prominent socialist features.

As with other clergymen of this period in the West, Woodsworth was also influenced by the Social Gospel. These problems that the immigrants in Winnipeg faced posed a "challenge to the church" that required it "not merely to preach to the people", but "to educate them and to improve the entire social conditions".[14] Unless the church were willing to minimize the importance of doctrinal orthodoxy, an orthodoxy with which Woodsworth found it increasingly difficult to profess agreement, it would not be an important social force. Woodsworth urged it to participate, not in a revolution, but in an extensive programme of education and social improvement.

By the time that he came to publish his next book, *My Neighbour,* in 1911, he was even more committed than he had been in *Strangers.* "*Someone* is responsible! Every unjustly treated man, every defenceless woman, every neglected child has a neighbour somewhere. Am I that neighbour?"[15] His work with the Mission in Winnipeg had begun to convince him that the increasing urbanization of the country would present society with problems which were increasingly difficult to solve. Moreover, these problems would be such that it was no longer possible to rely on virtues such as self-reliance and an individualistic morality. "Man has entered on an urban age. He has become a communal being." Cities differed from rural life because of the complex ties of interdependency. "City life is like a spider's web — pull one thread and you pull every thread."

The implications that were beginning to make themselves felt on Woodsworth were that the type of work that he was doing in Winnipeg, charitable work through the church in an attempt to alleviate the distress of individuals, was no longer adequate to the new problems which were arising as a consequence of the increasing trend toward urbanization. "[Injured workmen] are part of a system as we are part of the same system. We as individuals cannot help them as individuals. The whole system must be reckoned with — possibly completely changed."[16]

In spite of the suggestion that complete change might be necessary, Woodsworth was neither at this time in his life, nor later, a revolutionary, the abuse heaped on him by men who called him "a dirty bolshevist" or a "red rabble-rouser in the pay of Moscow" notwithstanding.[17] Rather, he repudiated socialism of "the doctrinaire variety so dear to the hearts of the self-styled 'scientific socialists'. [His] was kin to the socialism of the British Labour Party, a movement which had been fed from religious, ethical, co-operative and Fabian streams. . . . it was, in a new form, the building of the Kingdom of Heaven on earth." So Woodsworth tried to build an ideological understanding out of indigenous elements within Canada. His socialism would "spring from the soil of each locality, be rooted in its traditions and nurtured in its heart, adapt itself to its continually evolving mental and cultural climate." This argument reveals an appreciation of the openness of the Canadian political tradition to socialist ideas which we argued in Chapter II was an aspect of Canadian political life which distinguished it from the United States.

Woodsworth shrewdly appreciated that any attempt to import an exogenous ideology would not be fruitful. "Any effort to import the particular variety of socialism developed in Europe or elsewhere, he felt, would end only in futility and bitterness. Canadians must evolve their own type."[18] This understanding of socialism led him to reject the ideas of the more doctrinaire Marxists who had their utopias already sketched out. He did not want to discard what already existed if it could be made to work in the interests of the workers. "Our ideal ought to be not to create new organizations but rather to really socialize those already in existence." Only if this should prove impossible should they be relegated "to the scrap heap".[19]

As he became convinced that it was of central importance to the type of society he wished to see created in Canada that he enunciate a socialist political ideology, he became increasingly concerned with developing a doctrine that would repudiate privilege with sufficient vigour, while at the same time avoiding the theories of class war that classical socialism taught.

> We dream of a socialistic state and yet sympathize with Mr. Brooks when he says that "the Mecca of the Co-operative Commonwealth is not to be reached by setting class against class, but by bearing common burdens through toilsome stages along which all who wish well to their fellows can journey together." If there *must* be a fight then it is a fight for the rights of the many weak against the privileges of the strong few and we stand with the many weak. We believe in opportunism and compromise in securing practical reforms, but never when they involve the abandonment of the hope of attaining the ultimate goal, or the sacrifice of vital principles.[20]

This attack on privilege, shared partly by Canadian liberalism, together with a defence of opportunism and compromise set the future tone of both the CCF and the NDP. It goes a long way to explain why, in spite of the fact that both Canadian conservatism and Canadian socialism share collectivism as part of their ideological apparatus, the latter has more frequently allied with the Liberals in favour of pragmatic reform, than with the Conservatives. So strong is socialist hostility to Conservatism in this country that after the indecisive election of 1972, the leader of the NDP, David Lewis, was quick to indicate that he favoured the continuation in office of the Liberal government of Pierre Trudeau, in spite of its consistent record of favouring precisely those business interests which the NDP sought to restrict. This willing moderation, as we shall see, has been one of the greatest snares for Canadian socialists, because it has allowed the Liberals to characterize them, in Mackenzie King's immortal phrase, as "Liberals in a hurry." To the extent that they tailored their programme to what could be attained, they left it open to other parties, especially the Liberals, to adopt their policies when the times were ripe.

All this was for the future. It was not until 1921 that Woodsworth was first returned to the House of Commons for a Winnipeg constituency. In the interim, he had resigned his position with the Mission, taken a position with the provincial government, and been fired from it for his pacifist opposition to the Great War, and in particular, to conscription. The desperate financial condition he found himself in as a result led to his first and only direct participation in the life of the workingmen of Canada to whom he had dedicated his life; he worked for a time as a longshoreman in British Columbia. However, he soon began to give lectures, and it was as part of a lecture tour that he arrived back in Winnipeg on June 8, 1919, three weeks after the beginning of the Winnipeg General Strike.

The men who participated in the General Strike in Winnipeg can be divided into the three groups which we identified earlier. First, there were the liberals, the orthodox trade union leaders, who "approved of the existing system of trade unions, which they regarded as well designed to improve the position of labour. They envisaged no fundamental reconstruction of society, but instead orthodox efforts to raise wages and reduce hours within the framework of capitalist free enterprise."[21] In the opinion of one of the leaders of the international union movement in Canada, Tom Moore, the error of the syndicalists in the One Big Union was that they had attempted to usurp the power of the international union executives. These latter preferred a "policy of negotiation and the using of the strike weapon as a last resort only."[22] The second group, to which we will turn in a moment, was composed of those socialists, such as Woodsworth, who supported the moderate goals of the trade union leaders.

Most controversial, however, was the vocal minority from the Socialist Party of Canada who pressed the notion of the One Big Union. Most of the leaders of this movement were born and raised in the British Isles and they brought with them when they came to Canada certain ideas from British unionism and British socialism. It is in part because of the continuing influence of such men that we were unwilling in the second chapter to accept Horowitz' notion of a point of congealment in Canadian ideological development. Masters goes so far as to suggest that the "course followed by the western labour movement" could be regarded "almost as an extension of the British labour movement." In spite of the fact that the programme of the One Big Union was considerably less radical than its American counterparts, the International Workers of the World (I.W.W. or "Wobblies") and the Workers' International Industrial Union, it could not have come onto the stage in an historical situation more likely to cause panic in both business and governmental circles.[23]

Not only was there widespread industrial unrest in Canada at this time as a consequence of the demobilization after the Great War, there was also the inspiration of the Russian Revolution which "had aroused keen enthusiasm in the hearts of those who wanted direct and drastic economic action."[24] The government could not be reassured by suggestions put forward that the Russian Soviet system had been devised from the same source from which the OBU was derived. Nor would they feel secure when they heard the aggressive rhetoric of men such as Kavanagh when they explained the rationale behind the movement: "Political action comes through a political system and a political system is a class or slave system. Politics only exist where there are classes, and any act taken by a class in defence of its interests is political action. . . . any action used to control political power in order to utilize it for the benefit of that class; that is political action, and it matters not what method it takes."[25] As Robin summarizes their ultimate goal, only "a One Big Union, the living embodiment of the Class consciousness the socialist educators worked to create, could accomplish the revolution."[26] The preamble to the constitution of the One Big Union sets out clearly and concisely the social analysis which lay behind the movement.

> Modern industrial society is divided into two classes, those who possess and do not produce, and those who produce and do not possess. . . . Between these two

> classes a continual struggle must take place.... In the
> struggle over the purchase and the sale of labour power,
> the buyers are always masters — the sellers always
> workers. From this fact arises the inevitable class
> struggle.... Compelled to organize for self-defence, they
> are further compelled to educate themselves in prepara-
> tion for the social change which economic developments
> will produce whether they seek it or not.
>   The One Big Union, therefore, seeks to organize the
> wage worker not according to craft, but according to in-
> dustry; according to class and class needs; and calls upon
> all workers to organize irrespective of nationality, sex,
> or craft, into a workers' organization so that they may be
> enabled to more successfully carry on the everyday
> fight over wages, hours of work, etc. and prepare them-
> selves for the day when production for profit will be re-
> placed by production for use.[27]

All this was clear enough, but its very weakness lay in the
vigour and the determination with which its supporters pressed it.
It was not an ideology which was congenial to Canada. "Even a
brief description of the O.B.U. opinions will sound a number of
notes familiar to students of proletarian history in western Europe
and the United States."[28] The very fact that the ideology of the proponents of the O.B.U. was so close to the theories advanced by
continental and American socialists suggests that it was, in a Canadian setting, exogenous; as a consequence there was no reason to
suspect that Canaian workers, as distinct from those socialists who
had brought their socialist theories with them when they came to
Canada, should find these explanations either powerful or compelling. British trade unionist ideas might have a convenient point of
contact with the similar unionism in Canada, but the British socialism that the leaders of the O.B.U. were pressing on their Canadian
followers was Marxist, rather than the Fabian or Labour Party
variety.

Woodsworth's attitude was more in harmony with that of the
effective leadership of the General Strike. "His was a practical approach to a concrete situation." Although he took a sufficiently
active interest in the strike, particularly with regard to editing the
Western Labor News, that he was arrested (though he was never
finally tried), he was strongly opposed to the basic approach taken
by the O.B.U. supporters. He favoured, here as ever, "a solution by
peaceful legal means", and he "had no use for class war and re-
peatedly stated his belief that no society founded upon hatred could
endure. Instead of wanting to fasten the dictatorship of the prole-

tariat upon Canada, he talked of a new social order where each individual would have more freedom than was possible today."[29]

It was Woodsworth's approach, and that of the trade union leaders, founded as it was more securely in indigenous local roots, that proved the more enduring. Within a year after the General Strike the One Big Union was "no more than a small sect"[30] and within two years the Socialist Party of Canada "was reduced to a shambles of depleted, dispirited, and disorganized local groups."[31] Although the Communist Party of Canada, led by Tim Buck, was formed in 1921-2 the events of the aftermath of the Winnipeg General Strike established that mainstream socialist opinion would follow the peaceful, pragmatic and opportunistic course of the British Labour Party rather than the class wars of the Marxist doctrinaires.

Even if we accept this argument — that by 1921 Canadian socialism had chosen the road that it was to follow — it is clear that it had not selected the vehicle. "By 1921 there was a host of various labour parties in Canada, most with branches — some with headquarters — in the western cities." To name a few, there were the Dominion Labour Party, the Manitoba Independent Labour Party (ILP), the Saskatchewan ILP, the Farmer-Labour Party, the Canadian Labour Party, the Labour Representation League, the Federal Labour Party, the Workers' Party, and the Socialist Party of Canada. In spite of this wealth in numbers of parties, only twenty-nine labour/socialist candidates stood in the 1921 election, of whom only two, Woodsworth and William Irvine, were elected.[32]

The presence of these two men alone was not, of course, by itself a turning point for Canadian socialism. Although they both took radical stands on subjects such as civil liberties, especially on issues like the repeal of Section 98 of the *Criminal Code,* and on matters concerned with public ownership in the economy, Woodsworth's pragmatic strategy in a parliamentary setting was such that it hampered the development of a consistent and coherent socialist doctrine. Because the Labour Party group was so small, it was not in a position to press home its policies or its programmes. If it hoped to influence the course of events, it could only do so by pressing for measures, as it did with old age pensions in 1926, that were within the ideological scope of the Liberal Party. In spite of this tactical manoeuvring inside Parliament, at which Woodsworth, like Stanley Knowles after him, became adept, he would not modify his principles or the public expression of his beliefs in order to curry favour with the electorate. Like King, Woodsworth was a democrat, but unlike the prime minister, the Labour leader had a radically different perspective on time. King was convinced that he had to maintain power, both to accomplish his policies, and to prevent the Conservatives from implementing theirs. For King there was no end to this process; there was no foreseeable point at which the process of governing would come to an end. Woodsworth on the other hand, although his vision was certainly not apocalyptic, could imagine a time, once the Co-operative Commonwealth was established, when politics of the traditional sort would no longer be necessary. However, the post-political age could not be attained by a cynical manipulation of short-term electoral considerations, which Woodsworth consequently eschewed.

This hostility to political parties, and the correlative preference for considering Canadian socialism as a movement, came into Canadian socialism from the farmers' movements, such as the United Farmers of Alberta. In 1924 Woodsworth had succeeded in extending the ambit and influence of his leadership by forging increasingly close ties with a group of the more radical Progressives, the majority of whom came from Alberta; later they formed the Ginger Group. In an earlier chapter we pointed out that a majority of the Progressives, with Forke as their leader, were radical Liberals, who could find a relatively congenial home in the Liberal Party of Mackenzie King, once the social and economic conditions in the farming areas had improved sufficiently to take the edge off the need for a new ideological perspective. However, the more radical group, mostly from Alberta, were supporters of the ideas of Henry Wise Wood. Irvine himself had written a book, The Farmers in Politics (1920), "expounding the ideas of group government better than those ideas had ever been presented by Henry Wise Wood himself".[33]

As Irvine saw it the Great War had induced a dramatic alteration in social and economic circumstances in Canada, especially in the competitive system, for which the traditional parties were unable to present effective or compelling explanations. Farmers, Irvine believed, possessed a truly novel ideological vision. It was, therefore, "the privilege and duty of organized farmers to show the better way in politics and industry. All parties are alike to them. . . . In their economic oppression and political wandering, the farmers have discovered the new law and the new hope. They do not seek to destroy, but to fulfil, governments; they do not want to compete with exploiters for the lion's share of the plunder, but seek true co-operation in all things for the highest common good."[34]

The farmer was the ideal representative of the nation, of "the highest common good" because he transcended all divisions. "The farmer, in reality, combines in his own profession, the two antagonists. He is both capitalist and laborer." This union of the "two antagonists" was a symbol for the collectivism which he pursued. His plan was to rely on this aspect of the farmer's nature to replace individualism by a philosophy that treats "group organization" as "the first democratic unit" and proceeds from there to "cohesion, concentration, solidarity, united action, and co-operation". Farmers, organized on a class basis, would not have to "shape their minds to a previously made platform"; rather they could "shape their platform according to their collective mind".

If collectivism was one lodestar of Irvine's political thought, equality was the other. "The History of Canada is the record of the rise, development, and supremacy of class rule." Just as the Ontario election of 1919 had presented a "formidable challenge to partyism and privilege" so the rise of a national farmers' movement would put an end to privilege throughout the country. "The group policy, logically followed, will prevent *any* class from dominating. . . . Group organization does not imply class legislation. It is the negation of class legislation."

Although Irvine thought that his approach included everything that was valuable in bolshevism, syndicalism and guild socialism, the theory that he propounded in this book would not have been accepted by continental socialists as socialism at all. However it was perhaps all the more appropriate in a Canadian setting for that. Irvine's theory of group government, although addressed to farmers in the first instance, was not exclusive, and the grounds on which he sought to make his appeal — collectivism and equality — were ideals which had an attraction for Canadian socialists as well as to some politically minded members of the Canadian labour movement. Of special importance was the fact that these ideas, like Woodsworth's, were quite congenial to theories of the radical members of the UFA and the Progressives. Throughout the 1920's these men continued to work in increased harmony with the Ginger Group in spite of their diverse political backgrounds.

"By the end of the twenties some of the members [of the Ginger Group] had come to regard finance as the overshadowing issue of modern society. Unwittingly, by focusing public opinion in Alberta almost exclusively on the banking system, they were preparing the way for Aberhart and Social Credit".[35] Grace MacInnis' argument here, though plausible, is misleading. Irvine, whose beliefs by this time shared much in common with Social Credit,[36] was already inclined in that direction when he wrote *The Farmers in Politics*. More serious, however, is the overestimate implicit in this argument of the power of individual ideological thinkers or groups to effect a transformation of the ideological attitudes in the public at large. Although the repetition of the antibanking theories of the Ginger Group throughout the 1920's would have prepared the ground for Social Credit to the extent that it began to familiarize the people of Alberta with that sort of argument, it is more likely that the Depression, rather than the Ginger Group was the more important causal factor.

The Depression was significant, in the context we are presently considering, not so much because it worked such havoc with men's lives — there had in the past been plagues, famines and other natural disasters which did not induce men to begin a process of ideological introspection — but rather because it was inexplicable; it perplexed people. Many of the assumptions of the old individualism were brought into question. The notion that there were, in Shaw's phrase, "deserving poor", became more widespread. It became harder and harder to accept the belief that if a man were suffering, then it was the consequence of a lack of virtue — industry, prudence, thrift or the like — on his part. The Social Credit and socialist movements shared this in common: they both provided perspectives on what was happening that absolved the individual working man of the blame for his plight. There is no space in this volume to go into the ideas of Social Credit. What concerns us here is the impetus that the Depression gave to the congealing of the disparate socialist, labour and farmers' movements into the coalition that became known as the CCF.[37]

Woodsworth was the focus around which the movement centred. Throughout the twenties, and increasingly with the onslaught of the Depression, he spoke in defence of those who suffered and against vested interests and privilege. In 1930 he contended that "the present system is failing to function";[38] and by 1932 he was railing against the economic system as the cause of most of the evils which beset the nation: "The present capitalist system has shown itself unjust and inhuman, economically wasteful and a standing threat to peace and democratic government. . . ." Just as he had been sceptical about the usefulness of individual action to rectify such miseries in *My Neighbour,* so now he continued to promote the idea that it was only through concerted group action that any alleviation was possible. The aims of the movement were the same that Irvine sought — collectivism and equality: "We therefore look to the establishment in Canada of a new social order which will substitute a planned and socialized economy for the existing chaotic individualism, and which, by achieving an approximate economic equality among men in place of the present glaring inequalities, will eliminate the domination of one class by another."

This hostility to capitalism was critical, because it was perhaps the only thing that united the different groups that met first in Calgary in 1932 and then in Regina in 1933. The Calgary Programme of 1932 was laudably imprecise. The weakness of socialism in Canada previous to that time had not been that socialists believed in too little, but rather they believed doctrinally in too much. Their ideological quarrels not only split them from the labour movement and the farmers' movements, but even from each other. Hence a federation, the object of which would be to "promote co-operation between the member organizations and to correlate their political activities", with the purpose of establishing in Canada "a Co-operative Commonwealth in which the basic principle regulating production, distribution and exchange, will be the supplying of human needs instead of the making of profits" was not needlessly divisive.

At the famous convention in Regina the next year the task was more difficult. There it was necessary to spell out in some detail the principles of the Co-operative Commonwealth, but to do so without alienating the different elements — liberal, socialist, trade unionist, social credit — that were hoped would support the coalition. "The ideological disagreement that existed between the various elements could not have been reconciled within the framework of a single party. The federal structure meant that each constituent group could retain to a large degree its original doctrine under the broad umbrella of the Regina Manifesto."[39] The organizational structure then was one tack. The other was Woodsworth's attempt to appeal to the nationalist feelings of the delegates by trying to persuade them that the novelty of their undertaking implied that they ought to discard those aspects of their ideological understanding which found its roots in foreign sources. Here as before Woodsworth reiterated his belief that the only kind of socialism that could succeed in Canada was one which grew from indigenous roots. "Undoubtedly we should profit by the experience of other nations and other times, but personally I believe that we in Canada must work out our own salvation in our own way. Socialism has so many variations that we hesitate to use the class name. Utopian Socialism and Christian Socialism, Marxian Socialism and Fabianism, the Latin type, the German type, the Russian type — why not a Canadian type?"[40]

What Frank Underhill and his academic colleagues in the League for Social Reconstruction achieved in the Manifesto that was presented to and substantially endorsed by the convention that met at Regina was a relatively short and concise statement of the outlines of the Co-operative Commonwealth. For most Canadians, until the *Winnipeg Declaration of Principles* in 1956, the *Regina Manifesto*, with its clarion call for the eradication of capitalism, was the definitive answer to the question Woodsworth posed. If pressed that this was not socialism as it was known in other places, the CCF replied, "The C.C.F. is essentially socialistic. It does not wish to follow slavishly schools of thoughts [sic] in existence elsewhere but aims to develop a distinctively Canadian approach to socialism".[41] It is therefore worth looking for a moment at the details of the *Manifesto*.

The basic source of agreement between the diverse groups at Regina was a hatred of the excesses of capitalism, "the cancer which is eating at the heart of our society".[42] Two important things were wrong with capitalism, in addition to the fact that it did not appear to be an effective economic system in 1933. First it rested on the premise that men were competitors, rather than co-operators; in the Co-operative Commonwealth, economic planning would "supersede unregulated private enterprise and competition". The second objection to capitalism was just as serious and just as radical. Capitalism had an inexorable tendency to develop in such a way that "our principal means of production and distribution are owned, controlled and operated for the private profit of a small proportion of our population". This system should, and could, be replaced "by a social order from which the domination and exploitation of one class by another will be eliminated".

All this was for the future, though in the moral outrage and heady optimism of Regina there were doubtless many who expected the movement to make rapid strides towards both power and suc· cess. On the whole, however, this was a vision of the green and pleasant land which would ultimately come. Other problems needed more immediate attention. This was recognized in 1933, and brought out more clearly at the Winnipeg Convention in 1934, which prepared the "CCF Immediate Programme".

At no time was the CCF ever a revolutionary movement. One of the reasons for this was the absence of a revolutionary tradition in Canadian politics. Unlike many European countries, or even the United States, Canada has no history, except for minor incidents like the Rebellion of 1837 or Riel's Rebellions, of the use of violence to promote extensive changes in the country's political order. The absence of revolutionary rhetoric from the speeches of men like Woodsworth puzzled many of his political opponents, who often imputed to Canadian socialism violent designs drawn from continental experience. This preference for peaceful change was not derived from considerations of expediency, but rather from what Young has described as the rationalist nature of many of the CCF's assumptions. The CCF did not believe "in change by violence". Its members preferred to wait until enough people had been "inspired by the ideal of a Co-operative Commonwealth". In the interim it sought to appeal "for support of all who believe that the time has come for a far-reaching reconstruction of our economic and political institutions". If these supporters did not constitute a majority, then it was the task of those who believed in the ideal to proselytize and educate until this goal could be achieved "solely by constitutional methods".

This approach rested on one of two doubtful assumptions. First, it could assume that ideological conversion on a wide scale was a likely outcome of the CCF's vigorous "educational" activities. We have suggested in our general analysis in Chapter I that such an eventuality was unlikely. Second, it might have been based on the presumption that the socialist strain in Canada was powerful enough in its own right to allow the CCF to secure widespread electoral support. This assumption could plausibly support the apparently sincere charge that the CCF often made that the comparatively large sums of money available to the Liberals and Conservatives for election campaigns, obtained to a large extent from the business community, deceived the common voter. However, our argument in Chapter II suggests that Canadian socialists were incorrect when they foresaw a large number of voters to whom collectivism and equality were potent ideological principles. As we shall see, the CCF recognized both limitations implicitly in their frequent additions of liberal concepts to the CCF public doctrines.

The collectivist element in this programme does not need comment here additional to that we have made previously in this chapter. Worthy of note, though, is another feature which the CCF shared in common with their hated enemies, the Conservatives. As Bennett was to reassert in his abortive New Deal, economic forces could no longer be allowed free play. Politics was the primary activity, and the state had the right and the duty to control economic consequences where necessary. The CCF affirmed its belief that "the welfare of the community must take supremacy over the claims of private wealth". The insistent and often repeated demands for economic order and centralized planning were not only elements central to the faith of Canadian socialists; they were also reassuring ideological explanations which offered an appeal to all who felt disoriented by the economic crisis through which Canada was passing.

A final important element in this ideological mix must be separated, not only because it was discordant, but also because it was extremely important for an understanding of the later development of socialism in Canada. That element is liberalism. The Conservative prime minister in the election campaign of 1935 declared that there "is no room in the same country for socialism and liberty".[43] Here Bennett was working, probably unwittingly but certainly not disingenuously, a grave injustice on Canadian socialism. The *Manifesto* came out strongly and clearly in favour of: "Freedom of speech and assembly for all; repeal of Section 98 of the Criminal Code; amendment of the Immigration Act to prevent the present inhuman policy of deportation; equal treatment before the law of all residents of Canada irrespective of race, nationality or religious or political beliefs." The goal of these freedoms was to be the traditional liberal one of "a much richer individual life for every citizen." Their most notable rival for the distinction of being the champions of the oppressed was the Liberal Party of Mackenzie King. As we have seen in Chapter III, King succeeded in weaning Canadian Liberalism away from an exclusive reliance on negative liberty, and began to infuse a concern for positive liberty in the party.

This same problem concerned the CCF: "Genuine liberty for the masses of the people is impossible without economic equality".[44] The mistake that the CCF made, and it was one which caused them great heart-rending when they saw the Liberals implement what they thought were their policies, was to believe that they were the only party in Canada concerned, or even aware, of the preconditions of positive liberty. Although the requirement of "economic equality" was more radical than anything Mackenzie King ever spelled out, the CCF never made clear what they meant by that concept either, and we are left with the conclusion that it probably had no greater effective meaning for them than the equivalent notion of greater security might have had for King. What was important to the CCF was the belief that they were the only group in Canadian political life that cared about such matters. To achieve this, they charged that the "Liberal Party is, in fact, grooming itself to take the place of the Tories as the party of big business".[45]

Not only was the *Manifesto* an ideological compromise, it was also a social and economic compromise. If it hoped to have wide electoral support the CCF had to include provisions that would appeal to farm elements, the labour movement and the socialists. This problem meant that the programme had to contain a number of uneasy compromises, especially on matters relating to property holding. Although all groups could agree that finance and public utilities ought to be "socialized", it was very clear that the farmers especially were not in favour of an extensive policy of nationalization. Hence the programme acknowledged that "the family farm is the accepted basis for agricultural production in Canada", though it went on to encourage an extension of co-operative institutions. Labour also had to be offered policies which were attractive in the short-run, and the *Manifesto* promised a "National Labor Code to secure for the worker maximum income and leisure, insurance covering illness, accident, old age, and unemployment, freedom of association and effective participation in the management of his industry or profession".

In spite of the extensiveness of the appeal, both ideological and class, the voters of Canada appeared to have agreed that the choice in 1935 was between King and chaos. The Liberals won a landslide victory in the election of that year and the CCF returned a very disappointing seven MP's, three from British Columbia, two from Saskatchewan and two from Manitoba. They were shut out of Alberta completely in the face of the Social Credit landslide, and in national terms, they were overshadowed by Social Credit's seventeen seats, although more than doubling its popular vote. However if 1935 was not electorally a gratifying year, it was, intellectually, the highpoint of the CCF. It was in that year that the academics of the League for Social Reconstruction (LSR), including Frank Scott, Frank Underhill and Eugene Forsey, published what is probably the greatest single socialist work in Canadian history, *Social Planning for Canada*.

The LSR was created by academics from the University of Toronto and McGill, with a view to its playing a role similar to that played by the Fabian Society in the United Kingdom in relation to the Labour Party. However these intellectuals did not succeed in keeping their distance from the party and instead of remaining an independent source of ideas, they were involved with plotting the course the CCF would take from the very beginning. The LSR's Manifesto of 1932 announced that it would "support any political party insofar as its program furthers the principles it favoured", including public ownership of public utilities, the nationalization of banks, the development of agricultural co-operatives, social legislation, steeply graded income and inheritance taxes and the creation of a National Planning Commission.[46] When Woodsworth wrote in the Preface to *Social Planning for Canada* that, "on the whole this book is undoubtedly in line with the Regina Manifesto"[47] he was doing no more than acknowledging that the men who wrote the one had amplified their views into a "sustained academic critique that was a far cry from the more superficial criticisms of the farmers' organizations".[48]

There were, clearly, few doctrinal surprises to be expected from this work, but for the first time there was a document which would amplify and clarify (in spite of the dubious value of this process in terms of party unity) the principles of Regina. Throughout the book, the two main conflicting ideologies were juggled and blended. The socialist aspects came out most clearly in the critiques of contemporary capitalism, "a luxury we can no longer afford".[49] In all advanced industrial countries, the argument went, the forces of production had a strong tendency to become concentrated in increasingly fewer hands. A handful of businessmen could "dominate enterprises covering almost every imaginable economic activity".[50] The consequence of this economic development was the creation of a small class of privileged property owners who dominated the economic and political life of the country. But the concentration of economic power was the fruitful source of the capitalists' downfall and the necessary precondition of the Co-operative Commonwealth, since it was relatively easy, given the development of "monopoly capitalism" for the state to take over the existing business, and operate without the necessity of any far-reaching economic reorganization.[51]

At this point in the analysis, however, an important disagreement arose between the urban, intellectual socialists and the farmers' movement, whom the former acknowledged would, "because of voting power, be for a considerable time the senior partner".[52] The LSR thought that the economic state of affairs lent itself easily to placing "ultimate authority in the hands of the State".[53] The farmers' movements were not so sure that this was the right approach. As E .J. Garland said in the debate on the *Marketing Act* of 1934:

> ... the two most essential steps towards the building of a new state and a new social order in which through the encouragement and growth of cooperatives on the one side, collectively owning the essential basic industries, and direction by the State of the other essential secondary industries, we will have brought about what we are proposing in our Cooperative Commonwealth Federation Manifesto....
>
> I am not a socialist, I have never been a socialist....
>
> The organization to which I belong, the United Farmers of Alberta, constitutes the largest and most powerful part of [the CCF]. Our whole philosophy is based upon the development of cooperatives....
>
> We do not, particularly those of the U.F.A. which is the most powerful body in the Canadian Cooperative Federation, regard it as essential to undertake, say, vast dislocating series of socializations or nationalizations of industries. We do not believe it is necessary..[54]

Woodsworth tried to split the difference on this issue. "'[The CCF] does not advocate a bureaucratic state socialism. We recognize very clearly that there are certain matters which must be dealt with by the State; there are other matters that may be left to voluntary cooperative effort."[55] It is worth noting this disagreement because it indicates that right from the very beginning of the CCF there was a serious ideolgical division between those who leaned more to the egalitarian side of the ideological compromise, and favoured extensive state activity to that end, and those whose primary goal was the more explicitly liberal one of enhancing freedom.

The latter element was by no means absent from the LSR's thoughts. They sought a "full realisation of personal freedom", but argued that it could only come about through collectivism, through a "willing co-operation in concerted social action". True freedom could "only be enjoyed by people whose work and incomes secure against arbitrary disaster and afford them a reasonable chance of a decent living and leisure".[56] None of this was very far at all from the beliefs of positive liberalism, an ideology which the League believed had seduced "the disinherited groups". This "middle class optimism" was all the worse because it rendered "impotent the finer impulses".[57] This false consciousness on the part of "the classes which suffer most from the present chaos of monopoly capitalism" meant that the CCF had a formidable task of education in front of it. "No system of socialism will work without the support of a determined and instructed public behind it, and this work of public education is the more necessary in a democratic movement which does not contemplate a violent or forcible transition to the new order".[58] Even the theorists of the LSR, then, could not imagine a successful appeal to the people which did not embody elements of the liberal ideology which had struck such deep and extensive roots in the Canadian ideological soil. Or perhaps even these theoreticians could not themselves escape from the ideological snare of liberalism. One of their most distinguished number, Frank Underhill was to become increasingly an exponent of liberal ideas; and as we shall see, the trend of the development of the CCF, until its demise, was precisely the same as that of the Conservatives after Bracken: namely, towards a minimization of ideological differences with the Liberals.

Between 1935 and 1940 the CCF moved increasingly into the control of the urban, Eastern forces in the party, who began to consider it increasingly a labour party allied with the farmers' movements.[59] But for the most part the trade unions in Canada were content to continue the policy which they had pursued since the nineteenth century of avoiding specific commitments to any single party. King's masterfully cynical timing of the 1940 election made things incredibly awkward for a party committed to domestic reform. Although the party as a whole did not endorse Woodsworth's consistently pacifistic opposition to war, and announced that it was as determined "to bring the war to a successful conclusion" as the

Liberals and Conservatives, it was faced with the unlikely eventuality that the people of Canada would abandon King's Liberals during such a crisis. Although it gained one seat, its share of the popular vote remained static.

After that, however, its popularity surged. As people began increasingly to turn their attention to the problem of post-war reconstruction, the attractiveness of choosing a CCF government to carry out this process of reconstruction became more appealing. The end of the war presented an opportunity, even more than had the Depression, of choosing between ideological visions. Great changes were bound to be underfoot, and the question was: what shape would the post-war nature of Canada take. The first taste of success was in October 1941, with a strong showing in a British Columbia provincial election. This was quickly followed in 1942 when the CCF candidate, Noseworthy, defeated the redoubtable Arthur Meighen in South York in his attempt to regain entry into the House of Commons. 1943 was their highpoint. They won 34 seats in the Ontario provincial legislature where they had held none previously, and a Gallup poll in September showed them leading both the Liberals and Conservatives in popular support (29 per cent-28 per cent-28 per cent). Finally in 1944 they scored what turned out to be their only enduring electoral triumph when they swept to power in Saskatchewan.[60]

On Woodsworth's death in 1942 the party formally elected M. J. Coldwell as leader. He had been in effective control of the party from the beginning of Woodsworth's disability in 1940. Coldwell was born in England and as a young man emigrated to Canada where he settled in the West and became a school teacher. While in Saskatchewan he participated in labour politics at both the municipal and provincial level, and in 1935 he was elected to the Dominion Parliament. Coldwell had more of the politician's time perspective than had Woodsworth, the prophet. Under Coldwell's leadership the CCF lost some of its millenarian fervour and began to take into account more tactical electoral considerations. The successes of the early 1940's gave him and the other leading theorists of the CCF reason to hope that they were devising policies and drafting programmes which they would very soon be in a position to implement.

In 1943 David Lewis and Frank Scott collaborated in writing *Make This Your Canada* which Coldwell wrote "presents a faithful outline of the principles, history and organization of the CCF."[61] In this work there is clear evidence that the liberal elements in the party's ideological mix were beginning to take on an increased importance under the new regime. Ironically it was the more doctrinaire socialist elements in the party's economic analysis that drew them in that direction. Their understanding of the development of the Canadian economy taught them to isolate as a critical factor the remorseless tendency of that economic organization to concentrate power in the hands of increasingly fewer capitalists. If, as they speculated, the well-to-do Canada numbered no more than 10,500 families, or 0.6 per cent of the population,[62] the overwhelming majority, the 99.4 per cent of farmers, workers and middle class had a real and substantial interest in combining to end the rule of the wealthy. "Obviously, if the farmers, workers and middle class were allowed to recognize their common interests and to unite in an effective political party with a programme and a philosophy deriving from their own experience and needs, no power in the land could stop them from building together a free society based on the common welfare of all."[63] This analysis raises a difficult question: why include the middle class in this coalition, when according to the CCF's figures, farmers and workers together comprised 73.7 per cent of the total population? The answer can only be that the socialism of the CCF had grown from the collectivist theories of the Western farmers' movements. The CCF preferred an anlysis which would allow it to speak for virtually the whole country, rather than for class divisions within it. Provision had to be made within the doctrine and within the programme for measures which would appeal to middle class voters.

This development did not involve the leaders of the party in much personal soul searching, since, for the most part, they tended to be Eastern intellectuals, of a predominantly middle class bent themselves. Their preoccupations were more those of the middle class to whom they sought to appeal than of the farmers to whom they did appeal, and upon whom they relied for the bulk of their parliamentary representation. They continued to strive for a society which would provide an "opportunity for all the people to build and work cooperatively in an environment of democratic equality and fellowship";[64] but their overriding goal was the fundamentally liberal one of increased freedom. A "dynamic, progressive society" to them was one which allowed all to "express their *individual* personalities and initiative in accordance with their talents and aspirations. . . ."[65] Although they emphasized that individual rights "are not absolute, but are qualified by their communal purpose",[66] it is clear that they intended little more than a statement that the freedom about which they were concerned was not the freedom of the capitalists to the unregulated use of or control over their enterprises. What they were saying amounted to little more than the observation that the aims of positive liberalism could be attained better in an "organized society which reached far beyond the negative 'freedom from want' ".[67] Even the equality which they pursued was influenced by individualist assumptions. "Democratic equality rests on the basic right and value of every personality"[68]

Although this ideological development took place as a consequence of dynamics which had been present in the party since its birth, this style of political thought had been foreshadowed earlier in the century in England by men such as L. T. Hobhouse. Hobhouse rejected the old *laissez-faire* argument that practices like child labour and the 12-hour day were justified because they were based on freely made contracts between employer and employed. He concluded that the state had to intervene to rectify injustices which resulted from the unequal bargaining power of the parties. When the liberal came to terms with this necessity, he was impelled to make modifications in classic liberal doctrine. "[I]ndividualism, when it grapples with the facts, is driven no small distance along Socialist lines. Once again we have found that to maintain individual freedom and equality we have to extend the sphere of social control."[69] Hobhouse was well aware that his position might be criticized as not being liberalism at all, and to that he retorted: "Pursuing the economic rights of the individual we have been led to contemplate a Socialistic organization of industry. But a word like Socialism has many meanings, and it is possible that there should be a Liberal Socialism, as well as a Socialism that is illiberal."[70] It is our contention that although the CCF began at a starting point different from Hobhouse, it arrived at a similar ideological conclusion. Since it is this "Liberal Socialism" of which Hobhouse spoke that became the dominant form of liberalism in our society today, it is easy to understand why the CCF and later the NDP had a close but jealous relationship with the Liberal Party, and why the Liberals found it easy to adopt their rival's policies. Mackenzie King, whose beliefs led him in the direction of Hobhouse's liberalism, was the leader of a Liberal Party which included, even in the 1940's, many prominent supporters who were still concerned exclusively with negative liberty. The electoral threat which the CCF from time to time posed to the Liberals allowed King to use the opportunity that this presented him to introduce modest doses of the positive liberalism he favoured.

Coldwell's book, *Left Turn, Canada* (1944) took basically the same tack as Lewis and Scott. The individualism of the latter was there, but Coldwell, former school teacher as he had been, drew out even more the educational aspects of the CCF programme. Since socialism aimed at a new way of life, as well as new political and economic arrangements, Canadian socialists have long been concerned with education as a means of attaining it. It has become a traditional socialist policy in Canada to advocate that educational facilities ought to be expanded and opened equally to members of all social classes. As Coldwell explained, "The product of the school ought not to be a regimented automaton, but a self-reliant, thinking and co-operative person.... Such a society requires not only reliable information, but the ability of large masses of the people to make a critical analysis of known facts to provide the foundations for appropriate action."[71]

The next year, 1945, saw the CCF's greatest electoral success with 16 per cent of the popular vote and 28 members of Parliament, a number not exceeded by a socialist party in Canada until the NDP's 31 members in 1972. The cautiousness of the approach in 1945 is indicated by the title given to the programme, *Security with Victory*. It contained no ringing denunciations of capitalism, only a mild criticism of "the planlessness of capitalism and the restrictive power of private monopolies". Although it promised "to remove the glaring inequalities that still exist", the programme made only the modest request for "a new mandate for a further advance toward the Co-operative Commonwealth". What was foremost in the strategists' minds, and they expected, in the fears of the voters, was the spectre of massive unemployment consequent on demobilization, and to this end they made, as their "central aim" the scarcely uniquely socialist pledge of "jobs and an adequate income for all."[72]

From 1945 on, the liberal aspects of the party's ideology waxed while its electoral strength, on the whole, waned. Too little is known about the factors that induce voters to cast their ballots as they do to come to any firm conclusions that there is a link between the progressive liberalization and the decline. There is, though, reason to suspect that the more doctrinaire socialists were shrewd in their appreciation that if the people of Canada wanted liberalism, they would prefer to give their support to the Liberals, rather than to the CCF. As Carlyle King of the Saskatchewan CCF observed earthily in 1952: "The trouble is that socialist parties have gone a-whoring after the Bitch Goddess. They have wanted Success, Victory, Power; forgetting that the main business of socialist parties is not to form governments but to change minds. When people begin to concentrate on success at the polls, they become careful and cautious; and when they become careful and cautious, the virtue goes out of them."[73]

The 1949 programme *Security for All*, on which the CCF dropped to 13 per cent of the popular vote and 13 seats, was scarcely socialist at all. At least the socialist inspiration of many of the party's promises was heavily veiled behind liberal rhetoric. In fact the programme sought to hide any differences that might prove offensive to voters. Instead of providing a clear ideological choice, it announced: "In a land of Canada's resources, no person should go without the basic necessities of life. *All parties agree; therefore they promise these necessities.*"[74] In place of the social and economic analysis which figured prominently in 1945 and before, the CCF in 1949 was content with the cheap and banal charge that the "Old Parties can't fulfil their promises because those who provide their election funds, and therefore control them, are unwilling to pay the price."[75]

Security for All was probably the highpoint of liberal influence in the period in which the CCF was the vehicle for the expression of mainstream Canadian socialism. Walter Young has argued that the CCF's "liberalism kept them from being communists while their socialism prevented them from becoming liberals".[76] The 1953 election saw them winning 23 seats but falling to 11 per cent of the popular vote. It was at this time that Young's Law (above) came into force, and the party veered away, at perhaps the last moment, from its assimilation course with Liberalism. *Humanity First* spoke in more traditionally socialist terms of an economy "artificially bolstered by war production" in which "no one's future is secure"; and praised the determination of those "Canadians who are determined to put an end to the exploitation of the poor by the rich, of the weak by the strong — Canadians who believe in working co-operatively for the good of all instead of the dog-eat-dog method of every man for himself".[77]

The possibility that the CCF would merge with the Liberals, as had the Progressives in the 1920's, was the more likely of Young's two possibilities. For CCFers to become Communists would have involved them shifting from an indigenous ideology to an exogenous one. It would have meant, for most of them, becoming outsiders rather than insiders in Canadian politics. More, it would have involved the type of ideological move, with all the inherent difficulties that such a change involved, that we discussed in Chapter I: the replacement of one set of social and political presuppositions with an entirely different set. The CCF was democratic, liberal and socialist of a Fabian sort; the Labor-Progressives, led by the Communist Tim Buck, were authoritarian and favoured a Marxist socialism as modified by such Bolshevik theorists as Lenin.

Nonetheless, the Labor-Progressives were a constant embarrassment to the CCF, in much the same way that the British Labour Party suffered from the exaggerated zeal of the British Communist Party to affiliate. Time after time CCF members denied the accusation that they were themselves Communists, and the party platforms of 1949 and 1953 contained strong statements disassociating the CCF from Labor-Progressive offers of electoral alliance. To prevent infiltration of the CCF by individual Communists, the CCF carried out periodic small scale purges, and denied membership in their organization to any person who was already a member of another political party. Yet there can be little doubt that their position was misunderstood by many. The consistent agitation by Woodsworth and his allies against both the old Section 98 of the Criminal Code and the deportation powers of the government had granted itself during the Winnipeg General Strike, found a parallel in the CCF's opposition to the Liberal Government's desire to outlaw the Communist Party. The CCF realized the dilemma in which their apparent support for the Communists placed them from the electors' point of view, but felt that "democracy cannot exist where minorities do not have full protection against oppression, domination or encroachments on their legitimate freedoms."[78] With specific reference to Communism, and doubtless in full confidence that their position would be both misunderstood and cynically misrepresented, they stated:

> Although the CCF abhors communism and will continue to fight it, the CCF does not support proposals to outlaw it. The CCF has always contended that the way to fight communism is not to outlaw it, but to correct those social and economic injustices and wrongs on which communism thrives. To outlaw communism and to engage in "McCarthyism" and witch-hunting is to weaken the very freedoms we are trying to protect.[79]

In an attempt to continue to steer a course between the extremes of communism and liberalism the party drafted the *Winnipeg Declaration of Principles* of 1956[80] in an attempt to develop a new synthesis of liberalism and socialism as a contemporary restatement of what had been expressed in Regina in 1933. How it would have fared had it been attempted earlier will never be known. As it was it had the misfortune of running afoul of John Diefenbaker's compelling mixture of liberalism and conservatism, more accurately progressivism and nostalgia. Throughout the *Declaration* liberal and socialist concepts jostle one against another. The first sentence speaks in terms of the "co-operative commonwealth" and presses the primary importance of "supplying human needs and enrichment of life." Yet the very next sentence goes on to laud the importance of the quintessentially individualist notion of equality of opportunity. The third and fourth paragraphs deal with inequalities, which the CCF claimed resulted "in a virtual economic dictatorship by a privileged few." But nowhere is there an attempt to explain how a society in which equality of opportunity operates could fail to produce inequality, given the unequal distribution of talents within society, which is a primary justification for equality of opportunity.

Although the *Declaration* condemned Canadian society as "motivated by the drive for private profit and special privilege" it no longer sought a new form of property holding to eliminate what it repudiated as "basically immoral". The CCF "recognized" that private enterprise could make a "useful contribution to the development of our economy." When David Lewis took stock in 1956 he rejected nationalization as a cure-all for social and economic problems. Instead of this traditional socialist policy Lewis proposed a reliance on the Keynesian economic palliatives which had by then become the orthodoxy among Liberal economists. He spoke of the "use of fiscal and financial policies to influence the volume and direction of investments, to redistribute income, and to stimulate purchasing power."[81] Here was a policy which would not have been uncomfortable to any but the most unreconstructed supporters of negative liberalism.

The *Winnipeg Declaration* was meant to breathe new life into the party; yet within two years, its parliamentary strength had been reduced to eight, its lowest level since 1940, and only one more than had been elected in 1935. Clearly the CCF had failed in Winnipeg, and a few clues to this failure can be gleaned from the party's *Share Canada's Wealth!* (1957). An ideology, as we argued in Chapter I, has to provide answers to certain enduring questions about the polity if it is to be an adequate guide for its converts in their political activities. It was in this area that the CCF failed most clearly; the following passage is most instructive:

> The CCF presents an alternative to the people of Canada. It offers a program designed to ensure that every person — regardless of occupation, sex, colour or creed will have full opportunity to share in the nation's progress and to develop his talents in a society free from the exploitation of *man by man or class by class.*[82]

There is no clear answer in this passage to the question of whether men are to be competitors or cooperators. The ideal of the Co-operative Commonwealth would seem to imply the latter, as would the suggestion that men were to share in the nation's progress. Yet individualism and competition is present in the references to the development of talents and the insistence that prior membership in a group based on occupation (and this would have to be taken generally, as including farmers and workers) is deemed harmful. Another question which an ideology is supposed to treat — namely, the units of which society is composed — is also skirted. The focus is primarily economic, but the units involved might be individuals ("exploitation of man by man") or groups ("class by class").

There was, however, one clear area of difference between the CCF and the Liberals, and that was the question of the primacy of politics over economics. The Liberals, as we have seen, were content to allow the free play of economic forces in international trade, regardless of the consequences to such things as ownership of Canadian industry. The CCF was alarmed both at this attitude and at its consequences. They asserted that government had to play "a much more active part in the nation's economic life", especially to check the hold of American concerns in the Canadian economy which threaten "our economic, and even our political independence". This latter problem was, as we shall see, to become a matter of increasing importance to Canadian socialism. For the time being, however, it is of importance only to the extent that it indicates how little the CCF had succeeded in providing Canadians with a real ideological alternative; for the Progressive Conservative platform of 1957, *A New National Policy*, also took the same stand. It too talked about the importance of the "nation builders who made Confederation" and worried that the policies of the Liberal Party had exposed "future generations to the possible loss of national independence". John Diefenbaker's liberal conservatism, with its concern for "that equality of opportunity [which] must be assured to our people in every part of Canada" had, for the time being at least, pre-empted the ground which could be occupied by a party in Canada which was interested in mixing a form of collectivism with liberalism. The crushing defeat the CCF suffered in 1958 was clear proof that the party had outlived its usefulness, and a new party movement arose soon after the defeat to effect a "fundamental political realignment through the creation of a broadly based people's political movement embracing the CCF, the labour movement, farm organizations, professional people, and other liberally minded persons interested in basic social reforms and reconstruction through our parliamentary system of government".[83]

There were a number of advantages to founding a new party, rather than attempting to remould the remnants of the CCF into an acceptable ideological state. In the first place it appeared that the socialist "touch" in Canada of which Horowitz spoke and which we explained in an earlier chapter, did not comprise a sufficient proportion of the population to allow the CCF to maintain a high minimum representation in the House of Commons, sufficient to endow it with the tinge of success that would have convinced voters of the vigour of the alternative it offered. Second, a new party would not be tied, as the CCF had been, by the ideological compromises that had been arrived at in Regina in 1933, which hampered the restatement of Canadian socialism in Winnipeg in 1956. Third, and perhaps most important from the point of view of practical politics, if not from an ideological perspective, was that for the first time a significant number of Canadian trade unions were willing to abandon their traditional Gompersism — the refusal to align with one particular political party — in favour of supporting the new party. The CCF unlike the British Labour Party had survived in the absence of this stable trade union support, which provided for social democratic parties in the United Kingdom and elsewhere both stable electoral and financial support, especially in the period between elections. The CCF was proud of this financial independence, which it believed gave it the freedom to promote social justice without fear of the consequent wrath of the large corporations; but its relative poverty, at least compared to the Liberals and Progressive Conservatives, left it barely able to perform the task of socialist education which doctrine dictated was an essential precondition for social and economic transformation. Thus the CCFers followed the dictates of their ideology to one of its possible conclusions, and put an end to the party itself.

This development was made more likely by the amalgamation in 1956 of the two leading trade union groups in Canada, the Trades and Labour Congress and the Canadian Congress of Labour into the Canadian Labour Congress. Before this time the Gompersism of the TLC was too strong. It objected to the support of any one political party, and advocated strongly that the trade union movement support whomever was deemed most friendly to labour at the time. Yet the merging of these two bodies was not as fortuitous as it might seem. In Britain the Labour Party had been the creation of the trade union movement. In Canada the politicians in the CCF had taken an active and perhaps leading role in the creation of the Canadian Labour Congress, and had thereby prepared the way for an alliance between the unions and a social democratic political party.

The new party, subsequently christened the New Democratic Party at its founding convention in Ottawa, 31 July — 4 August 1961, was formed by the same groups that had founded the CCF in 1933 — farmers, labour, socialists. But in 1961 the second element in the triad loomed far larger than it ever had previously in the history of socialism in Canada. Canada, by comparison with European countries, is not heavily trade unionized and the support of the trade unions for the NDP has never been total. All the same the influx of large numbers of organized unionists had a major impact on party ideology. "A Job for Everyone" was the first item in the *Federal Programme*[84] adopted by the NDP's founding convention, reflecting, perhaps, Knowles' belief that unions are basically economic units. [85] The programme went on to outline a whole range of policies on investment, Canadian ownership, trade, automation; a national health plan, retirement plan, labour standards, and education, "a matter of sound economics"; co-operative federalism, an entrenched bill of rights; and co-operation for peace.

Yet the real ideological difference the unions made was to alter the time perspective of Canadian socialism. Practical men, concerned with this world rather than the next, the unionists in the past had found the millenarian aspects of the CCF unappealing. Their wish was not to educate for socialism, but to agitate for better conditions for their members. Some writers, noting this different attitude in the NDP, would prefer to describe it as a social democratic, rather than a socialist, party. Others prefer to distinguish between socialism as a goal and socialism as a process. The NDP was clearly of the latter stamp. Stanley Knowles set the tone in his *The New Party* (1961). There he argued strongly that socialism did not strive for a fixed and static final goal; rather it involved continual movement towards dignity, equality, social justice and economic and political freedom.[86] The conversion of the ideal of the Co-operative Commonwealth into an endless process was a vital part of the melding of socialism and trade unionism.

Knowles also succeeded, better than had anyone before him in Canada in reconciling the liberal and socialist elements in the NDP's official ideology. He achieved this by what superficially appears to be a minor change, but which in reality is one of great significance. Instead of attempting to attain equality, the NDP was to be content with "greater equality". This phrase was satisfactorily vague in that the NDP was not forced to choose whether it meant by that a strict economic equality as the socialists had traditionally preferred, or equality of opportunity, as the liberals in the CCF had favoured. "Greater equality" was consistent "economic security" and the "opportunity to develop the best that is in him",[87] as well as with a "society in which human dignity might be the lot of all". Knowles' phrase indicated the importance of the value of equality both to socialist theory and socialist practice in Canada without raising the issue in such a way as to be needlessly clear.

Clarity was provided by *Social Purpose for Canada*, essays by such leading theorists of socialism as George Grant, John Porter and Pierre Trudeau. However a collection of essays could not be expected to have the same force as the League for Social Reconstruction's 1935 study, since the tendency of the writers was to tackle different problems from an independent point of view. As a consequence Knowles' *The New Party* is a better statement of the NDP's ideological position than *Social Purpose for Canada* or any of the succeeding books published under the auspices of the University League for Social Reform.

Grant's essay in this volume is, as is usual with his work, a brilliant piece of philosophical writing in its own right; it pinpoints an essential problem that the NDP faced: did it still remain a socialist party? Grant's concern was to show the new party that its proper concern was equality, both material and moral. What Grant spoke of as "the old socialist ethic of egalitarian material prosperity" which the CCF had pursued was still necessary to solve a number of the quantitative problems which continue to plague Canadian society. But increasingly, Grant argued, these quantitative problems would diminish in importance, and qualitative problems would loom large which could not be solved by a society in which "production is inevitably directed to those things which can be produced privately at a profit at the expense of those goods which cannot be."[88] It was here that socialism was most important, because only socialism offers a "high and more realistic morality" that was "a better alternative to our present capitalist system and ethic".[89] The key to the new socialist vision of Canada would have to continue to be equality, rather than, as Grant showed in his later works, the liberal principle of freedom.

> Equality should be the central principle of society since all persons, whatever their condition, must freely choose to live by what is right or wrong. This act of choosing is the ultimate human act and is open to all. In this sense all persons are equal, and differences of talent are of petty significance.[90]

There was some evidence that the NDP might chart a course which highlighted this greater moral equality. The party's choice for its first leader was the successful CCF Premier of Saskatchewan, T. C. Douglas, who was persuaded to leave provincial politics to contest the leadership of the new federal party. His chief rival for the leadership, Hazen Argue, indicated his dissatisfaction with the ideological direction of the new party by defecting to the Liberals soon after his defeat by Douglas. A former Baptist minister, Douglas developed his political awareness in much the same way as Woodsworth: he came to the social gospel through a progressive dissatisfaction with the ability of the traditional church to do anything in a real way to alleviate suffering and hardship. To some extent, then, Douglas reintroduced into the party the millenarian aspects which had been progressively squeezed out under the Coldwell-Lewis regime. Yet even under Douglas, the new alliance with the trade movement kept the party from reversing its direction. And if not all trade union leaders, by any means, were liberals, there was little doubt that the bulk of the membership, reflecting the social composition of the country as a whole, were as sympathetic to individualism and increased liberty as to collectivism and equality.

In its first two elections, in 1962 and 1963, the NDP increased its share of the popular vote first to 13 per cent and then to 14 per cent, winning 19 and 17 seats respectively. Although its platforms were as comprehensive as those of its rivals, the party tended, in its election campaigns to concentrate on a single major issue fundamental to its concept of social justice. In 1962 the campaign focussed on the issue of "the right to health". Here is a good example of the way that ideology works to provide answers to important political and social questions.

We have seen that equality and collectivism are the key concepts which distinguish Canadian socialism from other ideologies. These two root ideas are reflected in the medical care plan that the NDP presented. It rejected, as the CCF had done many times in the past, anything that looked like a means test, on the grounds that such a requirement was always demeaning for those who had to apply: "Worst of all, it would be humiliating." This was an affirmation, as they saw it, of the dignity of man. Their plan would, therefore, not be a private one supplemented by government assistance to the needy: "It will be based on two fundamental principles." The first of these was equality: Services must be available to every citizen when needed, regardless of income." The second was collectivism: "The cost must be spread over society as a whole, each person contributing on the basis of ability to pay."[91]

External events took the issue of the 1963 campaign out of the control of the NDP. The question of nuclear warheads for the Canadian armed forces had brought down the minority Diefenbaker government in the House of Commons, and the central issues revolved around questions of foreign policy and Canadian independence, the latter because of the intervention of senior American military and government personnel in the campaign on behalf of the Liberals. The NDP at the time advocated the rejection of these arms, and spoke strongly in favour of an internationalist approach to foreign policy, a doctrine which implied paying less concern to the sensibilities and interests of the Americans. But on this issue their stance, though more righteous, was not easily distinguished from that of the Conservatives, especially as presented by the Secretary of State for External Affairs, Howard Green. In the event the voters preferred the continentalist defence policy of the Liberals.

There had, of course, been little time for ideological development between elections. What had happened was that the Liberals had moved more convincingly into the NDP's main campaign issue of the previous year, medicare. However the differences between the two plans are interesting. They indicate limitations on the theory that the NDP and the CCF before, function as a pressure group which spurs the Liberals on to enact progressive measures. We have seen that the NDP's plan relied heavily on principles we have identified as fundamental to Canadian socialism. In the same way the Liberals advanced a medicare plan, but it was one which differed significantly from what the NDP had proposed, and those differences are directly traceable to the two concepts central to liberalism in this country, liberty and individualism. As the Liberals said about their plan: "Their will be *no restrictive conditions*. The patient will be *free* to choose his doctor. The doctor will remain *free* to practice as he chooses. There will be no interference with the doctor-patient relationship. . . . The doctor will continue to receive his income on a fee for service basis."[92] Comparison of the two schemes indicates that the Liberals could be pressed by NDP pressure to adopt a liberal medicare programme, perhaps sooner than they might have otherwise; they could not be manoeuvred into bringing forth a socialist one.

The surprise election of 1965 saw the NDP still pressing for the same issue. But its rise to 18 per cent of the popular vote more likely reflected the dissatisfaction of some liberals for Lester Pearson's decision to call an election on the pretext that he needed a majority government. By 1968, however, things had changed significantly in all the major political parties in Canada. As we have seen the Liberals and the Conservatives chose new leaders; the NDP was soon to follow in 1971. But for the time being, the party had to content itself with the arrival of a new faction called the Waffle movement. Because the most widely controversial aspect of the Waffle was its violent anti-Americanism we shall analyze it as well in the next chapter; but it is appropriate to treat it here as well, because it offered a rival conception of socialism.

Ironically, the Waffle movement probably owes its impetus to a task force set up by the Liberal government of Lester Pearson to investigate foreign ownership in the economy, under the direction of Mel Watkins. After Watkins had submitted his committee's report in 1968, he began increasingly to associate with a group of the NDP who came to consider American ownership in the Canadian economy to be the most important barrier to the establishment of a socialist state in Canada. Their choice for an agent to break the power of the foreign corporations was the traditional socialist one, namely the state. Such a state, however, was sure to be a powerful institution, and to make sure that this powerful state was the servant and not the oppressor of the vast majority of the Canadian people, it would have to be a socialist state. The creation of "an independent socialist Canada" was their goal.

The Waffle only began to make its influence as a pressure group within the party felt at the Winnipeg Conference of 1969, but some of its preoccupations found their way into the platform upon which the party fought the election of the previous year. There it was announced, ignoring the earlier pronouncements of the CCF that "New Democrats have become convinced that recovering our economic independence is a crucial step in securing our future prosperity. This is not narrow nationalism. . . "[93] The spirit of 1968 was clearly infectious and the party began to talk consciously again, and with renewed assurance that there was the possibility of ideological conversion in Canada, a "new society in a new world", one in which "excessive privilege and wealth for the few will be replaced by equal opportunities for the many." In spite of the vigour of the 1968 programme the NDP found themselves losing out to Prime Minister Trudeau's promise to establish a Just Society. They should not have been surprised however, because Trudeau's Just Society bore certain striking resemblances, especially in regard to promises of greater equality of opportunity, to that put forward in the 1968 Regina Program. The NDP dropped in 1968 from 18 per cent to 17 per cent of the popular vote, though its parliamentary representation, the vagaries of the Canadian electoral system being what they are, rose from 21 to 22 seats. Douglas had not made the breakthrough in electoral terms that he had expected, and he gracefully stepped down as leader.

When the party met in Ottawa in 1971 to choose Douglas' successor, it was faced with a range of ideological choice at least as wide as that which met the Conservatives in 1967 and the Liberals in 1968.[94] Representing the more liberal aspects of the party ideology and closely identified with the trade union leaders was David Lewis, a man who had dedicated his life first to the CCF and then to the NDP. His chief rival, as it turned out, was the representative of the Waffle movement, James Laxer, a relative newcomer to NDP politics, but a man with considerable support especially among younger members of the party. John Harney, a York University English Professor, was a strong candidate, identified most clearly in the minds of most delegates as someone who would have a strong appeal in the province of Quebec. Ed Broadbent attempted to create a position for himself at the party's centre, between Laxer and Lewis, forging an appeal to both socialist and liberal elements: but, like all previous attempts the NDP or CCF had made in this direction, Broadbent's floundered. The last candidate in terms of the number of delegate votes he received at the convention was the British Columbia member, Frank Howard who exemplified, more than any other of the candidates, the party's traditional compassion and concern for the dignity of man.

The surprising strength of Laxer as the Waffle candidate was a clear indication that the fragile doctrinal unity which the party had always cherished was in danger of breaking down. The more doctrinaire socialists in the party — or, to put it less contentiously, those who believe more in socialism as a goal, than as a process — had normally been discontented with the compromises the party had customarily made with the aim in mind of attracting large segments of the liberal centre. These socialists were under no delusion concerning the difficulty of effecting ideological conversions. They were aware that the process which we described in Chapter I involved enormous expenditures of time and effort on what they chose to call educational activity; but they argued, as the CCF had argued in the 1930's, that only such an ideological conversion, and only a party elected by a majority of the citizenry which had previously been persuaded of the correctness of their positions, could succeed in achieving a socialist society. On this ground they were in clear conflict with the more ameliorationist minded trade unionists, who represented, for the time being anyway, a substantial portion of the NDP's electoral strength, and a growing portion of its finances.

This is not the place to deal with the events which led to the destruction of the separate Waffle caucus within the NDP in 1972. It is sufficient here to note that the new leader, David Lewis, thought that he could not fight a successful election campaign with the party in ideological disarray, and he chose the dangerous alternative of risking an open split by suppressing the Waffle movement as a separate group within the party.

When the 1972 election was finally called for October 30, Lewis thought to reunite the party by a campaign against the "corporate welfare bums", the corporations, many of which were foreign owned or controlled, that received grants and subsidies from the federal government. For Lewis this looked an ideal issue to reunite the party. He also had reason to anticipate that it would have wide appeal to the people of the country.

An attack on the corporations was sure to appeal to those who had supported or sympathized with the Waffle. After all, the

Waffle manifesto had complained: "Canadian development is distorted by a corporate capitalist economy. Corporate investment creates and fosters superfluous individual consumption at the expense of social needs."[95] The Waffle might support this attack for both socialist and nationalist reasons. Nonetheless the issue was perfect because it did not involve him in a compromise with them. By concentrating on the corporations he was choosing an issue that would not take him too far away from the mainstream of his party's preoccupations, nor was he likely to alienate the support of the trade union leaders. Lewis justified his stance by attacking the privileges that business had acquired: "gross inequities have continued to exist in our social and economic structure. We have laboured to make Canadians aware of these inequities."[96]

Of perhaps even greater interest than the substance of Lewis' tilting against the corporations was an admission he made near the end of his book concerning the difficulties of ideological change in Canada. The Waffle had urged the NDP to strive above all for an ideological victory: "The development of socialist consciousness, on which can be built a socialist base, must be the first priority of the New Democratic Party."[97] Lewis, conscious of the problems that democratic socialism has always faced in Canada — that ideological conversions take place only slowly, and only when the people can be persuaded that their previous understanding is no longer adequate, put the problem shrewdly and eloquently:

> Every day of our lives we arrive at a crossroad. Every day we make decisions that will affect the course of our lives to a greater or lesser degree. To choose the right road, we must first know where we want to go. We must identify our destination. Otherwise, we stand paralyzed at the crossroad, without progress in any direction.
>
> No decision of any moment is simple or without conflict. But no achievement of any merit was ever accomplished by shirking decision, by apathy, by timidity or lack of commitment to desired goals. Canadians must confront themselves with the evidence. They must weigh it carefully, because justice is not blind. Justice comes only to those who work for it, demand it, shout for it and proclaim its worth above other considerations.[98]

This passage, almost more than any other, points out the difficulties inherent in the task of converting a basically liberal country such as Canada to socialism. Although there are in this land socialist and tory touches, as Horowitz' argument outlined in Chapter II shows us, we are left with the conclusion that our argument in

Chapter I is basically correct, and that the political parties in Canada, different though they are in their ideologies, are fundamentally limited, in the short run in any event, by the social, economic and political beliefs already in the country. Lewis' vigorous campaign brought the party 31 seats, its highest total ever, but its percentage of the popular vote rose to only 18 per cent, the same level as the party had achieved under Douglas in 1965. Nonetheless, the only conclusion that can be drawn from our study is that, just as the Progressive Conservative party cannot wean itself from a heavy reliance on liberal ideas if it is to be electorally successful, so the NDP is equally reliant on a heady dose of liberalism in addition to that party's socialism. There can be little doubt that if the Waffle had seized control of the NDP, and had made it, as they wished, "a truly socalist party", purity of doctrine would have gone hand in hand with electoral decline, unless conditions arose which facilitated changes in ideological perspective. Such changes, however, are normally beyond the power of any group in the political life of the country to develop: all that is usually possible is to be ready to profit by them if the conditions arise.

There is, then, a gentle irony at the heart of current Canadian socialism. The mainstream of this tradition is, as Horowitz argued, peaceful, pragmatic and non-Marxist. Its chief concern is to move towards social equality through collectivism. To this end it has rejected the authoritarianism of the Communist Party, and has moved in paths first trod by the proponents of the Social Gospel, the Methodists and Baptists in Western Canada, of whom Woodsworth was the most influential. Yet the leading defender of this tradition, David Lewis, is an immigrant from central Europe, an untypical representative of men who were chiefly responsible for propagating doctrinaire Marxian socialism in both Canada and the United States.

This paradox, however, is only superficial, since Lewis' early associations in England with the Labour Party exposed him to a style of socialism more indebted to Methodism than to Marx. There has been throughout the history of the CCF and the NDP the union of liberalism and socialism which has often been a problem, and sometimes a reproach to their supporters. For Canadian socialism, though, this need constantly to juggle or balance sometimes incompatible ideological elements has reflected the ideological composition of the country itself. The tensions that this largely unsynthesized alliance from time to time produces accounts for the sometimes unpredictable swings the parties' ideologies have taken over time. For nationalism, though, to which we next turn, such alliances are dictated not only for the sake of electoral success, but also to provide ideological completeness.

[1] Paul Fox, "Early Socialism in Canada" in *The Political Process in Canada,* J. H. Aitchison, ed. (Toronto, © University of Toronto Press 1963) pp.79, 98.
[2] Doris French, *Faith Sweat and Politics,* (Toronto: McClelland and Stewart Limited, 1962) pp.22-30.
[3] *Palladium of Labour,* January 5, 1884. Quoted in Martin Robin, *Radical Politics and Canadian Labour, 1880-1930,* (Kingston: Industrial Relations Centre, Queen's University 1968) p.22.
[4] James Harding, "The New Left in British Columbia" in *The New Left in Canada* (ed.) Roussopoulos, (Montreal: Our Generation — Black Rose Books, 1970) p.19; Robin, p.34.
[5] Robin, p.34.
[6] Grace MacInnis, *J. W. Woodsworth: A Man to Remember,* (Toronto: Macmillan, 1953) p.6.
[7] Robin, p.34.
[8] MacInnis, p.11.
[9] Kenneth McNaught, *A Prophet in Politics,* (Toronto: University of Toronto Press, 1959) p.43; MacInnis, p.17.
[10] J. S. Woodsworth, *Strangers Within Our Gates* (Toronto: Missionary Society of the Methodist Church, 1909) p.217. Reprinted 1972 by the University of Toronto Press.
[11] *Ibid.,* pp.217-19.
[12] *Ibid.,* pp.206, 279.
[13] *Ibid.,* p.219.
[14] *Ibid.,* p.311.
[15] J. S. Woodsworth, *My Neighbour* (Toronto: Methodist Book Room, 1911) p.20. Reprinted 1972 by The University of Toronto Press.
[16] *Ibid.,* pp.29, 26, 21.
[17] McNaught, p.v.
[18] MacInnis, p.124.
[19] Woodsworth, *Neighbour,* p.332.
[20] *Ibid.,* p.88.
[21] D. C. Masters, *The Winnipeg General Strike,* Copyright, Canada, 1950 by University of Toronto Press, Toronto, pp.17-18.
[22] Robin, p.184.
[23] Robin, p.177, Masters, p.8.
[24] MacInnis, p.124.
[25] "The Origin of the O.B.U." Verbatim Report of the Calgary Labour Conference, 1919, p.47. Quoted in Robin, p.176.
[26] *See* generally Robin, pp.174-6.
[27] Quoted in Robin, pp.187-8.
[28] Master, pp.20-21.
[29] MacInnis, pp.147, 214.
[30] Robin, p.192.
[31] Fox, p.98.
[32] Walter Young, *The Anatomy of a Party,* (Toronto: University of Toronto Press, 1969) p.23.
[33] McNaught, p.157.
[34] From *The Farmers in Politics* (1920; pp.98-99, 101, 158, 157, 167, 198, 193, 207-2-8) by William Irvine reprinted by permission of The Canadian Publishers, McClelland and Stewart Limited, Toronto.
Our emphasis.

Political Parties and Ideologies

[35] MacInnis, p.223.
[36] Young, p.34.
[37] *See* Young, pp.34-6.
[38] J. S. Woodsworth, *A plea for Social Justice,* (Ottawa: CCF 1933), pp.4, 78, 79.
[39] Young, p.34.
[40] Quoted in MacInnis, p.274.
[41] Grace MacInnis and Charles Woodsworth, *Canada Through C.C.F. Glasses,* (Ottawa: CCF 1935), p.58.
[42] This and following quotes until otherwise noted are taken from the CCF programme, Regina, 1933.
[43] Carrigan, p.119.
[44] CCF Platform of 1935.
[45] *Ibid.*
[46] *Canadian Forum,* XII, No. 139, April 1932, p.250.
[47] J. S. Woodsworth, Preface to *Social Planning for Canada* (Toronto: Thomas Nelson and Sons 1935) p.v.
[48] Young, p.71.
[49] League for Social Reconstruction, *Social Planning for Canada,* p.53.
[50] *Ibid.,* p.85.
[51] *Ibid.,* pp.101, 266.
[52] *Ibid.,* p.475.
[53] *Ibid.,* p.266.
[54] House of Commons Debates (1934) pp.2558, 2559, 2563.
[55] House of Commons Debates (1932-1933) p.7.
[56] LSR, *Social Planning,* p.225.
[57] *Ibid.,* pp.32, 37.
[58] *Ibid.,* p.465.
[59] *See* Young, Chapter 4.
[60] For the preceeding, see Leo Zakuta, *A Protest Movement Becalmed,* (Toronto: University of Toronto Press, 1964) pp.154-6.
[61] M. J. Coldwell, "Introduction", David Lewis and Frank Scott, *Make This Your Canada,* (Toronto: Central Canadian Publishing Co., 1943).
[62] Lewis and Scott, *Make This Your Canada,* p.96.
[63] *Ibid.,* pp.99-100.
[64] *Ibid.,* p.34.
[65] *Ibid.,* Our emphasis.
[66] *Ibid.,* p.194.
[67] *Ibid.,* p.34.
[68] *Ibid.,* p. 195.
[69] L. T. Hobhouse, *Liberalism,* (Oxford: Oxford University Press, 1911) p.54.
[70] *Ibid.,* p.87.
[71] M. J. Coldwell, *Left Turn, Canada,* (New York: Duell and Sloane, 1944) pp. 180-94.
[72] *Security With Victory* (Ottawa: C.C.F., 1945). Reprinted in Carrigan, pp.143-50. To get the ideological moderation of this programme in perspective, it is worth noting that the Liberal platform of the same year promised equality of opportunity, "a wide-open chance to make a real success of [one's] life." In concert with the CCF's emphasis on industrial development, the Liberal platform asked, "Isn't that what you want — a chance to make your own way. In your own way?"
[73] Quoted in Young, p.127.
[74] *Security for All,* (Ottawa: CCF, 1949), Our emphasis. Reprinted in Carrigan, pp.168-78.
[75] *Ibid.*
[76] Young, p.137.
[77] *Humanity First,* (Ottawa: CCF, 1953) Reprinted in Carrigan, pp.198-205:
[78] *Ibid.*
[79] *Ibid.*

[80] *Winnipeg Declaration of Principles of the Co-operative Commonwealth Federation,* (Montreal: CCF, 1956). Reprinted in Carrigan, pp.215-22.

[81] David Lewis, "A Socialist takes Stock" in *Politics: Canada, 3rd. ed.,* Paul Fox, ed. (Toronto: McGraw-Hill Ryerson, 1970) pp.238-41.

[82] *Share Canada's Wealth!* (Ottawa: CCF, 1957) Our emphasis. Reprinted in Carrigan, pp.217-22.

[83] The wording is that of the Canadian Labour Congress Resolution, 1958, which can be found in CLC-CCF Joint National Committee, *A New Political Party for Canada,* (Ottawa: CLC 1959).
See also, Stanley Knowles, *The New Party,* (Toronto: McClelland and Stewart, 1961) p.20.

[84] *The Federal Program of the New Democratic Party,* (Ottawa: NDP, 1961), Reprinted in Carrigan, pp.271-83.

[85] Knowles, p.113.

[86] *Ibid.,* p.93.

[87] *Ibid.,* p.102.

[88] George Grant, "An Ethic of Community" in M. Oliver, ed. *Social Purpose for Canada,* Copyright, Canada, 1961, by University of Toronto Press, Toronto, p.9.

[89] *Ibid.,* pp.16, 17.

[90] *Ibid.,* pp.20-21.

[91] *Campaign Leaflet,* (Ottawa: NDP, 1962). Reprinted in Carrigan, pp.283-6.

[92] *The Policies of the Liberal Party,* (Ottawa: 1963). Reprinted in Carrigan pp.294-302.

[93] *New Democratic Party Program,* (Regina: NDP 1968). Reprinted in Carrigan, pp.342-8.

[94] It was also faced, as has become customary for the mainstream of socialism in Canada, with a raft of advice about how it should develop. *Essays on the Left,* ed. LaPierre *et al* contained a brilliant paper by Charles Taylor titled "The Agony of Economic Man", which along with Taylor's *Pattern of Politics* (Toronto: McClelland and Stewart, 1970) constitutes two of the most significant recent contributions to Canadian socialist thought. Taylor's penetrating critique of modern socialist thought begins with a rejection of the ubiquitous notion that modern society and social organization exists for the sole purpose of "transforming the surrounding natural world" and goes on to argue for a society in which contemplation rather than production is deemed the "highest activity of man." To this end Taylor calls for a rewriting of socialist theory "as complete and far-reaching as that of Karl Marx a hundred years ago." Taylor, "The Agony of Economic Man" in *Essays on the Left* edited by J. T. McLeod and L. Lapierre, (Toronto: McClelland and Stewart, 1971). pp.221-35.

[95] "Waffle Manifesto" in *Politics: Canada,* ed. Fox, pp.242-3.

[96] David Lewis, *Louder Voices: The Corporate Bums,* (Toronto: James, Lewis and Samuel, 1972), p.v.

[97] "Waffle Manifesto", Fox, p.242.

[98] Lewis, pp.117-18.

Chapter VI

Canadian Nationalism

The mixtures of liberalism and conservatism in the Conservative Party, and of liberalism and socialism in the CCF/NDP have been marriages of convenience rather than necessity. They reflect the need and the desire of politicians to ally with the pervasive liberalism of Canada rather than the impossibility of establishing a permanent, if small, Tory or Socialist party. Toryism or socialism possess a sufficiently comprehensive vision of society to sustain a continuing political party; they do not enjoy sufficiently comprehensive support to sustain a successful political party. The position of nationalism is in some ways the reverse.

Nationalism, concerned with the important but limited question of national identity and independence, is a less comprehensive ideology than liberalism, conservatism, or socialism — it accounts for a narrower range of social and political phenomena, and provides answers to fewer questions. There is no distinctive nationalist approach to many important political concerns, from local government to social policy and protection of the environment. While its concern for national identity or independence may have some relevance to many areas of policy, and may even dominate some — foreign policy or ownership and control of business — it is not sufficiently comprehensive to stand alone as a descriptive or prescriptive account of political phenomena in general.

In consequence nationalism has not found permanent embodiment in a particular political party — there has never been, nor is there likely to be a Nationalist Party in Canada, though there are parties whose attitudes to questions of public policy can be consistently described as liberal, liberal-conservative, or liberal-socialist, even if the fits between party and ideology are by no means perfect. Rather, nationalism has enjoyed an intermittent influence on all political parties, at different times and in varying degrees. This alliance has been forced on it in an attempt to remedy its lack of comprehensiveness and has created both nationalist variants of liberalism, conservatism and socialism as well as liberal, conservative and socialist forms of nationalism. The weakness of specifically nationalist political bodies is revealed in both the late nineteenth-century Canada First movement and the contemporary Committee for an Independent Canada, each of which has been limited to the status of special interest or pressure groups; or in Henri Bourassa's Nationalists or the Bloc Populaire of the Second World War, which lasted as full blown political parties for only a relatively short time.

This weakness of nationalism is not unique to Canada, but the bicultural nature of the Canadian state has produced a distinguishably Canadian variant of the nationalist pattern. To understand this development, it is necessary to turn to an examination of the nature of nationalism. Without being a little arbitrary, this would be a full study in itself, since nationalist doctrines are ubiquitous in the modern world, and have, in Europe at least, a history stretching back over one hundred and fifty years. We can, however, sketch the outer limits, and that done, we will be able to show that nationalist beliefs and attitudes in Canada fall between two rather different end points.

The first of these is what might be called "full-blown" nationalism, or in Carlton Hayes' term, integral nationalism.[1] The most cogent and lucid account of this variety is the brilliant study, *Nationalism*, by Elie Kedourie, a man who, incidentally, had an important influence on Pierre Trudeau's attitude to this question. He defines it as the doctrine which "holds that humanity is naturally divided into nations, that nations are known by certain characteristics which can be ascertained, and that the only legitimate type of government is national self-government."[2] In his view nationalism presents a truly ideological way of viewing the world, limited and incomplete. It sees the world in terms of a supposed division into nations, and seeks to remake politics in that image, regardless of the claims of history, economics, art or religion.

For Kedourie this nationalism has roots in philosophy, specifically in the Kantian argument that the essence of moral behaviour is the free individual acting in accord with an internalized moral law, the categorical imperative. As we suggested in Chapter I, although philosophy does not claim direct political application, it is always open to others to take philosophy's teachings, and to apply them, for better or worse, in the practical world. This is what happened to Kant's doctrines. His ideas were first put to the service of liberalism when some of his successors emphasized that the self-determination of the individual should be the hallmark of political morality. Subsequent thinkers like Fichte shifted the emphasis to the group and claimed that the universal, rather than the individual, consciousness was the source of order and rationality.

The final step in the conversion of this philosophic idea into a political doctrine came with the rise of romanticism. Especially in Germany men like Herder and von Humboldt praised the value of ethnic diversity, and inspired extensive ethnological and philological research. These inquiries persuaded many that there were natural divisions of mankind, marked out by linguistic differentiation. For the romantics the preservation and fostering of these differences became a necessity, the highest cultural value.

When this idea was joined to the doctrine of the moral value of group self-determination, it produced the nationalism which Kedourie describes, the overriding commitment to the realization of national self-determination. This doctrine, that any group sharing the same language and culture ought to be self-governing, and that such groups or "nations" are sovereign, embodying the highest earthly values for their members, has had a potent appeal. The moral strenuousness of Kantian moral philosophy which nationalism absorbed tended to give it a spiritual or even quasi-religious appeal, a point which has been well made in C. J. H. Hayes' *Nationalism: A Religion* which documents the sacralization of the nation and its various symbols — flag, anthem, heroes — as well as the "nationalization" of previously universal institutions like the Christian church. It is this appeal which provides the basis for nationalist fanaticism, which subordinates all other moral considerations to nationalist criteria, and has resulted in numerous instances of terrorism, war and violence in the name of the nation and its freedom.

This view of nationalism is not however universally accepted and many object that while it is valid in some circumstances it ignores genuine varieties of nationalist thinking which take a less extreme view both of the definition of the "nation", and the status of the moral claims which the nation makes on its citizens. Thus nation or nationality might be defined in terms of a common political allegiance, or domicile in a particular country rather than in more restrictive ethnic or linguistic terms. Likewise, the degree of identification of individual and nation, and the claims made by the nation on the individual's loyalties may be considerably less than absolute.

This sort of thinking is, by Kedourie's definition, hardly nationalist at all; it bears, as he points out, a greater resemblance to the relatively universal, and well-nigh immemorial human propensity to show love and affection for one's native land; in short, patriotism. And patriotism, in this sense, is not as exclusive or demanding as the more rigorous forms of nationalism, because it is not tied to a particular or restrictive view of nationality, nor is it invested with any special moral claims on the individual. It is merely one loyalty among others. As George Heiman has put it:

> . . . nationalism, as opposed to patriotism, commands the ultimate loyalty and devotion to the nation-state. Patriotism, on the other hand, is pluralistic in its inclinations. A patriot can have ties with other associations besides those he has with the nation. He may show loyalty towards a religious group, a political party, a trade union, not to mention the traditional ties of family and kin. These loyalties are not looked upon as being incompatible with the loyalty he shows towards the nation. Where patriotism rather than nationalism prevails, the political structure of the native land, the nation-state, does not encompass or subjugate all of the individual's interests.[3]

This moderate nationalism is more appropriate to a multiethnic and bilingual state like Canada. The more extreme nationalist doctrine which calls for one state with one language is clearly incompatible with the basis of the present Canadian Confederation; it has been taken up solely by those who have sought some sort of radical change in existing arrangements.

The proponents of this position, both French and English, have differed considerably over the extent of the desired change. Some have wished entirely to extinguish the cultural diversity and linguistic duality of Canada; the English by the assimilation or suppression of the French, the French by secession or separation. Others have merely wished for a modification of the terms of our duality. In any case we shall not attempt to draw sharp lines of demarcation between these two extreme positions.

Both the extremes of English assimilation and French separatism are profoundly ideological in nature; they attempt to remake the existing situation in the light of the limited perspective of nationality. It is the magnitude of the change they seek, the genuinely revolutionary character of their aims and the degree to which they would change Canada which has led most Canadians to reject these more extreme nationalist options. This has doubtless reduced the intensity and strength of nationalist feeling in Canada, because it has separated ethnic and linguistic loyalties from national loyalty. Canadian nationalists have had to appeal for support either to simple patriotic affection for the land and a shared past; or to the negative argument that nationalist measures are desirable merely to protect or preserve certain other values, such as bilingualism, which have little connection with nationalism. This tendency to moderation in most Canadian nationalism has been reinforced by the absence of ideological uniformity which we noted in Chapter II. Thus, unlike the identification of liberalism with "Americanism" in the United States, national and ideological loyalties in Canada have remained quite separate.

This moderate mainstream notwithstanding, the fact remains that Quebec or French-Canadian nationalists have pursued the goal of national self-determination and the erection of an independent French-speaking state; and that some English Canadians have sought a corresponding linguistic and cultural uniformity through assimilation rather than separatism because of their majority position. Assimilation was seriously mooted by Lord Durham in his *Report;* but the imperial government chose not to pursue that policy fully, and contented itself with the act of 1841 which provided for a modest extension of English-speaking influence by giving both Canada West and Canada East equal representation in the new legislature, in spite of the larger population of the latter.

Pressure for full-scale assimilation only became a significant political force in the last quarter of the nineteenth century. In the decade or so following the Riel Rebellion, an atmosphere of racial hostility, engendered by the crisis over Riel's execution, was exacerbated by the conflict over separate schools in Manitoba and the official recognition accorded the French language in the Northwest Territories. Some English Canadians advocated outright assimilation of the French, or failing that, at least a gradual reduction of the importance of the French fact in Canada.

Charles Mair, one of the original members of Canada First, spoke for many English Canadians in opposing the extension of any French language rights to the Northwest Territories: "How, then, if we wish ever to become a homogeneous people, can we extend the parliamentary use of a language which is limited of right to a certain Province."[4] Canada First however, despite its concern for cultural and racial uniformity[5] was overshadowed in its zeal for a British Canada by the imperial federation movement which rapidly gained momentum in the 1880's. Dalton McCarthy, president of the Imperial Federation League during the later 1880's, led a vigorous battle in 1889-1890 against French language rights in the Northwest, as well as the successful campaign for the abolition of separate schools in Manitoba. National unity demanded unity of language, and the complete assimilation of the French: they must "learn to cherish, not merely our institutions, but our glorious past, and to look forward with us to a still more glorious future".[6] By no means all of those connected with the imperial federation movement were hostile to the French in this way — George Munro Grant for example was both tolerant of French Canada, and indeed, appreciative of the merits of its conservative society; but even he was convinced that the French fact in Canada was bound to be a declining force.[7]

The problem of cultural duality was not the only one however to be faced by Canadian nationalism. If the approach of the imperial federationists or imperialists could not provide a theory that accounted satisfactorily for the aspirations of the major language groups in Canada, their theories provided more compelling answers to other problems. Indeed, the imperial federationists are the direct ancestors of most modern Canadian nationalists, and made a contribution to the development of nationalist thought in Canada which is still being felt today. All this may well appear paradoxical to a reader who associates "imperialism" with colonial subordination and wonders what possible connection this can have with nationalism. The fact is however that the movement for imperial federation — that is the closer integration of the British Empire and Britain itself with greater colonial participation in the imperial government — represented a direct repudiation of Canadian colonial status. Canada, its authors reasoned, had outgrown the colonial status, and was ready to assume greater responsibilities in the world; the Empire of which she was a part was the vehicle through which this enhanced national stature would be realized. The time had come for Canada to take her place in the world alongside the mother country, eventually with the same status and responsibilities. To become a co-imperial power Canada had to assume a proportionate share in the governance of the Empire. This was hardly colonialism; as Stephen Leacock, a convinced imperialist stated: "I . . . am an imperialist because I will not be a Colonial".[8]

The objection to this line of reasoning, both then and later, was that Canada's growing national stature ought more properly to result in independent national action. The imperialists rejected this suggestion outright — Canada, though maturing, was too small and weak to play a meaningful role in the world outside the imperial context. The imperialists correctly equated advocacy of greater Canadian independence from the Empire with a desire for isolationism, a stance which they believed unworthy of Canada's rising stature. R. B. Bennett clearly drew this conclusion in a speech of 1914:

> How can you and I think of independence, how can we be concerned about an independent Canada? Eight or nine million people could not discharge the responsibilities that have come down to us .... An independent Canada means this, that we Canadians are afraid of responsibility and obligation of power....[9]

Not only was isolationism unworthy of Canada; it was extremely dangerous. To abandon Europe and the Empire meant to abandon the British make-weight to the power and expansionism of the neighbouring United States. As the poet Wilfred Campbell pointed out, Canada had a choice between "two different imperialisms, that of Britain and that of the Imperial Commonwealth to the south";[10] the option of Canadian independence was a spurious one, merely disguising a move into the American orbit. Sir John A. Macdonald himself was in no doubt on this score: "As to independence, how long could we stand as an independent republic. . . .?"[11]

Indeed, the most lasting contribution of the imperialists to Canadian nationalism was a strong sense of the separate identity of Canada within North America and their very clear apprehension of the dangers to it from any form of continentalism. Campbell, for example, thought that entry of Canada into the American imperial system would mean "sheer annihilation of all our personality as a people".[12] The basis of this Canadian personality could obviously not be based on linguistic or ethnic uniformity, like much European nationalism, for the logic of linguistic or ethnic unity pointed towards continentalism, as the arguments of proponents of a united "Anglo-Saxondom" like Goldwin Smith clearly demonstrated.

The imperialists relied to a degree on the uniqueness of the Canadian physical setting, and particularly the invigorating northern climate, but placed a good deal of weight on the ideological differences between Canada and the United States. They saw the United States as a land in which liberty ran riot, producing lawlessness, social disorders, and political corruption. Canada on the other hand had inherited, through British institutions, a greater sense of social order and stability, and respect for law and authority. This social conservatism in Canada about which the imperialists were so enthusiastic fitted closely with their own conservative leanings, for they were the embodiment at the time of the tory strain in the Canadian ideological structure which we have already discussed. It is no accident that the imperial federation movement was closely connected with a great revival of interest in the United Empire Loyalists. Interestingly enough, the conservatism of the imperialists tended to soften their potential hostility to French Canada, for men like G. M. Grant thoroughly approved, and even idealized, the rural and conservative society of Quebec, in sharp contrast to liberal criticisms of French-Canadian society mounted by Lord Durham and Goldwin Smith.[13]

This alliance of nationalism and conservatism was not ideologically difficult for both shared a common concern for the collective aspects of political life. Collectivism forms a major part of the conservative ideology, and nationalism, concerned with a collectivity, the nation, shares that ground. In practice, the willingness of conservatives to subordinate economic considerations to politics lent itself admirably to the achievement of nationalist ends. The effectiveness of this alliance and the strength of conservative nationalism were strikingly evident in the first half century of Confederation, not only in the theoretical formulations and propaganda activities of the imperialists, but in the practical politics of the Conservative Party. The great nation-building policies of Macdonald, the National Policy and the CPR, his adamant opposition to continentalist policies of reciprocity, were all products of this school of conservative nationalism.

If Macdonald's policies were primarily internal and domestic, Sir Robert Borden's aspirations were to raise Canada's status in the world. Indeed Borden's drive for greater Canadian autonomy and influence represented the high point of the imperial federation movement and the most significant realization of its nationalist goals. To begin with, Borden (like Macdonald) was convinced that Canada could only maintain and develop her autonomy by remaining at arm's length from the United States through association with the Empire. He characterized the decision on reciprocity in the 1911 election as a choice between "the spirit of Canadianism or of Continentalism", and declared that rejection of the latter was a vote for "the maintenance of our commercial and political freedom, for the permanence of Canada as an *autonomous nation* within the British Empire".[14]

Canada's status demanded more than merely negative steps to repel external threats; national status within the Empire required that she assume the duties of a nation and receive the privileges which went with responsibility. In particular, Borden felt that Canada should assume a fairer share of the burden of imperial defence. Answering Laurier's reluctance to move in this direction and his willingness to shield Canada with the Monroe Doctrine, Borden retorted: ". . . if we have assumed that status of a nation in one respect, shall we adhere to the status of a Crown colony in other and still more important respects?"[15] National "self-respect" required in that Canada avoid the "humiliating" and "degrading" position of relying on Britain for her own defence, or worse, in "an appeal to the charity . . . of a great neighbouring nation"; rather she ought to "stand proud, powerful and resolute in the very forefront of the sister nations".[16] In return, Borden and other imperialists expected a corresponding share in imperial decision-making on an equal basis with Britain. As we saw in Chapter IV, Macdonald had distinguished between being British and being a tool of English foreign policy. Indeed there were those among the imperialists who took this a stage further and looked to the day when Canada would surpass Britain in size and power, and herself assume the leading position in the Empire. Borden's consistent pressure on Britain after 1911, for a greater Canadian voice in imperial foreign policy and in the conduct of the war, and for proper recognition of Canadian autonomy at the Peace Conference is too well detailed to re-require further treatment here.

Conservative nationalism succeeded then in fostering the realization that a distinctive Canadian nation existed, and that it should begin to assume, in its external as well as its domestic affairs, the powers and the responsibilities which went along with this status. This position however, while genuinely nationalist enough, was not entirely satisfactory for the Canadian situation, for it stressed the Englishness of Canada to an extent which practically excluded the French-Canadians. This in turn was potentially so disruptive to national unity as to negate the ends the nationalists sought. The imperial federationists were not content merely to stress the value of British political institutions, for instance, a subject upon which most French Canadians agreed in full. They went further and saw Canada as essentially British, or English, in language and culture: if only a minority were systematic assimilationists, even those most sympathetic to French Canada, like G. M. Grant, accepted the likelihood of a steady decline in French culture and language. Their vision of Canada was basically unicultural. Finally the imperialists' desire for active Canadian participation in world affairs in the framework of the Empire ran up against a deep isolationist current in French Canada heightened by the lack of any emotional ties between French Canadians and the Empire.

In time though, despite the racial friction imperialist nationalism caused, it might have become the dominant form of Canadian nationalism, had it not been for external events which doomed the imperial federation movement and many of the ideas which it involved. The Great War allowed Canada to exercise to the full her new-found national responsibilities, to consolidate her autonomy and her sense of national pride and identity. But the carnage of the Western Front led to a deep aversion to any further outside commitments and a strong tendency to isolationism. The ethnic conflict engendered during the war, especially over conscription, ended any possibility that the French Canadians might come to accept an attitude to Confederation and the position of Canada in the world that the conservative nationalists had envisioned. Furthermore, the war, by encouraging more vigorous French-Canadian nationalism dashed any hopes that the social conservatism common to most of French Canada and to many of the imperialists might bridge the other gaps between them. In this competition of ideologies, nationalism proved stronger than conservatism.

Above all however, the war marked an inexorable decline in the position of Britain in the world, and substantially diminished the attractiveness of the Empire as a field for the exercise of Canadian autonomy and national status. The imperialist argument was irretrievably lost — the fact of Canadian nationhood which they had done so much to establish remained; the particular national identity and place in the world which they had asserted was a fatal casualty of time and fortune. Canadians were forced to find a new focus for their nationalism after 1920, and the "new nationalism" of the 1960's and 1970's is in many ways a part of this search. That so much time passed without a resolution of the issue, and that it has fallen on the nationalism of the last decade to make such a significant contribution to the debate, can be attributed in large part to the deficiencies of the doctrine that was waiting in the wings as the conservative, imperialist nationalists departed. This successor was to hold sway for nearly forty years.

This alternative doctrine we shall call liberal nationalism, for it was basically an alliance of liberalism and nationalism; and the particular ideological mixture thus created was substantially reflected in the ways in which liberal nationalists pursued nationalist ends, and the degree to which they accepted them. It was associated almost exclusively with the Liberal Party. Just as the great nation-building policies of Macdonald — the National Policy and the CPR — and Borden's nationalist opposition to Unrestricted Reciprocity were shaped by the conservative willingness to subordinate economics to politics; so the nationalism of Laurier and King was expressed in terms of the Liberal Party's commitment to liberty and individualism.

From the beginning the marriage of liberalism and nationalism has been uneasy. The primary focus of nationalism is on the nation as a collectivity rather than on the individuals of whom the nation is composed. Nationalists have often drawn the conclusion that individual welfare can only be understood in terms of the collective whole. This nationalist tendency to subordinate individual interests to the nation may not sit well with the liberal concern for individual liberty. There is however a point of contact between the two ideologies: a common concern for liberty. Liberals both in Europe and Canada have been able to support nationalist goals on a number of occasions when it appeared that they were promoting increased national liberty.

Canada's position in the Empire was a case in point. To many liberals the Canadian status of partial subordination to Britain was an offence to liberty, because imperialism in any form implied the control of one nation by another. Liberal nationalists therefore sought greater autonomy and enhanced national status solely to advance the cause of liberty. Unlike their imperialist contemporaries who looked to greater national power and status through more equal participation in the Empire, the liberal nationalists preferred withdrawal from imperial participation. If anything, they favoured outright isolationism. As the Australians and New Zealanders showed, this was not an inevitable reaction of colonials to a former imperial master, and indeed many Canadians remained imperialists.

The liberal hostility to Europe as well as to Britain involved, as Borden's reminiscence in Chapter IV also revealed, a strong dislike for certain salient features of the European ideological mix. As Hartz has pointed out, Europe was ideologically diverse, possessing strong elements of privilege, hierarchy and collectivism which repelled Liberals who saw Europe as, in Laurier's words, "a vortex of militarism", created by a privileged aristocratic minority with nothing but contempt for individual liberty. All in all, Europe was a model to be kept at arm's length. They saw the Canadian imperialists' desire for participation in imperial affairs as an attempt to extend this nefarious system to the purer new world of North America. If the conservative nationalists thought largely in imperial terms, their liberal counterparts were as naturally attracted to the thoroughly liberal model immediately at hand, and turned in reaction to the United States and a continental perspective.

This anti-British orientation secured for the liberal nationalists the sympathy of French Canadians, who saw the conservative nationalists' desire for close ties with the Empire as evidence of their desire to anglicize Canada. The liberal nationalists' opposition to imperial involvement coincided with the natural inclinations of the French Canadians and overcame any misgivings the conservative French might have had about their liberalism. Laurier cemented this alliance in practice, and from his time the Liberal Party used it to claim a unique competence in preserving national unity.

Continentalism was not only an understandable product of Canadian liberal sympathy for the eminently liberal society of the United States; it also coincided with the liberal unwillingness to subordinate economics to politics, even if this imperative coincided with their nationalist impulses. We have already examined in Chapter III the consistent opposition from Brown to Laurier and beyond, of Liberals to the Conservative policies of economic nationalism which gave concrete expression to the feelings of patriotism and national pride felt by most Liberals. The logical drift of liberal thinking, once the counter-pressure of this patriotic sentiment was removed, was revealed clearly in the annexationism of Goldwin Smith, a sentiment which did not remain entirely academic; for as we have seen, as prominent a Liberal political figure as Sir Richard Cartwright in the later 1880's could entertain the possibility of continental union. In a sense, nationalist or patriotic feeling also acted to restrain the tendency in pure liberalism to be insensitive to ethnic or linguistic differences. While this tendency was sometimes overt, electoral necessity and the growing feeling of national pride in Canada's bicultural makeup effectively countered it in the twentieth century, although it has not made Liberals any readier to accept the collective aspects of cultural duality as the Trudeau approach to the question reveals.

This inherent tension in Liberalism between continentalism and nationalism undoubtedly contributed to the party's relative lack of success before 1920 since in those years it was in competition with a nationalism which possessed a more compelling vision of the national identity, and a more consistent approach to achieving it. For the majority of English Canadians, the distinctiveness of Canada lay in its Britishness within North America, and the Conservative Party offered the most clear and consistent defence of that national identity. It enjoyed power for the greater part of that period, and even during the Laurier period its nationalist policies were substantially maintained. Indeed, when Laurier attempted to diverge from them, in his naval policy and support of reciprocity, he met defeat at the polls.

After the war the situation changed substantially. The drastic decline in British power and prestige made increasingly irrelevant British-oriented ideas of the conservative nationalists, and the racial rift opened up in 1917 revealed the inadequacy of their views to ensure national unity. The imperial federation movement disappeared almost without trace. However the Conservative Party under leaders like Meighen approached the areas of nationalist concern as if nothing had changed; for this they paid the supreme political penalty. Equally they ignored the changing pattern of Canadian trade and foreign investment in an increasingly continentalist direction and could produce no improvements on the National Policy of 1879. Not surprisingly, Conservative nationalism in Canada gradually atrophied, and was replaced, except for pangs of nostalgia for the British connection, by the burgeoning forces of the liberal strain in the Conservative Party, a development we have analyzed in Chapter IV.

The years between 1920 and 1957 witnessed the triumph of

liberal nationalism with all its weaknesses. It saw Canada as a primarily North American nation sharing a common territory and a common set of liberal values with the United States. In this view, Liberal governments were supported by a continental school of Canadian history, led by the late Frank Underhill, and following in the traditions of Goldwin Smith (of whom Underhill was a keen student). Canada's destiny was to escape entirely from the evils of Europe and to realize the liberal values epitomized by United States President Franklin Roosevelt or later, President John Kennedy. The thrust of Canadian foreign policy under King, shaped by O. D. Skelton's almost pathological suspicion and dislike of Britain, was to escape from imperial or other international commitments into a North American fastness. Domestically, there was a steady policy of reducing ties (now largely of form rather than of substance) with Britain. This was not entirely unattractive to conservative nationalists, for they too had wished greater autonomy for Canada, though in a different world context. Thus St. Laurent's decision to end appeals to the Privy Council in civil cases in 1949 was an extension of Bennett's similar decision in criminal cases of 1933; and the inauguration of separate Canadian citizenship in 1947 was the logical development of a more limited form of separate status established by the Meighen government in 1920. The *Statute of Westminster* itself, the final recognition of Canadian legal independence, was passed by Britain and accepted by Canada in 1931 during Bennett's term in office.

In the area of trade and investment policy the liberal triumph reached new heights between 1935 and 1957. Few new national policies were devised to maintain the national east-west economic system constructed by Macdonald; either by influencing the flow of trade or the flow of investment, both of which were rapidly turning to a north-south orientation. By 1957 Canadian trade was predominantly with the United States rather than Britain and Europe, and American investment had displaced European in importance. Indeed the United States was rapidly attaining a level of ownership and control in Canada reached nowhere else in the world. This process of economic integration into the United States was tolerated and often encouraged by the King and St. Laurent governments. The attempt of the latter's chief lieutenant C. D. Howe to railroad through Parliament a measure to aid the exploitation of Canadian gas resources by Texas interests in the notorious "pipeline debate" of 1956 was only a dramatic reminder of a common occurrence. The process of north-south integration forecast and acclaimed by Goldwin Smith was well on the way to completion.

The abandonment of any attempt to preserve a national economic identity by the Liberals illustrated clearly the shortcomings of liberal nationalism. Liberalism had great difficulty in articulating any clear sense of national identity. The very notion of a nation, of a collective entity and interest superior in some respects to the individual was suspect and, to a doctrine which placed supreme reliance on individual rationality, the values of history and tradition upon which nationalism or patriotism were based were of dubious value. In particular, liberals found it difficult to perceive any clear differences from their co-ideologists to the south. Preoccupied with escaping British ties they were blind to the new bonds they were forging. The liberal commitment to individual liberty made them loath in the extreme to place restrictions on it for collective, nationalist ends. They consistently opposed restrictions on economic liberties which a policy of economic nationalism involved. Liberals could not see the ends, and denied themselves the means to achieve any satisfactory nationalist position.

The Canadian people however were by no means uniformly liberal in their outlook, and the liberalism of many was tempered by strong, if inarticulate sentiments of nationalism. By the mid 1950's the degree of American economic penetration and increasing American influence in various fields of Canadian life, from culture (radio, TV, books and magazines) to politics (the attempts of McCarthyites in the United States to interfere with Canadian foreign service officers) had aroused increasing concern and anxiety. John Diefenbaker's proposals for a Macdonald-style national development policy and trade diversification away from the south in 1957 struck a responsive chord and were a major factor in his upset victory.

At the same time, a new wave of French-Canadian nationalism was developing in Quebec, nurtured beneath the Duplessis veneer of calm, ready to burst forth in the Quiet Revolution of the 1960's. The French-Canadian nationalism, as we argued above, ran at cross purposes to the new current in English Canada for it asserted the existence of a distinctictive French-Canadian nation based on a common language and ethnic origin; and drew, in varying degree, the nationalist conclusion that this nation enjoyed rights of self-determination. We have already argued, this was a potentially revolutionary claim, for it threatened the basis of the existing Canadian state: the belief that a political community could exist independently of linguistic and ethnic uniformity. Paradoxically, French-Canadian nationalism flared up again in the 1960's when English Canada had apparently laid to rest the remnants of the assimilationist ideas which had previously threatened from the opposite direction, but on similar grounds.

Its roots however ran as deep as its extremist English counterpart. The rebellion of the *Patriotes* in 1837 was in part an expression of resentment against alien, English domination, though partly also a conservative reaction to the impingement of a liberal society and people on conservative Quebec.

As early as 1846, Etienne Parent, in a speech to the *Institut Canadien,* was urging French Canadians to organize their approach to political questions along nationalist grounds: "Our national consciousness must constantly be our beacon, our compass, our guiding star, as we pick our way through the stumbling-blocks of politics." This was not only a nationalist approach; it was a truly ideological stance — for Parent, nationality was the key, the window through which all political questions ought to be viewed, the ultimate standard against which to judge political priorities: "Our nationality should be our prime concern, then all the rest will automatically fall into place".[17]

At about the same time that Confederation was creating a political union of both French and English Mgr. L.-F.-R. Laflèche was linking language and nationality, and identifying a distinctive French-Canadian nation. Arguing on Biblical grounds, Laflèche maintained that before the Flood and the Tower of Babel, man was "able to maintain *unity of language* and therefore *national unity*". The multiplication of tongues after these events naturally created a variety of nationalities, a work in which he saw the hand of Providence, for he quoted with evident approval the opinion "that God himself created different nationalities".[18] Applying this to French Canada, Laflèche had no difficulty in concluding that:

> French Canadians in this country are a real *nation,* and ... the vast expanse of territory irrigated by the majestic St. Lawrence is their own legitimate *homeland.*
>
> For here we have a population of close to one million rising up as one man upon hearing their name called out, speaking the same language, confessing the same faith.
>
> ... we French Canadians have become a *nation.*[19]

At this point, the final factor in the nationalist equation, the call for self-determination for this French-Canadian nation, was missing, but by the turn of the century, the development of nationalist thinking had rectified the omission. The successive French-English conflicts surrounding the Riel Rebellion and the Manitoba schools crisis doubtless contributed to this process by providing proof for extreme nationalist claims that English Canada was bent on assimilating the French. As J.-P. Tardivel put in 1904:

The partisans of a great, unified Canada, whatever their political affiliation, Liberal or Tory, want to make the Dominion of Canada an exclusively English-speaking country with English customs and English traditions ... when they act, it is always with a view toward the anglicizing of the great whole.[20]

This militant English nationalism Tardivel found "quite natural"; his answer was to encourage French nationalism to the ultimate end of separation:

We have been working ... toward the development of a French-Canadian national feeling: what we want to see flourish is French-Canadian patriotism; our people are the French-Canadian people; ... *the nation we wish to see founded at the time appointed by Providence is the French-Canadian nation.*[21]

By the 1920's, following the further crises over conscription and regulation XVII in Ontario, separatism was discussed explicitly and in some detail. J.-M.-R. Villeneuve, writing in 1922, provides a good example of this. He identified nationality closely with race and language; four elements combined to form a nation, "origin, language, territory, and form of government", but "these elements are of unequal importance: the first two are the soul, the last two the body, of a nation. As the soul by far transcends matter, so must unity of origin and community of language be much more important."[22] For Villeneuve, the differences between English and French in Canada were insurmountable — "there is not the slightest meeting-point between our languages, social traditions, religious aims, habits of mind, spiritual formation, public institutions, or civil laws",[23] and separation was inevitable: "Whether we like it or not, Canada is bound to split up."[24] National self-determination for French Canada was now a real possibility: "That a French and Catholic State should, during the course of the present century, be established in the St. Lawrence valley is, according to many people, no longer a utopian dream, but a viable ideal, a hope founded in reality."[25] Furthermore, separation by Quebec would be in the best interests of the French minorities outside Quebec: "A strong French State, practically homogeneous and completely free in its activities, would be the surest guarantee of the survival and integrity of our people of the Diaspora."[26] Antonio Perrault, writing about the same time, and like Villeneuve, connected with the conservative and clericalist *Action Francaise* movement, also stressed the gulf between English and French in Canada (both attributed this

in part to the growing Americanization of the English provinces)
and unequivocally stated the goal of their group: "the establishing
of a French State in eastern Canada".[27]

Separatist nationalism in Quebec waned after the 1920's. Perhaps
the main reason for this was the increasingly conservative and
Catholic cast of nationalist thinking, which justified French Canada's existence as much on grounds of religious vocation as linguistic differentiation; and which ignored or attempted to repel the
intrusions of liberal and technologically dynamic social forces into
Quebec. The hand of time could not be stayed, though, and the
concerns of the traditional nationalists, whether their notion of
the Catholic and apostolic vocation of French Canada or their neglect of the needs of a secular urban, industrial society, came to be
increasingly irrelevant to much of the population. During the 1940's
and 1950's, the nationalists fought the battles of the past; the federal government and its supporters seized the initiative in attacking pressing social and economic problems. Nationalism in Quebec
was on the defensive, within the ramparts of the "siege mentality",
and the movement towards independence was abandoned in favour
of a rearguard action to protect the existing position of the government of Quebec. Premier Duplessis became the symbol and the
focus of French Canadian nationalism during this period.

Nationalism in French Canada took the offensive again when
it succeeded in forging new ideological alliances which allowed it
to rectify its previous weaknesses. As we argued in Chapter II, as
Quebec became increasingly integrated into the liberal economic
structure of North America, the traditional "feudal" or conservative
ideology was largely displaced; either by the dominant liberalism
of North America; or by socialism which developed from the collectivism of the old conservatism. Nationalism followed suit, and
largely exchanged its conservative ally for either liberalism or
socialism. Thus rearmed, nationalism returned to the battle im-
mensely reinforced, as English Canada increasingly came to realize
after 1960. Its new liberal and socialist weapons allowed it to make
great inroads among the economic, political and intellectual elites of
Quebec and to reverse the defensive posture of the government of
that province.

Throughout these changes however, the fundamental nationalist
concerns remain. The political lodestar remains the nation defined
in terms of language and ethnicity. Jean-Marc Leger, for instance,
writing in 1964 of néo-nationalisme in French Canada, talks as did
Laflèche or Tardivel, of the "French-Canadian nation". Similarly,
Marcel Chaput in 1961 called for a "Quebec sovereign unilingual
state of French language".[28] Likewise the conclusion drawn from the

premise of the existence of the nation is the same — it must possess a very substantial degree of political self-determination. The end of the new nationalism, as Leger calls it is "the definition and erection of a national State", the "recognition of Quebec as the political expression of the French-Canadian nation, that is, as a national State".[29] What is new is the determination to include within the purview of nationalism the "fundamental realities of the economic and social spheres",[30] and to promote state intervention, whether along lines of socialism, or positive liberalism, to allow French Canada real national self-determination in these areas, to "regain the mastery of its destiny."[31]

The new nationalism has had as its main vehicle of expression since 1969, the Parti Québecois, the product of the merger of a number of smaller separatist groups together with separatist dissidents from the older parties like its leader and main spokesman René Lévesque. The PQ's relative success in the 1970 Quebec election was due not only to the united front it presented, and the attractiveness of its leader, but to the new ideological alliances it had forged. The PQ united nationalism with that mixture of socialism and positive liberalism perhaps most commonly known as "social democracy".

As we have already argued, such alliances are necessary for any nationalist ideology, to remedy its inherent lack of comprehensiveness — the PQ was fortunate in broadening its ideology in a way which had a wide appeal in contemporary Quebec, particularly among the young and in urban areas. In its 1970 election programme the PQ combined both the long-standing nationalist concern for the ethnic-linguistic nation with this new concern for its economic and social, as well as cultural, development. "Language is the prime factor of identity, the foundation and expression of the culture of the nation", and Quebec is "the land of a people whose language is French". Consequently the PQ promised to make French "the sole official language of the land".[32] But independence promised far more than being merely the "end-point of a long defensive process of survival".[33] It promised the means of rectifying the economic and social shortcomings of Quebec society. It is significant that economic matters are given first place in the PQ programme; more traditional cultural concerns are placed towards the end. The new nationalism seeks to employ all the powers of the modern state:

> In the economic realm as in others, progress requires that this fundamental condition for an appropriate policy be first realised: ONE complete government, given the whole range of powers and machinery required for the development of a society at once modern and unique.[34]

Thus the PQ has succeeded in re-asserting an all-encompassing ideological view of politics by providing a set of overriding nationalist goals to guide political action:

> Quebec nationalism, which inspires the programme of the Parti Québecois, possesses a profound function to restore to Quebecers the consciousness of a national homeland, to open to them all possible opportunities to assert themselves on the national and international levels, to make a modern nation of a territory still a prey to the constraints of a colonial domination.[35]

That the péquistes espouse a classical variety of nationalism is clear: that it has radical consequences within the context of Canadian Confederation requires neither tight analysis nor even close attention. At their party's conference in late February 1973 the PQ made it clear that they would take the election of their party as a mandate for the immediate withdrawal of Quebec from Confederation. At the same time the Gendron Commission brought in a report favouring increased emphasis upon French as the language of Quebec.

Others in Quebec have not been as patient as the péquistes or as confident as the Gendron Commission that the problems of Quebec nationalism are susceptible to moderate reforming measures. Chief among these more extreme nationalists was the apparently loosely organized Front de Libération du Québec (FLQ). The felquistes, one of whose cells kidnapped the British trade commissioner James Cross, and another of whose cells kidnapped and murdered the Quebec cabinet minister Pierre Laporte in October 1970, had been engaged in sporadic terror since 1963.

Yet the main focus of the felquistes as their leading theorist Pierre Vallières indicated in *White Niggers of America* was socialist rather than nationalist: "It is a question of making men equal, not only in law but in fact."[36] The felquistes were nationalists, not from intrinsic reasons, but because, contingently, Quebecers happened to be, in their view, a particularly oppressed class. Vallières makes it clear that nationalism, for him, is a means rather than an end in itself. In *L'Urgence de choisir* published in 1971 after he had repudiated the FLQ's violent road to Quebec independence, he wrote: "In Quebec, the establishment of a national independent state is the necessary condition for all economic development and all social progress".[37] His support for the Parti Québecois stemmed from his belief that: "In fact, from the permanent confrontation of social struggles and political crises in Quebec in the last ten years there has only arisen one type of coherent political action, as a real alternative to gain power for the white niggers of Quebec: and that's the Parti Québecois".[38]

Whether the Parti Québecois will become, as Vallières clearly wishes, a socialist party that harnesses nationalist emotions or whether it will remain a nationalist party espousing socialist principles as well is for the future to decide. What is significant from the point of view of our analysis is the apparently secure alliance between nationalism and socialism in Quebec. It is this accommodation which poses the greatest threat to the present Canadian Confederation since it endows the péquiste ideology with greater explanatory force and hence greater appeal and staying power than a simple, unalloyed nationalism would allow it.

The development of the socialist nationalism in Quebec has been paralleled by the resurgence of the wider Canadian nationalism whose stirrings we saw in the Diefenbaker campaign of 1957. This "new" nationalism which has been an increasingly important feature of Canadian politics since 1957 incorporates a number of different strands. At bottom it is rooted in simple patriotic sentiment, love of the country and its past and concern for its present and future. And it is important to realize that this is patriotic, and not in the extreme sense of the word, nationalist feeling, for there has been little attempt to give it any particular ethnic or linguistic bias though a tendency to minimize the importance of the French fact is present in some English nationalists. The existence of this sentiment in itself is not a sufficient explanation of the new nationalism; for patriotism is probably a permanent feature of human existence, and is certainly widespread in the Canadian population. What is important is to recognize the influences which have shaped the contemporary form, the intensity it has assumed, and the particular demands it has made on politicians.

One of the most important of these has been the recasting of the old conservative nationalist tradition, whose greatest contribution now, as in the past, is the sense of a distinctive Canadian identity, particularly within North America. It should not be surprising that the architects of this view are to be found primarily in the ranks of the historians, for a sense of national identity is largely the result of an appreciation of national history, of the process through which the nation became what it is. What is mildly surprising is that the first of these architects was an economic historian, Harold Innis, though surprise should perhaps be tempered by recalling that conservative nationalists like Macdonald or Borden were deeply concerned with economic questions.

Innis went directly in the face of the prevailing economic orthodoxy and argued that east-west economic links following national rather than continental lines, were just as "natural" as those along a series of north-south axes. In particular Innis offered an economic justification of the economic system developed under the National Policy, of the east-west, national economy which tied the St. Lawrence-Great Lakes area to the hinterlands of the east and west. Innis' defence of a national economic identity in turn exercised a powerful influence on general historians, and in particular, on Donald Creighton, who placed this identity into a wider historical context. This "empire of the St. Lawrence" was in Creighton's view the foundation upon which Macdonald built, and provided a major theme for his definitive biography of Macdonald.[39] Creighton's writing has not only evoked a sense of national destiny, and stimulated Canadian awareness and pride in its past, but has, both in his strictly historical, and his later and more polemical works[40] restated the old conservative nationalist doctrine and used it to criticize the shortcomings of liberal nationalists since 1920.

In addition Creighton and another leading conservative historian W. L. Morton have helped to create an appreciation of the ideological differences between Canada and the United States, and by implication our ideological diversity. Morton's *The Canadian Identity* (1961) points out both the greater respect for order and authority in Canada and the collectivist strain which has been apparent in our politics. Creighton's plea in *Canada's First Century* for vigorous government intervention to increase our economic independence reflects the old conservative willingness to subordinate economics to politics. Like their imperialist predecessors they attribute much of the distinctiveness of Canada from the United States to its British past, and particularly to its inherited British institutions. Morton argues that the monarchy has been a powerful force for national unity because of its neutrality in the face of ideological, regional and linguistic divisions; and Creighton too is a well-known defender of the Canadian crown.

It is this aspect of the "new" conservative nationalism which many find difficult to accept, especially as emotional ties to Britain dwindle. However, the wider sense which the conservative historians convey that Canada is not simply a North American nation, that there is a European-ness (if only partly British) about Canada which is not present in the United States has found wide acceptance. A good deal of the enthusiasm for the encouragement or preservation of a multiethnic society, the mosaic rather than the melting pot, derives from this and indeed, draws on the conservative toleration for diversity, ideological or ethnic which we have noted in Chapter IV. Finally, the Conservatives have contributed to the new nationalism their collectivist willingness to see the state intervene in wide areas of national life for nationalist ends. In this, conservatives like Creighton or Morton represent only one of the strands in the Conservative Party, the tory element. Because of the strength which the liberal strand in the party has enjoyed in recent years which we have already examined in Chapter IV, their views have by no means been reflected by the party though they have inspired a growing nationalist element.

Another important force in the new nationalism is the other bearer of collectivism in the Canadian political tradition, socialism. As we have argued conservatism, socialism, and nationalism all share a common collectivist orientation in various forms. Socialists are predisposed to appreciate the value of group or collective ties among men as well as to use collective means to protect and further group interests; and when nationalist or patriotic sentiment led them to see the nation as one of more important of such groups or ties socialist nationalism quickly developed. In addition, the socialist hostility to privilege has contributed to this process in Canada for socialists had consistently identified privilege with the interests of business; and as Canadian business became increasingly foreign owned and controlled (especially from the United States) nationalism was seen to be an effective means of attacking privilege.

Socialism has only contributed to Canadian nationalism in fairly recent times for it has only been a serious political force since the 1930's; and the contribution has never been made without reservation by the CCF or NDP. For the latter has its own liberal strand, perhaps found most strongly in the labour elements of the party, which has a long-standing commitment to international (i.e. continental) unionism and a consequent reluctance to endorse nationalist measures. Indeed, the proposed application of nationalist measures to international unions, and recent attempts to create national unions in their stead have provoked fierce resistance and a potential ideological division within the party. Nevertheless, the CCF sounded a distinctly nationalist note in the 1957 election campaign, and nationalism has remained a major concern of the party since, even after the attempted suppression of the Waffle group which had developed socialist nationalism to its most extreme point.

Paradoxically, the last factor in the nationalist revival is liberalism itself whose shortcomings from the new nationalism's viewpoint are legion. However, liberals who for many years had been preoccupied with freeing Canada from any vestiges of a colonial relationship with Britain belatedly began to realize that the new relations they had forged, or allowed to develop, with the United States bore an uncomfortable similarity to the colonial status they had so long fought. Such a realization was long overdue for ties with Britain had ceased to be anything more than symbolic by the 1920's, in sharp contrast to the ties to the south. Nor has this feeling been universal among Canadian liberals, least of all in the Liberal Party. Nevertheless it does exist and combined with rising patriotic feelings has given birth to a nationalist faction within the Liberal Party which in turn assisted the transition to nationalism among liberals in the Conservative or New Democratic Parties.

French Canada has provided both an opportunity and a problem for the new nationalism. On one hand, the French fact has become recognized as an important part of the Canadian identity, and the protection of the French language and cultural duality has become an important nationalist goal. On the other hand, rising French-Canadian nationalism and particularly separatism is diametrically opposed to the interests of Canadian nationalism. Efforts by Quebec to obtain greater autonomy are resented by Canadian nationalists for they promised to reduce the power of the national government to protect Canadian identity and sovereignty. The consequent feelings of frustration have led some nationalists to advocate drastic solutions: some, like Creighton or Morton would uphold federal power in direct conflict with French-Canadian nationalism if necessary; others, like some in the NDP, would avoid conflict and maintain a strong national government at the same time by granting Quebec special status, or acquiescing in secession, while increasing Ottawa's power in relation to the other provinces.

However, not all French Canadians are French-Canadian nationalists, nor have they always been so in the past. As emotional ties with Britain have faded, and English Canadians have become more responsive to the French fact and its rights, it has become a good deal easier for French Canadians to embrace a wider Canadian nationalism. Henri Bourassa consistently took such a position more than fifty years ago, and today, most French-Canadian "federalists" would see little to criticize in Bourassa's classic reconciliation of French-Canadian and wider Canadian national interests (made in answer to the extreme nationalism of Tardivel in 1904):

> Our own brand of nationalism is Canadian nationalism, based on the duality of the races and the special traditions this duality imposes. We are working towards the development of Canadian patriotism, which in our eyes is the best guarantee of the existence of two races and of the mutual respect they owe each other. Our people ... are the French Canadians; but the Anglo-Canadians are not foreigners, and we view as allies all of them who respect and desire, as we do, the full

> maintenance of Canadian autonomy. Our homeland is all
> of Canada.... The nation we want to see develop is the
> Canadian nation, made up of French Canadians and Eng-
> lish Canadians, that is, two elements separated by their
> language ... but united by brotherly affection and a
> common love for a common homeland.[41]

Finally, some nationalists see the new nationalism as an effective means of strengthening these sentiments, and combatting separatism. A Canada prepared vigorously to assert and protect its identity and independence would, they argue, be an inherently more attractive focus of loyalty for French Canadians, particularly since nationalist efforts in this direction would be directed against the same American influences that threaten French-Canadian society.

The various strands which make up the new nationalism were all beginning to emerge in 1957; the defeat of the essentially anti-nationalist Liberal Government in that year was certainly due in part to the success of John Diefenbaker in appealing to nationalist feeling. By 1957 also, the main areas of nationalist concern were becoming clear, areas which have remained constant to the present day. Most obviously there was disquiet about the erosion of Canadian political sovereignty; the attempts of American McCarthyites to hunt out subversion in the Canadian diplomatic service, the virtual fusion of continental defence efforts, and after 1960, American attempts to forbid the Canadian subsidiaries of American corporations to trade with Cuba and China all raised questions about the real area of Canadian political independence.

Others pointed out though that this was but the tip of the iceberg; that political independence could not be separated either from cultural or economic independence. As early as 1951, a Royal Commission headed by Vincent Massey (subsequently the first Canadian-born Governor General) emphasized the importance of cultural factors to national identity and survival:

> It is the intangibles which give a nation not only its es-
> sential character but its vitality as well. What may seem
> unimportant or even irrelevant under the pressure of
> daily life may well be the thing which endures, which
> may give a community its power to survive.[42]

"Our military defences must be made secure", the Commission concluded, "but our cultural defences equally demand national attention".[43] Five years later, in 1956 another royal commission, investigating Canada's economic prospects sounded a warning about foreign domination of the Canadian economy and recommended among other things that foreign controlled corporations be required to sell an "appreciable interest" in their equity to Canadians.[44] The head of the Commission, Walter Gordon, later to become the leading nationalist in the Pearson cabinet, had fired the first shot on the economic front which was to become the most important sector of the nationalist campaign.

Nationalist hopes which were focussed on Diefenbaker in 1957 were largely dissipated by the time of his defeat in 1963 by the almost complete inaction of his administration in this area. Even those who supported his stand against American interference in the 1963 election campaign (against Diefenbaker's refusal to accept American nuclear warheads for Canada's Bomarc missiles) damned with faint praise. George Grant, for example, in *Lament for a Nation* made it clear that Diefenbaker did not really understand the complexities of the problem of Canadian independence and had totally ignored economic and cultural factors which in effect determined the purely political question. Grant's brilliant study served further to stimulate the growing debate on economic and cultural nationalism which accompanied the career of Walter Gordon as Minister of Finance in the Pearson government from 1963 to 1965.

The Liberals had returned to power having acquired in opposition a nationalist wing, headed by Gordon, whose beliefs ran counter to the traditional liberalism of the bulk of the party. The result was an intra-party conflict over nationalism which has continued for the past ten years. The nationalists have always been in a minority; the Liberal governments of Pearson and Trudeau have consistently followed the traditional Liberal pursuit of the economic integration of Canada with the United States. Both Pearson and Trudeau possessed the deep suspicion of the nineteenth-century liberal for nationalism; for Pearson this was reinforced by his experience as a diplomat. Indeed one of the first concerns of his government was to restore the tradition of "quiet diplomacy" with the United States shattered by Diefenbaker's confrontation over nuclear weapons.

In this atmosphere, the Liberal nationalists had little success; the wonder is that they had any at all. The nationalist economic legislation passed under Pearson between 1963 and 1968, which restricted foreign ownership and control of banks and certain other financial institutions, newspapers, and broadcasting; and provided minor incentives to increase Canadian equity participation in foreign-controlled companies, owed its success to Pearson's tendency to compromise between the warring sections of the cabinet. Trudeau would not tolerate this sort of dissent in his cabinet, and the meagre nationalist measures which it produced owed their existence to the growing weight of nationalist opinion in the country at large.

The upsurge in nationalism which first became evident with the Diefenbaker triumphs of 1957-8 had scored some modest successes in the years up to 1966, in the growing commitment of the NDP to economic nationalism and in Walter Gordon's struggle within the Liberal Government. At the end of 1965 however, the outlook for nationalism was by no means bright as the NDP was far from power, Gordon had resigned from the cabinet, and his ideas had obviously been rejected by most Liberals. The Conservatives for their part were preoccupied with the bitter party warfare surrounding the leadership, and in any case were under strong pressure from the liberal, business elements in the party to eschew nationalism.

The downturn proved deceptive. It soon became clear that the arguments the nationalists had been making, particularly in the key area of economics, were beginning to strike home. The fundamental premise of economic nationalism was that foreign (largely American) penetration and influence of the Canadian economy would weaken both the Canadian identity and Canadian sovereignty. In short, a certain degree of economic independence was essential to a separate national existence for Canada — sharing a continent with a huge and powerful neighbour. The argument has several facets: foreign ownership and control drain profits out of the country and they may be used to alter the terms of trade between foreign parent and Canadian subsidiary, so as artificially to lower the price of Canadian exports or raise the price of imports of goods or technologies of management and production.

In either case, the Canadian balance of payments is affected. Foreign ownership may well result in reliance on imported technology and a neglect of Canadian research and development. In an age when technology is more and more the key to economic development and prosperity, such reliance may mean effective economic serfdom. In addition it may severely restrict the career prospects for Canadians in many fields, or force them to emigrate. Indeed, when foreign control results in integration of industry on a continental basis, many high-level jobs may be closed to Canadians unwilling to spend much of their lives outside of Canada. The continental integration of economic elites which often follows on foreign control threatens large-scale assimilation or breaking-down of Canadian values and attitudes in an important segment of the population. More directly, it may mean the extension of foreign domestic law, extraterritorially to Canada, through foreign parent corporations.

These specific arguments were joined by a more indeterminate conviction that economic integration with the United States was bound to lead to eventual political integration, and the destruction of Canada as an independent state. The close relationship of economic and political independence perceived by Macdonald in the 1880's was put concisely in the mid-1960's by George Ball, a senior American diplomat and proponent of continental union:

> Sooner or later, commercial imperatives will bring about free movement of all goods back and forth across our long border. When that occurs, or even before it does, it will become unmistakably clear that countries with economies so inextricably intertwined must also have free movement of the other vital factors of production — capital, services, labour. The result will inevitably be substantial economic integration, which will require for its full realization a progressively expanding area of common political decision.[45]

The message was made abundantly clear in December of 1965 when the American government in effect ordered American corporations to have their Canadian subsidiaries reduce investment and increase the repatriation of funds to the United States to improve its balance of payments.

Within a month, economic nationalism had made a prominent convert in the person of Eric Kierans, then a Quebec cabinet minister, subsequently a candidate for the Liberal leadership in 1968, and for a time a Trudeau cabinet minister. Kierans denounced the measures as a "tightening of the American grip on our economy that threatens the attainment of our own economic objectives and are an infringement of our political sovereignty".[46] Kierans' action was important psychologically, for he had led the battle against Walter Gordon's abortive attempt to discourage foreign takeovers in the 1963 budget, while head of the Montreal Stock Exchange.

Since 1966 Kierans has developed a nationalist economic policy which attempts to work within the existing private enterprise system, providing incentives for the ordinary market mechanisms to produce a higher degree of economic sovereignty.[47] Tariffs would be substantially eliminated to remove the attraction for foreign producers of establishing uneconomic branch-plants in Canada. Corporate tax rates would be lower for Canadian owned and controlled companies, providing a positive incentive to take over foreign businesses, and creating what Kierans calls a "buyer's market" for the assets of foreign subsidiaries. His nationalist critique of the tax system extends also to the extensive system of tax allowances allowed for resource-exploitation companies. Not only is this inequitable, but unwise, for it encourages investment in an area which provides few jobs, and encourages the "squandering" of natural resources for short term gains. Kierans bitterly attacks re-source sell-outs, and indeed resigned from the Trudeau government on this general issue. Resources are:

> A trust received from the past, to be husbanded by the present and to be passed on to future generations. A generation that deliberately squanders a nation's natural wealth to enhance its own standard of living, to live high off the hog, will have much to answer for. A govern-ment that deliberately pursues a policy of selling off the natural wealth of its people to achieve short run gains in GNP breaks faith with its own future.[48]

Kierans' preference to use market mechanisms to achieve nation-alist ends, and to avoid direct government intervention in the form of restrictions or prohibitions reveals a curious mixture of liberalism and nationalism. His liberalism verges on the radical — his attacks on certain corporate tax privileges coincided with David Lewis' as-sault on "corporate welfare bums" (and led him to write the intro-duction to Lewis' *Louder Voices*): but he retains a belief in the in-dispensibility of the business community for realizing economic independence, and a faith that they will seek that end given proper incentives. It illustrates the strength of his nationalist feelings for we have seen that nationalism and liberalism do not make the most congenial partners. Kierans is perhaps the exception that proves the rule.

Shortly after Kierans' conversion, Gordon returned to the fray, publishing *A Choice for Canada: Independence or Colonial Status* in 1966. In many ways this provided a model for economic national-ism which has predominated ever since. In the first place, Gordon, like Kierans, accepted the existence of a basically private enterprise, capitalist economy, and sought to modify its operation rather than to replace it on socialist lines. That this should be the dominant Canadian approach is hardly surprising for both Conservatives and Liberals accepted a capitalist economy even if differing at times on its regulation, and conservatism and liberalism together occupy much of the ideological stage in Canada. Gordon was not as much of a liberal as Kierans however, and his solution placed less faith in the operations of the market, and more in direct government intervention or supervision. He favoured a government agency to ensure that pricing and purchasing policies, profit margins, and ex-port policies of foreign controlled companies were in the best Cana-dian interests.[49] Further, direct measures should be taken to dis-courage foreign takeovers (e.g. a revival of the ill-fated takeover tax of 1963),[50] and the government should set up the Canada Development Corporation to funnel Canadian savings into Canadian equities.[51] Kierans for his part had little faith in the efficacy of such measures — he was convinced that success would only come through by employing market incentives to secure the "united efforts of all elements in the business and financial community".[52] This liberal faith in the market was not shared to the same degree by the strong conservative strain in the Canadian political tradition nor by many nationalists who distrusted what the market left to itself had done before, and who were prepared to override at least some of their liberal qualms to defend the national collectivity.

Thus Canadian economic nationalism has reflected fairly closely the ideological mix of the nation: its predominant concern for realising an economy both capitalist and Canadian, through a moderate degree of government intervention mirrors the way in which the dominant liberalism of Canada is sharply tempered by both conservatism and nationalism. Kieran's unique brand of liberal nationalism stands a little to one side; the full-blown socialist variety we will examine shortly stands a good deal to the other.

In December of 1966, Gordon, whose support in the Liberal Party had remained significant, returned to the cabinet on the condition that the government commission a study on the foreign domination of the economy, and ways it might be reduced. Accordingly a "Task Force on the Structure of Canadian Industry" was established, headed by Melville Watkins, an economist who had achieved a certain notoriety by challenging the conventional *laissez-faire* wisdom of most academic economists. The proposals in its report, *Foreign Ownership and the Structure of Canadian Industry,* which appeared in February 1968, were not significantly different from Gordon's earlier proposals, though set out in greater detail, and backed by a good deal more research. The report barely hinted at the more radical stand that Watkins was soon to take, and the Watkins proposals followed the path set by Gordon — a modest amount of government intervention within the context of an essentially private enterprise economy.

Although the Watkins Report appeared in the midst of the Liberal leadership campaign it was generally ignored or rejected by the candidates, and found no place in the subsequent Trudeau election campaign. Nor was it better received by the Conservatives. Its significance was not its immediate consequences, but rather its implications. It suggested a way to create a new, forward looking liberal-nationalism. We have seen that liberal-nationalism was preoccupied with the question of freedom from foreign control, and that traditional Liberal policy had pursued this with systematic vigour against the remnants of British influence in Canada. Yet through time liberal-nationalism has succumbed to the same ideological weaknesses that we analyzed in the Conservatives in the 1920's in Chapter IV: the problems with which it was meant to cope were no longer pressing.

Watkins offered an apparently plausible alternative. He suggested that new restrictions on Canadian national autonomy and liberty of action has arisen from the increasing foreign (mainly American) control of Canadian businesses, notably manufacturing, mining and smelting and petroleum and natural gas. Washington and New York were plausible modern substitutes for Whitehall and the City. The multinational corporation shifting production, investment, research and development from country to country as its global interests dictate represented a novel but serious threat to the development of a vigorous, independent economy. The Watkins Report, with its recommendations for a government regulatory agency, the establishment of the Canada Development Corporation, tariff reductions, stricter antitrust laws to control multinational oligopolies and measures to encourage Canadian research and development, probably represented the limits to which liberal-nationalism could be pushed without submerging the liberal elements in the mix.

For some, including, apparently, Watkins himself, it was ideologically inadequate. Only the NDP, following the CCF's pronouncements of 1957, endorsed the report, despite the fact that it contained few if any distinctively socialist measures. However, though the party's stand satisfied the nationalist feelings of its liberal wing, it was questioned and rejected after the election by the more radical socialism of the emerging Waffle faction.

The Waffle group, as we argued in Chapter V, grew out of frustration with the moderate, liberal-socialist mix of the NDP. It sought to replace the party's ideological diversity with socialist purity; to make the NDP "a truly socialist party" which would seek a "socialist transformation of society". For the Waffle, this end was inextricably connected with nationalism; national independence and socialism went together: "Our aim . . . is to build an *independent* socialist Canada". The primary obstacle to the realization of this goal was the threat posed to Canada's very existence by the domination of the Canadian economy by "American corporate capitalism".[53] This tied Canada to the American empire, committing her to American foreign politics which were both racist and militaristic, and to a domestic capitalism which subordinated human needs and the general good of the Canadian community to the profit motive and the value-system which accompanies it. Both nationalism and socialism had a common interest in breaking the bonds of the American empire, and to this extent they were allies: "Canadian nationalism is a relevant force on which to build to the extent that is anti-imperialist."[54] Indeed, the Waffle believed that real nationalism is impossible without that socialism, for the ideas of individual economic liberty and the primacy of individual private gain implicit in capitalism effectively counteracted the nationalist commitment to the national collectivity. This was revealed clearly in their approach to nationalist policies.

Unlike the other solutions to the problem of economic independence which we have examined, the Waffle's rejected the Canadian business community as a possible ally. Canadian capitalists, the Waffle argued, had only been nationalist when it was profitable to be so in the nineteenth century; now their interests lay in continentalism, denials by some businessmen notwithstanding: "any lingering pretentions on the part of Canadian businessmen to independence lack credibility."[55] This in turn ruled out the old-line parties as possible sources of a nationalist policy for they were too closely tied to their corporate allies. The Waffle rejected policies based on "substituting Canadian capitalists for American capitalists, or ... to make foreign corporations behave as if they were Canadian corporations".[56] This ruled out most previous proposals, including ironically, those which Watkins himself (now one of the chief architects of the Waffle programme) had promoted eighteen months previously.

The Waffle's mixture of socialism and nationalism, based on the element of collectivism common to both, was not subject to the check imposed on other nationalists by their attempt to reconcile nationalism with capitalism, with the ideological problems this posed. The Waffle was able to put forward a much more unambiguously nationalist set of proposals than Gordon, Kierans, or the Watkins Task Force. Such a potent combination has probably not been seen since Macdonald's blending of conservatism and nationalism; and Macdonald was restrained by the need to conciliate the liberal elements in the Liberal-Conservative Party. The Waffle had no ideological need to persuade, entice or reward Canadian capitalists to act in nationalist ways; they were simply to be replaced by direct and sweeping state intervention. The Canadian economy was to be recaptured by frontal assault, with "extensive public control over investment and nationalization of the commanding heights of the economy, such as the key resource industries, finance and credits, and industries strategic to planning our economy".[57] Regulatory agencies, takeover taxes, tax credits were merely redundant.

The Waffle believed that their programme of socialism and nationalism would also solve the problem of national unity, by forging ideological bonds between English and French. Both have a common interest in repelling American capitalism, and this "common perception of 'two nations, one struggle' " while not extinguishing linguistic and cultural differences, would at least create "common aspirations that would help tie the two nations together once more".[58] The watering-down of the traditional socialist hostility to nationalism and its commitment to internationalism is a good indication of the strength of the nationalist appeal to the Waffle, and the genuineness of the alliance they forged between nationalism and socialism.

The Waffle attempt to turn the NDP sharply to the left, and to undo the party's traditional mixture of socialist and liberal elements, precipitated a running battle with the more moderate majority in the NDP in which the first major encounter was the party's biennial convention in October 1969. Though it was not the last, it is of interest for the arguments used then by David Lewis to attack the Waffle and to defend the more moderate alternative put forward by the party council (unkindly christened the "marshmallow" resolution). This mentioned nationalization only briefly (under the euphemism of "public ownership") and in the context of a number of more familiar proposals — tax changes, the Canada Development Corporation, and laws to regulate foreign investment. Lewis rejected the ideological uniformity of the Waffle — it would put the NDP into an "ideological strait-jacket" — and attacked its pure socialist doctrine as foreign to the Canadian experience, in terms strikingly reminiscent of Woodsworth:

> To bury this central problem of independence in a general statement of analysis, to bury it in words which are foreign to the Canadian people, to clothe it in incomprehensible language and to put around it a lot of other issues is . . . to confuse the people of Canada.[59]

And, Lewis might well have added, alienate those NDP supporters who were attracted by its strand of radical liberalism.

Lewis clearly perceived the threat which the Waffle posed to the existing ideological balance of the party and to its support by the more liberally-inclined trade unionists, and led the majority of the NDP in forcing the Waffle to disband as a group within the party in the summer of 1972. Their action served to reinforce the conclusion that the mainstream of economic nationalism in Canada was to continue to be restrained by the powerful influence of the liberal substratum in the Canadian political tradition.

This was evident in the brand of economic nationalism emerging in the Conservative Party. At a policy conference held in Niagara

Falls in October of 1969 Eddie Goodman, a prominent Toronto Conservative, (soon to be a principal organizer of the Committee for an Independent Canada) proposed a modest nationalist programme. Its primary provision was for the division of Canadian business into three sections for purposes of regulating foreign control. In the first, which "would include communications and finance in its broadest sense" present foreign ownership would be limited to 20 per cent; in the second, containing resource and "certain of the heavy or strategic industries", *future* foreign investment would be limited to 50 per cent of the equity capital; and in the third, containing the rest, there would be no restrictions.[60]

The tide of nationalism was also rising within the Liberal Party, though with little apparent effect on the Trudeau government. In March of 1970, a rising Liberal backbencher, Alastair Gillespie, wrote that "if we do nothing in the next five years the process will be irreversible and the result inevitable". Gillespie's proposals were an expanded version of Gordon's: prohibition of further foreign takeovers, restrictions on expansion of existing foreign ownership, creation of the Canada Development Corporation, and requirements that future resource developments be 50 per cent Canadian owned.[61] It is perhaps a measure of the increasing weight of nationalist feeling in Canada (and even in the Liberal Party) that in December 1972, Gillespie was made Minister of Industry, Trade and Commerce in the Trudeau government which had entirely ignored his proposals of 1970.

This was brought home by the report in August of 1970 of a Commons committee headed by another Liberal backbencher, Ian Wahn, which followed the now-familiar liberal-nationalist path. Like Watkins the Wahn Report pressed for a government agency to co-ordinate actions with respect to the multinational corporation, for the establishment of the Canada Development Corporation, and for measures (though not an agency) to deal with American extraterritorial jurisdiction over Canadian subsidiaries. It followed Gillespie in advocating a ban on takeovers in "key" sectors of the economy, and government consideration and consent for all other takeovers. The Wahn committee also dealt with the neglected area of foreign control of Canadian unionism through international (in effect American) unions, and concluded that "the development of a fully independent Canadian identity and the need that Canadian interests be always uppermost in every sphere of activity require that Canadian branches of international unions quickly gain the fullest possible autonomy and freedom of action". While not recommending specific legislation to reach this end, the committee did set certain "general objectives", including recognition of separate Canadian sections, election of Canadian officers by Canadians, and complete autonomy over funds, staff, and collective bargaining.[62]

The Wahn committee represented nationalist opinion from all three major parties, and was indicative of a growing tendency for nationalists of different political allegiance to stand together on the basis of a shared ideological commitment to nationalism. As we have already argued, nationalism by itself does not provide a sufficiently comprehensive ideological vision to support a full-scale political party, and at no time has this tendency of nationalists to stand together presented the threat of a breakaway nationalist party.

It has produced one significant inter-party nationalist organization, the Committee for an Independent Canada, which was formed to promote nationalist measures on a non-partisan basis. Emerging in 1970, the CIC included Conservatives like Eddie Goodman and Flora Macdonald, Liberals Mel Hurtig and Ian Wahn, and New Democrat Abraham Rotstein, as well as independents like Peter Newman. It is based explicitly on the premise that the nationalist concern for Canadian independence is sufficient grounds for common action by those otherwise divided by party allegiance:

> We have enough in common in our concern for an independent Canada to work together effectively on a concrete program to reduce foreign control of the economy, foster the creative arts, assure more Canadian content in the media and in our educational system, and counter the deterioration of our environment.[63]

Like interest groups in other areas, the CIC has attempted to impress its views on government both from within, and by means of a publicity and education or propaganda campaign including public meetings and forums, and publications like *Independence: The Canadian Challenge,* (1972).

By 1970, the obvious upsurge in nationalist feeling could no longer be ignored by the Trudeau government, which until then had almost completely neglected it in accord with the prime minister's well-known antipathy to nationalism. Apart from tidying up some loose ends from the Pearson years, the Trudeau government had for the most part continued policies inherited from King and St. Laurent, reducing formal or ceremonial links with Britain. All the while, American ownership of Canadian industry increased inexorably, and the prime minister, and J. J. Greene, then Minister of Energy and Resources, talked enthusiastically of continental sharing of oil, gas, water and other resources.

Responding to rising nationalist opinion the Trudeau government altered its priorities outwardly at any rate, and belatedly turned its attention to problems of economic independence. Two large takeover bids (in oil and uranium mining) were blocked, and a cabinet task force under Herb Gray was charged with producing yet another report on foreign economic domination. In the meantime, the long-awaited Canada Development Corporation was set up in 1971, to funnel Canadian savings into Canadian industry, though in its first two years of existence it made little apparent impact apart from assuming control of several existing Crown corporations.

The Gray Report was never officially made public, but a substantial portion was "leaked" to the *Canadian Forum* and published in December 1971. Its primary recommendation was for a screening agency to exercise control over all foreign investment in Canada, considering takeovers, new foreign investment, and expansion of existing foreign-controlled firms in the light of their effect on productivity, regional development, competition, and any overall industrial strategy the government might formulate. This was hardly a novel policy, but the government's initial reaction was merely to offer a bill in the spring of 1972 giving the cabinet power to forbid takeovers alone. The bill died on the order paper when Parliament was dissolved, and had to be strengthened when re-introduced by the minority Trudeau government in January 1973 to meet the objections of the NDP. A separate agency responsible to the cabinet was now to be established, with authority to consider new investment in addition to takeovers. This remained Trudeau's only significant answer to the problem of American economic domination, though the appointment of a nationalist-inclined Minister of Industry, Trade and Commerce (Gillespie) may mean the eventual formulation of an independent industrial development strategy.

The prospects of this are not, in the short run at least, encouraging. We have seen time and time again that Liberalism's preoccupation with liberty and individualism makes any alliance with nationalism a temporary, contingent one, lasting only so long as the threat of foreign control is acknowledged. Canadian Liberalism seems unwilling to make the substitutions in the formula of its traditional nationalism that the Watkins Report first outlined, and which later liberal-nationalists have pressed. The liberal reluctance to interfere with economic forces, and the implicit belief that these forces represent a rational policy choice, lends strength to the contention of the Waffle that no party in which liberalism is the dominant ideological force can adequately come to terms with foreign ownership and the multinational corporation.

The Gray Report did break new ground in one respect by examining the relationship of economic to cultural dependence. It emphatically denied that the question of cultural identity could be separated from economic dependence: "There is no such compartmentalization. . . . There can be little doubt that economic activity, as organized in the modern corporation, has a profound impact on culture. . . ."[64] A vicious circle existed; cultural similarity between Canada and the United States facilitated American investment, yet that same investment strengthened and emphasized those common features. American social, cultural, political and economic ideas were exported to Canada along with American investment and technology to the detriment of other facets of the Canadian ideological mosaic. The technologies of production or management rarely take local needs or values into account, and produce a standardized product. The incompatibility of this process with the classical nationalist respect for the values of national identity and diversity is obvious.

It is here that the problems of the cultural diversity and linguistic duality of Canada which bedevilled the imperial federationists again arises. Classical nationalism had traced cultural differences between nations to linguistic divisions, and had drawn the conclusion that all who spoke the same language should belong to the same state. Modern Canadian cultural nationalists clearly want to avoid just that consequence. Yet because French and English in Canada share a common state, but not a common culture, they pull back from pursuing the clear cultural differences between Canada and the United States, for fear of clarifying the equally obvious differences between English and French Canada.

One solution to this dilemma long predated the Gray Report. That proposal was to see the government increase its support for the arts and letters throughout Canada by the creation of the Canada Council. In itself this suggestion, advanced by the Massey Commission in 1952 was not necessarily nationalistic. Their concern was for the arts in their universal rather than strictly Canadian forms, and their interest was limited to "high culture" — classical music, ballet and the like — rather than the sum of all the traditions, customs and attitudes which distinguish Canadians. The Council, however, has increasingly turned its attention to Canada's history and to the social, political and religious attitudes of Canadians throughout the country and to their local customs and folkways.

The logic of cultural nationalism has pushed beyond public support for high culture to protection of a whole complex of institutions which contribute to a national culture. In this view the desire for a Canadian business community is an integral part of the cultural nationalists' struggle. Understandably a good deal of interest has been focussed on the various communications media, particularly in view of the flood of American content available in books, magazines, radio and television.

Broadcasting was one of the first targets, and action was secured from the Pearson government in 1968, in a revision of the *Broadcasting Act* which effectively prohibited any significant financial ties between Canadian and foreign broadcasters, and strengthened the regulatory agency (the CRTC) to enable it to enforce this rule and stricter Canadian content rules. Since then the CRTC has vigorously pursued both objectives, though forced to slow down the increase in Canadian content in television due to financial problems experienced by private broadcasters. The predominance of the commercial element and profit motive in Canadian broadcasting, which gives advertising demands a heavy influence on programme content, is a prime cause of this problem. Since many advertisers are American-controlled corporations intent on maximizing the sale of consumer goods, programming has tended to be "bland, slick, escapist, . . . intellectually timid and uninventive, repetitive . . . and essentially unrepresentative of the national life and culture".[65]

Previous to 1968, legislation was also passed which prevented foreign ownership of Canadian newspapers, and forestalled foreign magazines from draining advertising revenue from Canadian magazines. The latter attempt was only partly successful since American government pressure on the Pearson government secured the exemption of *Time's* Canadian edition and the *Reader's Digest* from this measure. Again this problem is compounded by considerable American ownership of advertising agencies, and the tendency of American subsidiaries to place advertising through the Canadian branch of their parent company's agency, rather than a Canadian agency.

Next to the communications media, the Americanization of the Canadian education system has become the prime concern of cultural nationalists. The increasing use of American textbooks and teaching materials at the primary and secondary levels has gone along with a neglect of specifically Canadian subjects, particularly Canadian history. The result has been a spate of nationalist demands for more and better teaching of Canadian subjects, and for more Canadian books and other teaching materials. This in turn has brought attention to bear on the Canadian publishing industry, which includes a substantial number of American subsidiaries. Here the government of Ontario has taken the lead, assisting the Canadian publisher McClelland and Stewart out of temporary financial straits, acting to reduce American control of book distribution in Ontario, and appointing a committee in 1972 to investigate the publishing industry. The committee's report, made public in February, 1973, recommended a screening agency to prevent further foreign penetration of the industry, and a system of government aid to Canadian publishers.

In the universities, the debate has been even more bitter, because of the substantial numbers of Americans in Canadian faculties. It has been estimated that the proportion of Canadians on university faculties declined from 75 per cent in 1961 to closer to 50 per cent by 1968,[66] as the result of substantial immigration to satisfy university expansion needs. Furthermore, foreigners have been concentrated in areas like political science, sociology, economics, history and English which are more culturally sensitive than the physical sciences. In some cases, whole departments contained few Canadians, and consequently offered little Canadian content. To make things worse, American departmental chairmen responsible for hiring have often reinforced the imbalance.

This situation has produced a strong, and sometimes bitter campaign, for the "Canadianization" of university faculties, led by James Steele and Robin Mathews of Carleton University, who first gave the issue public prominence. Demands for preferential treatment for Canadians, or quotas, have been resisted by many academics, some legitimately concerned about a nationalist "witch-hunt"; others exhibiting the liberal hostility to national differentiation, or exalting the "universality" of learning and the irrelevancy of nationality to it.

Finally, cultural nationalism has to some extent taken under its wing the promotion of regional and minority cultural diversities. The Canadian cultural mosaic has been identified as an important part of the national identity, and efforts to preserve various of its parts, such as the Gaelic culture of Cape Breton or the Ukrainian culture on the prairies, are often seen as a proper nationalist concern. The presence of these local cultures which differ conspicuously from the pervasive and dissolvent American culture may indeed prove to be an important factor in the survival of an independent Canada.

Canadian nationalism then has become steadily more active and influential during the last decade and there are no signs at present that the immediate future will reverse this trend. On the contrary, insistent American demands for access to Canadian resources promise to raise with increasing acuteness the very questions about our economic relationship to the United States which are the nationalists' chief concern. This concern, we have argued, is not new — nationalism as an ideology in Canada, French and English, has roots deep in the nineteenth century; and the questions which

Political Parties and Ideologies

Canadian nationalism raises today are in substance, if not in detail, the same as those which Canadians faced in 1878 over the National Policy, in 1891 over commercial union, and in 1911 on reciprocity. Nationalism also remains, today as then, an ideology of limited comprehensiveness, raising questions and providing answers on a fairly limited range of concern, and forced to seek alliances with other ideologies. The future course and nature of Canadian nationalism will depend to a considerable extent on the nature of the alliances it makes. Nationalism in Canada's first half-century had a predominantly conservative flavour. Today, it enjoys close relations with its ideological half-brothers conservatism and socialism, and is flirting vigorously with some of its estranged liberal cousins.

Paradoxically, this weakness of nationalism, its need for allies, has probably widened its influence, for through alliances it has been able to appeal in one way or another across the whole ideological spectrum in Canada. Thus while only an intermittent participant in the ideological conversation, nationalism has contributed a good deal to its vitality, by raising questions about Canadian identity and independence to which all of the other participants have been forced to address themselves. This nationalist contribution has been particularly marked in the last decade or so, — indeed, it has certainly been the major factor in producing the debate over the nature and purpose of the Canadian polity which is the central preoccupation of our ideologies today. Nationalism can with justice claim the ideological leadership of the 1970's.

[1] See C. J. H. Hayes, Essays on Nationalism, (New York: Russell, reprint of 1926 edition) and Nationalism: A Religion (New York: Macmillan, 1960).

[2] E. Kedourie, Nationalism, (London: Hutchinson & Co., 1966) p.9.

[3] George Heiman, "The Nineteenth Century Legacy: Nationalism or Patriotism" in P. Russell, ed. Nationalism in Canada, (Toronto: McGraw-Hill Ryerson, 1966).

[4] Charles Mair, "The New Canada: Its Resources and Productions" in The Canadian Monthly and National Review (August, 1875) p.160.

[5] See Berger, The Sense of Power, (Toronto: University of Toronto Press, 1969) p.66. Berger's incisive study of the imperialist movement in Canada before 1914, and its nationalist overtones, provides an invaluable insight into this period.

[6] Berger, p.135 (Equal Rights Association of Ontario: D'Alton McCarthy's Great Speech Delivered at Ottawa, December 12th, 1889, Toronto, n.d.)

[7] See Berger, op. cit., pp.135-47.

[8] Stephen Leacock, "Greater Canada: An Appeal", in University Magazine, Vol. II, no. 2, April 1907, p.133.

[9] Empire Club of Canada: Addresses Delivered to the Members During the Sessions of 1912-3 and 1913-4, (Toronto: 1915) in Berger, p.231.

[10] Wilfrid Campbell, "Imperialism in Canada", Empire Club Speeches: Being Addresses Delivered Before the Empire Club of Canada During its Session of 1904-05, Toronto, 1906 in Berger, p.170.

[11] *Empire*, 2 October 1890, reprinted in Berger, p.169.
[12] Wilfrid Campbell, *op. cit.*, in Berger, p. 170.
[13] *See Berger*, pp.136-47.
[14] From campaign message, Halifax, 19 September 1911, in *Robert Laird Borden, His Memoirs*, (1969, Vol. I, p.157) by R. L. Borden, abridged and edited by H. Macquarrie, reprinted by permission of The Canadian Publishers, McClelland and Stewart Limited, Toronto.
[15] *House of Commons Debates*, 29 March 1909, p.3523, 1st Session — 11th Parliament, Vol. XC.
[16] *House of Commons* Debates, 12 January 1910, pp.1747, 1761, 2nd Session, 11th Parliament, Vol. XCIII.
[17] Etienne Parent, "Industry as a Means of Survival for the French-Canadian Nationality", *Le Répertoire National,* Montreal, 1893, translated and reprinted in Ramsay Cook, ed., *French-Canadian Nationalism* (Toronto: Macmillan, 1969) p.84.
[18] Mgr. L.-F.-R. Laflèche, *Quelques Considérations sur les rapports de la société civile avec la religion et la famille,* (Trois Rivières: 1866) translated and reprinted in Cook, p.93.
[19] *Ibid.*, p.96.
[20] J.-P. Tardivel, in *La Verité,* 1 June 1904, translated and reprinted in Cook, p.151.
[21] *Ibid.*, p.147.
[22] J-M.-R. Villeneuve, "Et nos frères de la dispersion" in *Notre Avenir Politique: Enquête de L'Action française,* Montreal, 1923, translated and reprinted in Cook, p.208.
[23] *Ibid.*, pp.206-7.
[24] *Ibid.*, p.204.
[25] *Ibid.*, p.202.
[26] *Ibid.*, p.205.
[27] Antonio Perrault, "Enquête sur le nationalisme" in *L'Action francaise,* February, 1924, translated and reprinted in Cook, p.220.
[28] Marcel Chaput, "The Secession of Quebec from Canada" in Canadian Commentator, July-August, 1961, in Paul Fox, ed. *Politics: Canada,* 3rd ed., (Toronto: McGraw-Hill Ryerson, 1970) p.46.
[29] Jean Marc Léger, "Le Néo-nationalisme, où conduit-il?" in *Les Nouveaux Quebecois,* Quebec, 1964 translated and reprinted in Cook, p.311.
[30] *Ibid.*, p.310.
[31] *Ibid.*, p.311.
[32] La Solution: Le Programme du Parti Québecois présenté par René Lévesque, (Montreal: Jacques Herbert, 1970) p.81. Our translation.
[33] *Ibid.*, p.9.
[34] *Ibid.*, p.20.
[35] *Ibid.*, p.7.
[36] Pierre Vallières, *White Niggers of America,* (Toronto: McClelland and Stewart, 1969) p.57.
[37] Pierre Vallières, *L'Urgence de Choisir,* (Montréal: Editions Parti Pris, 1971) p.40. Our translation.
[38] *Ibid.*, p.117.
[39] D. G. Creighton, *John A. Macdonald, 2 vols.,* (Toronto: Macmillan, 1952, 1955).
[40] See D. Creighton, *Empire of the St. Lawrence* (Toronto: Macmillan, 1953); *Canada's First Century* (Toronto: Macmillan, 1970).
[41] Henri Bourassa in *Le Nationaliste,* 3 April 1904, translated and reprinted in Cook, *op. cit.*, pp.149-150.
[42] *Report of the Royal Commission on National Development in the Arts, Letters and Sciences 1949-51,* (Ottawa: King's Printer, 1951) pp.4-5. Reproduced by permission of Information Canada.
[43] *Ibid.*, p.275.
[44] See *Report of the Royal Commission on Canada's Economic Prospects,* (Ot-

tawa: Queen's Printer, 1957).

[45] George Ball, *The Discipline of Power*, (Boston: Atlantic-Little, Brown, 1968) p.113.

[46] Speech at Montreal, March, 1966, quoted in D. Godfrey and M. Watkins, eds. *Gordon to Watkins to You*, (Toronto: New Press, 1970) p.51.

[47] *See* Eric W. Kierans "Towards a New National Policy" in *Canadian Forum*, Jan.-Feb. 1972, pp.52-5.

[48] *Ibid.*, p.54.

[49] *See* Walter L. Gordon, *A Choice for Canada*, (Toronto: McClelland and Stewart, 1966) pp.111-14.

[50] *See ibid.*, pp.114-17.

[51] *See ibid.*, pp.119-20.

[52] Kierans, p.53.

[53] Resolution 133, New Democratic Party Federal Convention, Winnipeg, 30 October 1969.

[54] *Ibid.*

[55] *Ibid.*

[56] *Ibid.*

[57] *Ibid.*

[58] *Ibid.*

[59] Debate at NDP Convention, 30 October 1969, reprinted in Godfrey, pp.115-16.

[60] Recommendations of sub-committee at Niagara Falls Progressive Conservative Conference, 12 October 1969, reprinted in Godfrey, pp.190-92.

[61] Toronto *Daily Star*, 2 March 1970.

[62] 11th Report of the Standing Committee on Defence and External Affairs, p.60.

[63] A. Rotstein, and G. Lax, "Introduction", in *Independence: The Canadian Challenge*, (Toronto: McClelland and Stewart, 1972), pp. xii-xiii.

[64] Gray Report, *Canadian Forum*, December 1971, pp.30-32.

[65] F. Peers, "Oh, Say Can You See", in I. Lumsden, ed. *Close to the 49th Parallel, etc., The Americanization of Canada*, (Toronto: University of Toronto Press, 1970).

[66] *See* J. Steele and R. Mathews, "Universities: Takeover of the Mind", in Lumsden, pp.170-77.

Chapter VII

Conclusion:
Whither are We drifting?

Arthur Meighen posed this question in 1935, and it is more than ever a pressing one today. For the last decade or so, those who have reflected on the future of the Canadian polity have manifested a deep pessimism. The expectations of a new vision and destiny for Canada of which the elections of 1957 and 1958 had been false harbingers have given rise first to disenchantment with John Diefenbaker, and then to dissatisfaction with politics itself as his successors have done little better.

In 1965 George Grant published *Lament for a Nation* with its brilliant argument that Canada was a "branch-plant" colony of the United States; and was moving remorselessly towards assimilation: as Taché had said a hundred years before, we were on an inclined plane, rolling insensibly to union with the United States. In 1967, amid the growing optimism surrounding Centennial Year, John Robarts convoked the Confederation of Tomorrow Conference on the assumption that the country's second century would call for a new constitution for Canada. This marked the beginning of what seemed an interminable series of constitutional conferences over the next five years, which have in the end, produced nothing but falsely raised expectations. These conferences, Donald Creighton wrote, were "begun in confusion and irresolution, with conflicting purposes and no common goal in sight .... the failure of this unavailing effort was certain to bring continentalism one long stage further towards its final triumph".[1]

More recent events like the October Crisis have added to the despair. Donald Smiley confessed that his recently-published study of federalism had been "delayed by two periods in which I ceased work because of the judgement that the federation would not last as long as it would take to finish the manuscript".[2] Denis Smith concluded his penetrating analysis of the October Crisis with the wistful remark that "if confidence and trust have disappeared, our hearts will bleed in vain. And so will Canada".[3]

What has produced this sense of drift and disquiet, this sense of foreboding for the future? Why in particular has it appeared so strongly in the last ten or fifteen years? The last question is of some moment for while the threat posed by a resurgent French-Canadian nationalism to Canada's future has only become acute since 1960, the more serious threat of absorption by the United States has been growing steadily since 1920, and in the economic area, reached a peak rate of growth in the later 1940's and 1950's. Yet despite apparent indications that the rate of American takeovers reached its highest point in the mid-1950's, widespread concern did not really arise for nearly ten years. The threat to Confederation from extreme provincial-rights positions was as well developed by Hepburn in the 1930's or Duplessis after 1944, as by any of the provincial leaders of the 1960's.

One is driven to the conclusion that what has changed in the 1960's is not the nature or the intensity of the problems facing Canada's future, but our perception of them, and the nature of the concerns that they raise in us. In the 1960's Canada has seen continuing problems in a new light. Why?

Our argument is that the situation of ideological diversity which we have described in the preceding chapters, the ideological "conversation" which characterized the Canadian political tradition, has taken on a new lease of life since 1957 — has become livelier, and at times, more like an argument than a conversation. The result is that previously accepted policies and attitudes have been subjected to new and searching criticism. This development is the result of the breaking of the liberal spell woven by Mackenzie King over Canadian politics after 1920, and which survived in his heir and successor, Louis St. Laurent.

King skilfully exploited the position of liberalism as the dominant ideology which was shared to a degree by his political opponents on both left and right as well as ruling unchallenged in the Liberal Party. On the left, with the Progressives and later the CCF, he minimized the differences between the Liberal Party and these other "Liberals in a hurry". By denying major differences between his ideology and that of the Progressives, he succeeded where the clearer and more forceful Meighen failed, in securing their adhesion in the delicate circumstances of the early 1920's. Later he managed to incorporate most of them in the Liberal Party. In the late 1940's and early 1950's, the same tack almost succeeded with the CCF, but as we argued in Chapter V, that party's socialism narrowly succeeded in veering it, at the last moment, from its assimilationist course with the Liberals.

On the right, with the Conservatives, King's tactic was to empha-size the ideological differences, to stress the toryism of the Con-servative Party, and try to detach the liberal elements from the party. Here his success was ensured by the alliance between lib-eralism and Quebec nationalism which Laurier had forged, and which the Conscription Crisis of 1917 had cemented. Largely de-prived of any significant support in Quebec, the Conservatives were placed at a tremendous electoral disadvantage. Successive defeats convinced many in the party that King's argument was right, that their toryism placed them in an inferior position, and that their best course of action was to imitate success, and stress the liberal ele-ment in the Conservative Party. Again the end result was to mute the ideological conversation.

The dominance of liberalism also tended to silence the nationalist voice. Electoral defeat led Conservatives to minimize their tradi-tional (and apparently unsuccessful) nationalism along with their toryism. Behind the facade of liberal nationalism, and its token at-tacks on symbols of the British connection, King and St. Laurent pursued continentalist policies virtually undisturbed. Thus the coun-try was deprived of the influence that the ideological differences of the Conservatives and the CCF/NDP as well as of nationalism, ought to have offered it. Their voices in the ideological conversa-tion were muted if not silenced. The mould was broken in 1957 however, and the indecisive elections of the last ten years give reason to suspect that this period of Canadian history is finally over, as liberalism has been unable to re-establish its predominant position contrary to Liberal expectations in 1962 and 1963.

With the renewal of this ideological conversation, we have been made aware of new perspectives both on our past and our future. Conservative, socialist, and nationalist critiques have revealed de-ficiencies in liberal thinking, providing us with some idea of what we have lost in the past through too much ideological uniformity, and indicating new alternatives for the future. This critique of lib-eralism has largely centred on its neglect of the collective aspects of political life. This is hardly surprising since collectivism is a feature shared by all three of liberalism's ideological rivals, and has consequently allowed their criticisms to reinforce one another.

The most important aspect of the clash of collectivism and liberal individualism has undoubtedly arisen out of the nationalist revival of the last fifteen years or so. We have already examined the growth of both conservative and socialist nationalism in this period in Chapter VI, and we have seen how their telling criticisms of Liberal continentalist policies have in turn led some Liberals to seriously modify their liberalism in favour of growing support for the national collectivity. The renewed vigour of French-Canadian nationalism after 1960 is another variant of this phenomenon.

Nationalism, whether Canadian or *Canadien,* is not the only example of a collectivist reaction to liberalism however. The tendency of liberalism to ally itself with technology, and the consequent drive to increasing standardization and homogeneity, on a national, continental, or world scale, has been brilliantly exposed by George Grant (following the French social theorist Jacques Ellul). This has in turn produced a sharp reaction in those who stand to be homogenized and assimilated. Thus, regions within Canada, local ethnic cultures, rural and small-town communities, neighbourhoods in our large cities, Indians and Eskimos have all attempted to throw sand in the works of the technological society, and to impede its movement in the direction of the "universal and homogeneous state" as Grant warns. These phenomena indicate the strength of collectivist ideas, if at times inchoate and unarticulated, in Canada; and along with the wider nationalist revival have both contributed to and benefited from more explicit and self-conscious collectivist critiques.

This "revolt of the collectivities" is the loudest, but not the only dissenting voice. Thus the individualist aspects of the liberal "positive liberty" ideas have been strongly criticized by socialism, which as we have seen desires equality of condition, as well as merely equality of opportunity for individual enterprise. Our brief analysis in Chapter V of the different ideological underpinnings for medicare in the mid-1960's is a case in point. Although both Liberals and NDP were promising the Canadian voters programmes with identical names, real and essential differences were masked under these similarities.

Canadian conservatism for its part has mounted a vigorous defence of our inheritance from the past, traditions and institutions, like the Canadian Crown and the House of Commons. Conservatives like John Diefenbaker and Donald Creighton are determined that in Richard Hooker's words, "We have not loosely through silence permitted things to pass away as in a dream."[4] Their criticism has in turn forced liberals both to justify their actions, and to examine them more deeply than they would have if they had gone more or less unchallenged.

Conservatives and socialists alike have pressed the notion that the Canadian polity ought to possess and pursue a vision of the common good higher than the mere maximization of individual freedom of action, and individual material gratification. Indeed in some senses this is their most important contribution to the conversation of ideologies in Canada; for it is clear from the period of Liberal dominance between 1920 and 1957, when such a vision was conspicuously absent, that Canada cannot long survive without it. As Grant reminds us, the Fathers of Confederation, and particularly Macdonald and Cartier, believed that they were creating a nation which was distinguished from the United States by precisely such a vision: the tory vision of an ordered, stable, and lawful society, prepared to use its collective powers to suppress socially harmful individual actions, and to further the collective good. Socialists in the twentieth century have supplemented that vision by insisting that the collective good requires the pursuit of equality, and the suppression of privilege, but they have not rejected it. It is for this reason that the renewal of our ideological conversation is a cause for some optimism about the future of Canada. If it does not ensure that Meighen's question, "whither are we drifting" will be definitely answered, it at least assures us that there is an answer to the question, and that Canada need not drift any longer.

[1] D. G. Creighton, *Canada's First Century,* (Toronto: Macmillan, 1970) p.356.
[2] D. V. Smiley, "Introduction" to *Canada in Question: Federalism in the Seventies,* (Toronto: McGraw-Hill Ryerson, 1972).
[3] Denis Smith, *Bleeding Hearts, Bleeding Country,* (Edmonton; Hurtig, 1971) p.150.
[4] Richard Hooker, "Preface" to *The Laws of Ecclesiastical Polity,* (1593).

Select Bibliography

PRIMARY SOURCES

General

Carrigan, D. O., ed. *Canadian Political Party Platforms*, 1867-1968. Toronto: Copp Clark, 1968.

Durham. *Lord Durham's Report*. Edited by G. M. Craig, Toronto: McClelland and Stewart, 1963.

Waite, P. B., ed. *Confederation Debates in the Province of Canada*. Toronto: McClelland and Stewart, 1963.

Liberalism

King, Mackenzie, *Industry and Humanity*. New York: Houghton Mifflin, 1918.

Pickersgill, J. W. *The Liberal Party*. Toronto: McClelland and Stewart, 1962.

Smith, Goldwin, *Canada and the Canadian Question*. Introduction by C. Berger. Toronto: University of Toronto Press, 1971.

Trudeau, P. E. *Federalism and the French Canadians*. Toronto: Macmillan, 1968.

Conservatism

Faribault, Marcel. *Unfinished Business*. Toronto: McClelland and Stewart, 1967.

Hogan, George. *The Conservative in Canada*. Toronto: McClelland and Stewart, 1963.

Meighen, Arthur. *Unrevised and Unrepented*. Toronto: Clarke, Irwin, 1949.

Wilbur, J. R. H., ed. *The Bennett New Deal*. Toronto: Copp Clark, 1968.

Report of the Round Table on Canadian Policy, Port Hope Conference, 1942.

Socialism

CCF. *Regina Manifesto*. Regina: CCF, 1933.

CCF. *Winnipeg Declaration of Principles*. Montreal: CCF, 1956.

Irvine, William. *The Farmers in Politics*. Toronto: McClelland and Stewart, 1920.

Knowles, Stanley. *The New Party*. Toronto: McClelland and Stewart, 1961.

League for Social Reconstruction. *Social Planning for Canada*. Toronto: Thos. Nelson & Sons, 1935.

Lewis, Davis and Frank Scott. *Make this Your Canada*. Toronto: Central Canada Publishing Company, 1943.

LaPierre, L., J. T. McLeod, C. Taylor, and W. Young., eds. *Essays on the Left*. Toronto: McClelland and Stewart, 1971.

Taylor, Charles. *The Pattern of Politics*. Toronto: McClelland and Stewart, 1970.

Woodsworth, J. S. *My Neighbour*. Toronto: Methodist Book Room, 1911. Reprinted 1972 by the University of Toronto Press.

Nationalism

Borden, R. L. *Robert Laird Borden: His Memoirs*. 2 vols., ed. H. Macquarie. Toronto: McClelland and Stewart, 1969

Cook, R. ed. *French Canadian Nationalism*. Toronto: Macmillan, 1969.

Creighton, Donald. *Canada's First Century*. Toronto: Macmillan, 1970.

Conclusion: Whither Are We Drifting?

Grant, George. *Lament for a Nation.* Toronto: McClelland and Stewart, 1965.
Lévesque, René. *Option for Quebec.* Toronto: McClelland and Stewart, 1968.
Russell, Peter, ed. *Nationalism in Canada.* Toronto: McGraw-Hill Ryerson, 1966.
Vallières, Pierre. *L'Urgence de choisir.* Montréal: Editions Partis pris, 1971.
Vallières, Pierre. *White Niggers of America.* Translated by J. Pinkham. Toronto: McClelland and Stewart, 1971.

INTERPRETATIONS

General

Glazebrook, G. P. de T. *A History of Canadian Political Thought.* Toronto: McClelland and Stewart, 1966.
Horowitz, Gad. *Canadian Labour and Politics.* Ch. 1. Toronto: University of Toronto Press, 1968

Liberalism

Careless, J. M. S. *Brown of the Globe.* 2 vols. Toronto: Macmillan, 1959, 1963.
Hutchison, B. *The Incredible Canadian.* Toronto: Longmans Green, 1952.
Morton, William. *The Progressive Party.* Toronto: University of Toronto Press, 1950.
Newman, Peter. *The Distemper of our Times.* Toronto: McClelland and Stewart, 1968.
Skelton, O. D. *Life and Letters of Sir Wilfred Laurier,* 2 vols. Toronto: McClelland and Stewart, 1965.

Conservatism

Creighton, Donald. *Sir John A. Macdonald,* 2 vols. Toronto: Macmillan, 1952, 1955.
Graham, Roger. *Arthur Meighen,* 3 vols. Toronto: Clarke Irwin, 1960, 1963, 1965.
Granatstein, J. L. *The Politics of Survival.* Toronto: University of Toronto Press, 1967.
Newman, Peter. *Renegade in Power.* Toronto: McClelland and Stewart, 1963.

Socialism

French, Doris. *Faith, Sweat and Politics.* Toronto: McClelland and Stewart, 1962.
Masters, William. *The Winnipeg General Strike.* Toronto: University of Toronto Press, 1950.
Robin, Martin. *Radical Politics and Canadian Labour.* Kingston: Centre for Industrial Relations, 1968.
Young, Walter. *The Anatomy of a Party: The National CCF, 1932-1961.* Toronto: University of Toronto Press, 1969.
Zakuta, L. *A Protestant Movement Becalmed: A Study of Change in the CCF.* Toronto: University of Toronto Press, 1964.

Nationalism

Berger, C. *The Sense of Power.* Toronto: University of Toronto Press, 1969.
Creighton, Donald. *Canada's First Century.* Toronto: Macmillan, 1970.
Godfrey, D. and M. Watkins, eds. *Gordon to Watkins to You.* Toronto: New Press, 1970.
Grant, George. *Technology and Empire.* Toronto: House of Anansi, 1969.
Kedourie, E. *Nationalism.* London: Hutchison, 1966.
Rotstein, A. and G. Lax, eds. *Independence: The Canadian Challenge.* Toronto: Committee for an Independent Canada, 1972.

Index

DATE DUE

GAYLORD			PRINTED IN U.S.A.